AUTOMATIC WEALTH III

The Attractor Factor

Including:

- **The Power of Your Subconscious Mind by Joseph Murphy**

- **How to Attract Money by Joseph Murphy**

- **Thought Vibration or the Law of Attraction in the Thought World by William Walker Atkinson**

- **Feeling Is The Secret by Neville**

Cover Desing: Jose Andres Neuman Vaisman

© Copyright 2006 – BN Publishing

www.bnpublishing.com

info@bnpublishing.com

Printed in the U.S.A.

The Power of
Your Subconscious Mind

Dr. Joseph Murphy

How This Book Can Work Miracles in Your Life

I have seen miracles happen to men and women in all walks of life all over the world. Miracles will happen to you, too—when you begin using the magic power of your subconscious mind. This book is designed to teach you that your habitual thinking and imagery mold, fashion, and create your destiny; for as a man thinketh in his subconscious mind, so is he.

• Do you know the answers?

Why is one man sad and another man happy? Why is one man joyous and prosperous and another man poor and miserable? Why is one man fearful and anxious and another full of faith and confidence? Why does one man have a beautiful, luxurious home while another man lives out a meager existence in a slum? Why is one man a great success and another an abject failure? Why is one speaker outstanding and immensely popular and another mediocre and unpopular? Why is one man a genius in his work or profession while the other man toils and moils all his life without doing or accomplishing anything worthwhile? Why is one man healed of a so-called incurable disease and another isn't? Why is it so many good, kind religious people suffer the tortures of the damned in their mind and body? Why is it many immoral and irreligious people succeed and prosper and enjoy radiant health? Why is one woman happily married and her sister very unhappy and frustrated? Is there an answer to these questions in the workings of your conscious and subconscious minds? There most certainly is.

• Reason for writing this book

It is for the express purpose of answering and clarifying the above questions and many others of a similar nature that motivated me to write this book. I have endeavored to explain the great fundamental truths of your mind in the simplest language possible. I believe that it is perfectly possible to explain the basic, foundational, and fundamental laws of life and of your mind in ordinary everyday language. You will find that the language of this book is that used in your daily papers, current periodicals, in your business offices, in your home, and in the daily workshop. I urge you to study this book and apply the techniques outlined therein; and as you do, I feel absolutely convinced that you will lay hold of a miracle -working power that will lift you up from confusion, misery, melancholy, and failure, and guide you to your true place, solve your difficulties, sever you from emotional and physical bondage, and place you on the royal road to freedom, happiness, and peace of mind. This miracle-working power of your subconscious mind can heal you of your sickness; make you vital and strong again. In learning how to use your inner powers, you will open the prison door of fear.

• Releasing the miracle-working power

A personal healing will ever be the most convincing evidence of our subconscious powers. Over forty-two years ago I resolved a malignancy—in medical terminology it was called a sarcoma—by using the healing power of my subconscious mind, which created me and still maintains and governs all my vital functions. The technique I applied is elaborated on in this book, and I feel sure that it will help others to trust the same Infinite Healing Presence lodged in the subconscious depths of all men. Through the kindly offices of my doctor friend, I suddenly realized that it was natural to assume that the Creative Intelligence which made all my organs, fashioned my body, and started my heart, could heal its own handiwork. The ancient proverb says, "The doctor dresses the wound and God heals it."

• Wonders happen when you pray effectively

Scientific prayer is the harmonious interaction of the conscious and subconscious levels of mind scientifically directed for a specific purpose. This book will teach you the scientific way to tap the realm of infinite power within you enabling you to get what you really want in life. You desire a happier, fuller, and richer life. Begin to use this miracle-working power and smooth your way in daily affairs, solve business problems, and bring harmony in family relationships. Be sure that you read this book several times. The many chapters will show you how this wonderful power works, and how you can draw out the hidden inspiration and wisdom that is within you. Learn the simple techniques of impressing the subconscious mind. Follow the new scientific way in tapping the infinite storehouse. Read this book carefully, earnestly, and lovingly. Prove to yourself the amazing way it can help you. It could be and I believe it will be the turning point of your life.

• Everybody prays

Do you know how to pray effectively? How long is it since you prayed as part of your everyday activities? In an emergency, in time of danger or trouble, in illness, and when death lurks, prayers pour forth—your own, and friends. Just read your daily newspaper. It is reported that prayers are being offered up all over the nation for a child stricken with a so-called incurable ailment, for peace among nations, for a group of miners trapped in a flooded mine. Later it is reported that when rescued, the miners said that they prayed while waiting for rescue; an airplane pilot says that he prayed as he made a successful emergency landing. Certainly, prayer is an ever-present help in time of trouble; but you do not have to wait for trouble to make prayer an integral and constructive part of your life. The dramatic answers to prayer make headlines and are the subject of testimonies to the effectiveness of prayer. What of the many humble prayers of children, the simple thanksgiving of grace at the table daily, the faithful devotions wherein the individual seeks only communion with God? My work with people has made it necessary for me to study the various approaches to prayer. I have experienced the power of prayer in my own life, and I have talked and worked with many people who also have enjoyed the help of prayer. The problem usually is how to tell others how to pray. People who are in trouble have difficulty in thinking and acting reasonably. They need an easy formula to follow, an obviously workable pattern that is simple and specific. Often they must be led to approach the emergency.

• Unique feature of this book

The unique feature of this book is its down-to-earth practicality. Here you are presented with simple, useable techniques and formulas, which you can easily apply in your workaday world. I have taught these simple processes to men and women all over the world, and recently over a thousand men and women of all religious affiliations attended a special class in Los Angeles where I presented the highlights of what is offered in the pages of this book. Many came from distances of two hundred miles for each class lesson. The special features of this book will appeal to you because they show you why oftentimes you get the opposite of what you prayed for and reveal to you the reasons why. People have asked me in all parts of the world and thousands of times, "Why is it I have prayed and prayed and got no answer?" In this book you will find the reasons for this common complaint. The many ways of impressing the subconscious mind and getting the right answers make this an extraordinarily valuable book and an ever-present help in time of trouble.

• What do you believe?

It is not the thing believed in that brings an answer to man's prayer; the answer to prayer results when the individual's subconscious mind responds to the mental picture or thought in his mind. This law of belief is operating in all religions of the world and is the reason why they are psychologically true. The Buddhist, the Christian, the Moslem, and the Hebrew all may get answers to their prayers, not because of the particular creed, religion, affiliation, ritual, ceremony, formula, liturgy, incantation, sacrifices, or offerings, but solely because of belief or mental acceptance and receptivity about that for which they pray. The law of life is the law of belief, and belief could be summed up briefly as a thought in your mind. As a man thinks, feels, and believes, so is the condition of his mind, body, and circumstances. A technique, a methodology based on an understanding of what you are doing and why you are doing it will help you to bring about a subconscious embodiment of all the good things of life. Essentially, answered prayer is the realization of your heart's desire.

• Desire is prayer

Everyone desires health, happiness, security, peace of mind, true expression, but many fail to achieve clearly defined results. A university professor admitted to me recently, "I know that if I changed my mental pattern and redirected my emotional life, my ulcers would not recur, but I do not have any technique, process, or modus operandi. My mind wanders back and forth on my many problems, and I feel frustrated, defeated, and unhappy." This professor had a desire for perfect health; he needed knowledge of the way his mind worked which would enable him to fulfill his desire. By practicing the healing methods outlined in this book, he became whole and perfect.

• There is one mind common to all individual men (Emerson)

The miracle-working powers of your subconscious mind existed before you and I were born, before any church or world existed. The great eternal truths and principles of life antedate all religions. It is with these thoughts in mind that I urge you in the following chapters to lay hold of this wonderful, magical, transforming power, which will bind up mental and physical wounds, proclaim liberty to the fear-ridden mind, and liberate you completely from the limitations of poverty, failure, misery, lack, and frustration. All you have to do is unite mentally and emotionally with the good you wish to embody, and the creative powers of your subconscious will respond accordingly. Begin now, today, let wonders happen in your life! Keep on, keeping on until the day breaks and the shadows flee away.

Contents

Chapter 1: The Treasure House Within You

Infinite riches are all around you if you will open your mental eyes and behold the treasure house of infinity within you. There is a gold mine within you from which you can extract everything you need to live life gloriously, joyously, and abundantly.

Many are sound asleep because they do not know about this gold mine of infinite intelligence and boundless love within themselves. Whatever you want, you can draw forth. A magnetized piece of steel will lift about twelve times its own weight, and if you demagnetize this same piece of steel, it will not even lift a feather. Similarly, there are two types of men. There is the magnetized man who is full of confidence and faith. He knows that he is born to win and to succeed. Then, there is the type of man who is demagnetized. He is full of fears and doubts. Opportunities come, and he says, "I might fail; I might lose my money; people will laugh at me." This type of man will not get very far in life because, if he is afraid to go forward, he will simply stay where he is. Become a magnetized man and discover the master secret of the ages.

• The master secret of the ages

What, in your opinion, is the master secret of the ages? The secret of atomic energy? Thermonuclear energy? The neutron bomb? Interplanetary travel? No—not any of these. Then, what is this master secret? Where can one find it, and how can it be contacted and brought into action? The answer is extraordinarily simple. This secret is the marvelous, miracle-working power found in your own subconscious mind, the last place that most people would seek it.

• The marvelous power of your subconscious

You can bring into your life more power, more wealth, more health, more happiness, and more joy by learning to contact and release the hidden power of your subconscious mind. You need not acquire this power; you already possess it. But, you want to learn how to use it; you want to understand it so that you can apply it in all departments of your life.

As you follow the simple techniques and processes set forth in this book, you can gain the necessary knowledge and understanding. A new light can inspire you, and you can generate a new force enabling you to realize your hopes and make all your dreams come true. Decide now to make your life grander, greater, richer, and nobler than ever before.

Within your subconscious depths lie infinite wisdom, infinite power, and infinite supply of all that is necessary, which is waiting for development and expression. Begin now to recognize these potentialities of your deeper mind, and they will take form in the world without.

The infinite intelligence within your subconscious mind can reveal to you everything you need to know at every moment of time and point of space provided you are open-minded and receptive. You can receive new thoughts and ideas enabling you to bring forth new inventions, make new discoveries, or write books and plays. Moreover, the infinite intelligence in your subconscious can impart to you wonderful kinds of knowledge of an original nature. It can reveal to you and open the way for perfect expression and true place in your life.

Through the wisdom of your subconscious mind you can attract the ideal companion, as well as the right business associate or partner. It can find the right buyer for your home, and provide you with all the money you need, and the financial freedom to be, to do, and to go, as your heart desires.

It is your right to discover this inner world of thought, feeling, and power; of light, love, and beauty. Though invisible, its forces are mighty. Within your subconscious mind you will find the solution for every problem, and the cause for every effect. Because you can draw out the hidden powers, you come into actual possession of the power and wisdom necessary to move forward in abundance, security, joy, and dominion.

I have seen the power of the subconscious lift people up out of crippled states, making them whole, vital, and strong once more, and free to go out into the world to experience happiness, health, and joyous expression. There is a miraculous healing power in your subconscious that can heal the troubled mind and the broken heart. It can open the prison door of the mind and liberate you. It can free you from all kinds of material and physical bondage.

• Necessity of a working basis

Substantial progress in any field of endeavor is impossible in the absence of a working basis, which is universal in its application. You can become skilled in the operation of your subconscious mind. You can practice its powers with a certainty of results in exact proportion to your knowledge of its principles and to your application of them for definite specific purposes and goals you wish to achieve.

Being a former chemist, I would like to point out that if you combine hydrogen and oxygen in the proportions of two atoms of the former to one of the latter, water would be the result. You are very familiar with the fact that one atom of oxygen and one atom of carbon will produce carbon monoxide, a poisonous gas. But, if you add another atom of oxygen, you will get carbon dioxide, a harmless gas, and so on throughout the vast realm of chemical compounds.

You must not think that the principles of chemistry, physics, and mathematics differ from the principles of your subconscious mind. Let us consider a generally accepted principle: "Water seeks its own level." This is a universal principle, which is applicable to water everywhere.

Consider another principle: "Matter expands when heated." This is true anywhere, at any time, and under all circumstances. You can heat a piece of steel, and it will expand regardless whether the steel is found in China, England, or India. It is a universal truth that matter expands when heated. It is also a universal truth that whatever you impress on your subconscious mind is expressed on the screen of space as condition, experience, and event.

Your prayer is answered because your subconscious mind is principle, and by principle I mean the way a thing works. For example, the principle of electricity is that it works from a higher to a lower potential. You do not change the principle of electricity when you use it, but by co-operating with nature, you can bring forth marvelous inventions and discoveries, which bless humanity in countless ways.

Your subconscious mind is principle and works according to the law of belief. You must know what belief is, why it works, and how it works. The law of your mind is the law of belief. This means to believe in the way your mind works, to believe in belief itself. The belief of your mind is the thought of your mind—that is simple—just that and nothing else.

All your experiences, events, conditions, and acts are the reactions of your subconscious mind to your thoughts. Remember, it is not the thing believed in, but the belief in your own mind, which brings about the result. Cease believing in the false beliefs, opinions, superstitions, and fears of mankind. Begin to believe in the eternal verities and truths of life, which never change. Then, you will move onward, upward, and Godward.

Whoever reads this book and applies the principles of the subconscious mind herein set forth; will be able to pray scientifically and effectively for himself and for others. Your prayer is answered according to the universal law of action and reaction. Thought is incipient action. The reaction is the response from your subconscious mind which corresponds with the nature of your thought. Busy your mind with the concepts of harmony, health, peace, and good will, and wonders will happen in your life.

• The duality of mind

You have only one mind, but your mind possesses two distinctive characteristics. The line of demarcation between the two is well known to all thinking men and women today. The two functions of your mind are essentially unlike. Each is endowed with separate and distinct attributes and powers. The nomenclature generally used to distinguish the two functions of your mind is as follows: The objective and subjective mind, the conscious and subconscious mind, the waking and sleeping mind, the surface self and the deep self, the voluntary mind and the involuntary mind, the male and the female, and many other terms. You will find the terms "conscious" and "subconscious" used to represent the dual nature of your mind throughout this book.

• The conscious and subconscious minds

An excellent way to get acquainted with the two functions of your mind is to look upon your own mind as a garden. You are a gardener, and you are planting seeds (thoughts) in your subconscious mind all day long, based on your habitual thinking. As you sow in your subconscious mind, so shall you reap in your body and environment.

Begin now to sow thoughts of peace, happiness, right action, good will, and prosperity. Think quietly and with interest on these qualities and accept them fully in your conscious reasoning mind. Continue to plant these wonderful seeds (thoughts) in the garden of your mind, and you will reap a glorious harvest. Your subconscious mind may be likened to the soil, which will grow all kinds of seeds, good or bad. Do men gather grapes of thorns, or figs of thistles? Every thought is, therefore, a cause, and every condition is an effect. For this reason, it is essential that you take charge of your thoughts so as to bring forth only desirable conditions.

When your mind thinks correctly, when you understand the truth, when the thoughts deposited in your subconscious mind are constructive, harmonious, and peaceful, the magic working power of your subconscious will respond and bring about harmonious conditions, agreeable surroundings, and the best of everything. When you begin to control your thought processes, you can apply the powers of your subconscious to any problem or difficulty. In other words, you will actually be consciously co-operating with the infinite power and omnipotent law, which governs all things.

Look around you wherever you live and you will notice that the vast majority of mankind lives in the world without; the more enlightened men are intensely interested in the world within. Remember, it is the world within, namely, your thoughts, feelings, and imagery that makes your world without. It is, therefore, the only creative power, and everything which you find in your world of expression has been created by you in the inner world of your mind consciously or unconsciously.

Knowledge of the interaction of your conscious and subconscious minds will enable you to transform your whole life. In order to change external conditions, you must change the cause. Most men try to change conditions and circumstances by working with conditions and circumstances. To remove discord, confusion, lack, and limitation, you must remove the cause, and the cause is the way you are using your conscious mind. In other words, the way you are thinking and picturing in your mind.

You are living in a fathomless sea of infinite riches. Your subconscious is very sensitive to your thoughts. Your thoughts form the mold or matrix through which the infinite intelligence, wisdom, vital forces, and energies of your subconscious flow. The practical application of the laws of your mind as illustrated in each chapter of this book will cause you to experience abundance for poverty, wisdom for superstition and ignorance, peace for pain, joy for sadness, light for darkness, harmony for discord, faith and confidence for fear, success for failure, and freedom from the law of averages. Certainly, there can be no more wonderful blessing than these from a mental, emotional, and material standpoint.

Most of the great scientists, artists, poets, singers, writers, and inventors have a deep understanding of the workings of the conscious and subconscious minds. One time Caruso, the great operatic tenor, was struck with stage fright. He said his throat was paralyzed due to spasms caused by intense fear, which constricted the muscles of his throat. Perspiration poured copiously down his face. He was ashamed because in a few minutes he had to go out on the stage, yet he was shaking with fear and trepidation. He said, "They will laugh at me. I can't sing." Then he shouted in the presence of those behind the stage, "The Little Me wants to strangle the Big Me within."

He said to the Little Me, "Get out of here, the Big Me wants to sing through me."

By the Big Me, he meant the limitless power and wisdom of his subconscious mind, and he began to shout, "Get out, get out, the Big Me is going to sing!"

His subconscious mind responded releasing the vital forces within him. When the call came, he walked out on the stage and sang gloriously and majestically, enthralling the audience.

It is obvious to you now that Caruso must have understood the two levels of mind—the conscious or rational, and the subconscious or irrational level. Your subconscious mind is reactive and responds to the nature of your thoughts. When your conscious mind (the Little Me) is full of fear, worry, and anxiety, the negative emotions engendered in your subconscious mind (the Big Me) are released and flood the conscious mind with a sense of panic, foreboding, and despair. When this happens, you can, like Caruso, speak affirmatively and with a deep sense of authority to the irrational emotions generated in your deeper mind as follows: "Be still, be quiet, I am in control, you must obey me, you are subject to my command, you cannot intrude where you do not belong."

It is fascinating and intensely interesting to observe how you can speak authoritatively and with conviction to the irrational movement of your deeper self bringing silence, harmony, and peace to your mind. The subconscious is subject to the conscious mind, and that is why it is called subconscious or subjective.

• Outstanding differences and modes of operation

You will perceive the main differences by the following illustrations: The conscious mind is like the navigator or captain at the bridge of a ship. He directs the ship and signals orders to men in the engine room, who in turn control all the boilers, instruments, gauges, etc. The men in the engine room do not know where they are going; they follow orders. They would go on the rocks if the man on the bridge issued faulty or wrong instructions based on his findings with the compass, sextant, or other instruments. The men in the engine room obey him because he is in charge and issues orders, which are automatically obeyed. Members of the crew do not talk back to the captain; they simply carry out orders.

The captain is the master of his ship, and his decrees are carried out. Likewise, your conscious mind is the captain and the master of your ship, which represents your body, environment, and all your affairs. Your subconscious mind takes the orders you give it based upon what your conscious mind believes and accepts as true.

When you repeatedly say to people, "I can't afford it," then your subconscious mind takes you at your word and sees to it that you will not be in a position to purchase what you want. As long as you persist in saying, "I can't afford that car, that trip to Europe, that home, that fur coat or ermine wrap," you can rest assured that your subconscious mind will follow your orders, and you will go through life experiencing the lack of all these things.

Last Christmas Eve a beautiful young university student looked at an attractive and rather expensive traveling bag in a store window. She was going home to Buffalo, New York, for the holidays. She was about to say, "I can't afford that bag," when she recalled something she had heard at one of my lectures which was, "Never finish a negative statement; reverse it immediately, and wonders will happen in your life."

She said, "That bag is mine. It is for sale. I accept it mentally, and my subconscious sees to it that I receive it."

At eight o'clock Christmas Eve her fiancé presented her with a bag exactly the same as the one she had looked at and mentally identified herself with at ten o'clock the same morning. She had filled her mind with the thought of expectancy and released the whole thing to her deeper mind, which has the "know-how" of accomplishment.

This young girl, a student at the University of Southern California, said to me, "I didn't have the money to buy that bag, but now I know where to find money and all the things I need, and that is in the treasure house of eternity within me."

Another simple illustration is this: When you say, "I do not like mushrooms," and the occasion subsequently comes that you are served mushrooms in sauces or salads, you will get indigestion because your subconscious mind says to you, "The boss (your conscious mind) does not like mushrooms." This is an amusing example of the outstanding differences and modes of operation of your conscious and subconscious minds.

A woman may say, "I wake up at three o'clock, if I drink coffee at night." Whenever she drinks coffee, her subconscious mind nudges her, as if to say, "The boss wants you to stay awake tonight." Your subconscious mind works twenty-four hours a day and makes provisions for your benefit, pouring all the fruit of your habitual thinking into your lap.

• How her subconscious responded

A woman wrote me a few months ago as follows: "I am seventy-five years old, a widow with a grown family. I was living alone and on a pension. I heard your lectures on the powers of the subconscious mind wherein you said that ideas could be conveyed to the subconscious mind by repetition, faith, and expectancy.

"I began to repeat frequently with feeling, 'I am wanted. I am happily married to a kind, loving, and spiritual-minded man. I am secure!'

"I kept on doing this many times a day for about two weeks, and one day at the corner drugstore, I was introduced to a retired pharmacist. I found him to be kind, understanding, and very religious. He was a perfect answer to my prayer. Within a week he proposed to me, and now we are on our honeymoon in Europe. I know that the intelligence within my subconscious mind brought both of us together in divine order."

This woman discovered that the treasure house was within her. Her prayer was felt as true in her heart, and her affirmation sank down by osmosis into her subconscious mind, which is the creative medium. The moment she succeeded in bringing about a subjective embodiment, her subconscious mind brought about the answer through the law of attraction. Her deeper mind, full of wisdom and intelligence, brought both of them together in divine order.

Be sure that you think on whatsoever things are true, whatsoever things are honest, whatsoever things are just, whatsoever things are pure, whatsoever things are lovely, whatsoever things are of good report; if there be any virtue, and if there be any praise, think on these things.

• Brief summary of ideas worth remembering

1. The treasure house is within you. Look within for the answer to your heart's desire.

2. The great secret possessed by the great men of all ages was their ability to contact and release the powers of their subconscious mind. You can do the same.

3. Your subconscious has the answer to all problems. If you suggest to your subconscious prior to sleep, "I want to get up at 6 A.M.," it will awaken you at that exact time.

4. Your subconscious mind is the builder of your body and can heal you. Lull yourself to sleep every night with the idea of perfect health, and your subconscious, being your faithful servant, will obey you.

5. Every thought is a cause, and every condition is an effect.

6. If you want to write a book, write a wonderful play, give a better talk to your audience, convey the idea lovingly and feelingly to your subconscious mind, and it will respond accordingly.

7. You are like a captain navigating a ship. He must give the right orders, and likewise, you must give the right orders (thoughts and images) to your subconscious mind, which controls and governs all your experiences.

8. Never use the terms, "I can't afford it" or "I can't do this." Your subconscious mind takes you at your word and sees to it that you do not have the money or the ability to do what you want to do. Affirm, "I can do all things through the power of my subconscious mind."

9. The law of life is the law of belief. A belief is a thought in your mind. Do not believe in things to harm or hurt you. Believe in the power of your subconscious to heal, inspire, strengthen, and prosper you. According to your belief is it done unto you.

10. Change your thoughts, and you change your destiny.

Chapter 2: How Your Own Mind Works

You have a mind, and you should learn how to use it. There are two levels of your mind—the conscious or rational level, and the subconscious or irrational level. You think with your conscious mind, and whatever you habitually think sinks down into your subconscious mind, which creates according to the nature of your thoughts. Your subconscious mind is the seat of your emotions and is the creative mind. If you think good, good will follow; if you think evil, evil will follow. This is the way your mind works. The main point to remember is once the subconscious mind accepts an idea, it begins to execute it. It is an interesting and subtle truth that the law of the subconscious mind works for good and bad ideas alike. This law, when applied in a negative way, is the cause of failure, frustration, and unhappiness. However, when your habitual thinking is harmonious and constructive, you experience perfect health, success, and prosperity.

Peace of mind and a healthy body are inevitable when you begin to think and feel in the right way. Whatever you claim mentally and feel as true, your subconscious mind will accept and bring forth into your experience. The only thing necessary for you to do is to get your subconscious mind to accept your idea, and the law of your own subconscious mind will bring forth the health, peace, or the position you desire. You give the command or decree, and your subconscious will faithfully reproduce the idea impressed upon it.

The law of your mind is this:

You will get a reaction or response from your subconscious mind according to the nature of the thought or idea you hold in your conscious mind.

Psychologists and psychiatrists point out that when thoughts are conveyed to your subconscious mind, impressions are made in the brain cells. As soon as your subconscious accepts any idea, it proceeds to put it into effect immediately. It works by association of ideas and uses every bit of knowledge that you have gathered in your lifetime to bring about its purpose. It draws on the infinite power, energy, and wisdom within you. It lines up all the laws of nature to get its way. Sometimes it seems to bring about an immediate solution to your difficulties, but at other times it may take days, weeks, or longer. . . . Its ways are past finding out.

• Conscious and subconscious terms differentiated

You must remember that these are not two minds. They are merely two spheres of activity within one mind. Your conscious mind is the reasoning mind. It is that phase of mind which chooses. For example, you choose your books, your home, and your partner in life. You make all your decisions with your conscious mind. On the other hand, without any conscious choice on your part, your heart is kept functioning automatically, and the process of digestion, circulation, and breathing are carried on by your subconscious mind through processes independent of your conscious control.

Your subconscious mind accepts what is impressed upon it or what you consciously believe. It does not reason things out like your conscious mind, and it does not argue with you controversially. Your subconscious mind is like the soil, which accepts any kind of seed, good or bad. Your thoughts are active and might be likened unto seeds. Negative, destructive thoughts continue to work negatively in your subconscious mind, and in due time will come forth into outer experience which corresponds with them.

Remember, your subconscious mind does not engage in proving whether your thoughts are good or bad, true or false, but it responds according to the nature of your thoughts or suggestions. For example, if you consciously assume something as true, even though it may be false, your subconscious mind will accept it as true and proceed to bring about results, which must necessarily follow, because you consciously assumed it to be true.

• Experiments by psychologists

Innumerable experiments by psychologists and others on persons in the hypnotic state have shown that the subconscious mind is incapable of making selections and comparisons, which are necessary for a reasoning process. They have shown repeatedly that your subconscious mind will accept any suggestions, however false. Having once accepted any suggestion, it responds according to the nature of the suggestion given.

To illustrate the amenability of your subconscious mind to suggestion, if a practiced hypnotist suggests to one of his subjects that he is Napoleon Bonaparte, or even a cat or a dog, he will act out the part with inimitable accuracy. His personality becomes changed for the time being. He believes himself to be whatever the operator tells him he is.

A skilled hypnotist may suggest to one of his students in the hypnotic state that his back itches, to another that his nose is bleeding, to another that he is a marble statue, to another that he is freezing and the temperature is below zero. Each one will follow out the line of his particular suggestion, totally oblivious to all his surroundings, which do not pertain to his idea.

These simple illustrations portray clearly the difference between your conscious reasoning mind and your subconscious mind, which is impersonal, non-selective, and accepts as true whatever your conscious mind believes to be true. Hence, the importance of selecting thoughts, ideas, and premises, which bless, heal, inspire, and fill your soul with joy.

• The terms objective and subjective mind clarified

Your conscious mind is sometimes referred to as your objective mind because it deals with outward objects. The objective mind takes cognizance of the objective world. Its media of observation are your five physical senses. Your objective mind is your guide and director in your contact with your environment. You gain knowledge through your five senses. Your objective mind learns through observation, experience, and education. As previously pointed out, the greatest function of the objective mind is that of reasoning.

Suppose you are one of the thousands of tourists who come to Los Angeles annually. You would come to the conclusion that it is a beautiful city based upon your observation of the parks, pretty gardens, majestic buildings, and lovely homes. This is the working of your objective mind.

Your subconscious mind is oftentimes referred to as your subjective mind. Your subjective mind takes cognizance of its environment by means independent of the five senses. Your subjective mind perceives by intuition. It is the seat of your emotion and the storehouse of memory. Your subjective mind performs its highest functions when your objective senses are in abeyance. In a word, it is that intelligence which makes itself manifest when the objective mind is suspended or in a sleepy, drowsy state.

Your subjective mind sees without the use of the natural organs of vision. It has the capacity of clairvoyance and clair-audience. Your subjective mind can leave your body, travel to distant lands, and bring back information oftentimes of the most exact and truthful character. Through your subjective mind you can read the thoughts of others, read the contents of sealed envelopes and closed safes. Your subjective mind has the ability to apprehend the thoughts of others without the use of the ordinary objective means of communication. It is of the greatest importance that we understand the interaction of the objective and subjective mind in order to learn the true art of prayer.

• The subconscious cannot reason like your conscious mind

Your subconscious mind cannot argue controversially. Hence, if you give it wrong suggestions, it will accept them as true and will proceed to bring them to pass as conditions, experiences, and events. All things that have happened to you are based on thoughts impressed on your subconscious mind through belief. If you have conveyed erroneous concepts to your subconscious mind, the sure method of overcoming them is by the repetition of constructive, harmonious thoughts frequently repeated which your subconscious mind accepts, thus forming new and healthy habits of thought and life, for your subconscious mind is the seat of habit.

The habitual thinking of your conscious mind establishes deep grooves in your subconscious mind. This is very favorable for you if your habitual thoughts are harmonious, peaceful, and constructive.

If you have indulged in fear, worry, and other destructive forms of thinking, the remedy is to recognize the omnipotence of your subconscious mind and decree freedom, happiness, and perfect health. Your subconscious mind, being creative and one with your divine source, will proceed to create the freedom and happiness, which you have earnestly decreed.

• The tremendous power of suggestion

You must realize by now that your conscious mind is the "watchman at the gate," and its chief function is to protect your subconscious mind from false impressions. You are now aware of one of the basic laws of mind: Your subconscious mind is amenable to suggestion. As you know, your subconscious mind does not make comparisons, or contrasts, neither does it reason and think things out for itself. This latter function belongs to your conscious mind. It simply reacts to the impressions given to it by your conscious mind. It does not show a preference for one course of action over another.

The following is a classic example of the tremendous power of suggestion. Suppose you approach a timid-looking passenger on board ship and say to him something like this: "You look very ill. How pale you are! I feel certain you are going to be seasick. Let me help you to your cabin." The passenger turns pale. Your suggestion of seasickness associates itself with his own fears and forebodings. He accepts your aid down to the berth, and there your negative suggestion, which was accepted by him, is realized.

• Different reactions to the same suggestion

It is true that different people will react in different ways to the same suggestion because of their subconscious conditioning or belief. For example, if you go to a sailor on the ship and say to him sympathetically, "My dear fellow, you're looking very ill. Aren't you feeling sick? You look to me as if you were going to be seasick."

According to his temperament he either laughs at your "joke," or expresses a mild irritation. Your suggestion fell on deaf ears in this instance because your suggestion of seasickness was associated in his mind with his own immunity from it. Therefore, it called up not fear or worry, but self-confidence.

The dictionary says that a suggestion is the act or instance of putting something into one's mind, the mental process by which the thought or idea suggested is entertained, accepted, or put into effect. You must remember that a suggestion cannot impose something on the subconscious mind against the will of the conscious mind. In other words, your conscious mind has the power to reject the suggestion given. In the case of the sailor, he had no fear of seasickness. He had convinced himself of his immunity, and the negative suggestion had absolutely no power to evoke fear.

The suggestion of seasickness to the other passenger called forth his indwelling fear of seasickness. Each of us has his own inner fears, beliefs, opinions, and these inner assumptions rule and govern our lives. A suggestion has no power in and of itself except if you accept it mentally. This causes your subconscious powers to flow in a limited and restricted way according to the nature of the suggestion.

• How he lost his arm

Every two or three years I give a series of lectures at the London Truth Forum in Caxton Hall. This is a Forum I founded a number of years ago. Dr. Evelyn Fleet, the director, told me about an article which appeared in the English newspapers dealing with the power of suggestion. This is the suggestion a man gave to his subconscious mind over a period of about two years: "I would give my right arm to see my daughter cured." It appeared that his daughter had a crippling form of arthritis together with a so-called incurable form of skin disease. Medical treatment had failed to alleviate the condition, and the father had an intense longing for his daughter's healing, and expressed his desire in the words just quoted.

Dr. Evelyn Fleet said that the newspaper article pointed out that one day the family was out riding when their car collided with another. The father's right arm was torn off at the shoulder, and immediately the daughter's arthritis and skin condition vanished.

You must make certain to give your subconscious only suggestions, which heal, bless, elevate, and inspire you in all your ways. Remember that your subconscious mind cannot take a joke. It takes you at your word.

• How autosuggestion banishes fear

Illustrations of autosuggestion: Autosuggestion means suggesting something definite and specific to oneself. Herbert Parkyn, in his excellent manual of autosuggestion, records the following incident. It has its amusing side, so that one remembers it. "A New York visitor in Chicago looks at his watch, which is set an hour ahead of Chicago time, and tells a Chicago friend that it is twelve o'clock. The Chicago friend, not considering the difference in time between Chicago and New York, tells the New Yorker that he is hungry and that he must go to lunch."

Autosuggestion may be used to banish various fears and other negative conditions. A young singer was invited to give an audition. She had been looking forward to the interview, but on three previous occasions she had failed miserably due to fear of failure. This young lady had a very good voice, but she had been saying to herself, "When the time comes for me to sing, maybe they won't like me. I will try, but I'm full of fear and anxiety."

Her subconscious mind accepted these negative autosuggestions as a request and proceeded to manifest them and bring them into her experience. The cause was an involuntary autosuggestion, i.e., silent fear thoughts emotionalized and subjectified.

She overcame it by the following technique: Three times a day she isolated herself in a room. She sat down comfortably in an armchair, relaxed her body, and closed her eyes. She stilled her mind and body as best she could. Physical inertia favors mental passivity and renders the mind more receptive to suggestion. She counteracted the fear suggestion by saying to herself, "I sing beautifully. I am poised, serene, confident, and calm." She repeated this statement slowly, quietly, and with feeling from five to ten times at each sitting. She had three such "sittings" every day and one immediately prior to sleep. At the end of a week she was completely poised and confident. When the invitation to audition came, she gave a remarkable, wonderful audition.

• How she restored her memory

A woman, aged seventy-five, was in the habit of saying to herself, "I am losing my memory." She reversed the procedure and practiced induced autosuggestion several times a day as follows: "My memory from today on is improving in every department. I shall always remember whatever I need to know at every moment of time and point of space. The impressions received will be clearer and more definite. I shall retain them automatically and with ease. Whatever I wish to recall will immediately present itself in the correct form in my mind. I am improving rapidly every day, and very soon my memory will be better than it has ever been before." At the end of three weeks, her memory was back to normal, and she was delighted.

• How he overcame a nasty temper

Many men who complained of irritability and bad temper proved to be very susceptible to autosuggestion and obtained marvelous results by using the following statements three or four times a day—morning, noon, and at night prior to sleep for about a month. "Henceforth, I shall grow more good-humored. Joy, happiness, and cheerfulness are now becoming my normal states of mind. Every day I am becoming more and more lovable and understanding. I am now becoming the center of cheer and good will to all those about me, infecting them with good humor. This happy, joyous, and cheerful mood is now becoming my normal, natural state of mind. I am grateful."

• The constructive and destructive power of suggestion

Some illustrations and comments on heterosuggestion: Heterosuggestion means suggestions from another person. In all ages the power of suggestion has played a part in the life and thought of man in every period of time and in each country of the earth. In many parts of the world it is the controlling power in religion.

Suggestion may be used to discipline and control ourselves, but it can also be used to take control and command over others who do not know the laws of mind. In its constructive form it is wonderful and magnificent. In its negative aspects it is one of the most destructive of all the response patterns of the mind, resulting in patterns of misery, failure, suffering, sickness, and disaster.

• Have you accepted any of these?

From infancy on the majority of us have been given many negative suggestions. Not knowing how to thwart them, we unconsciously accepted them. Here are some of the negative suggestions: "You can't." "You'll never amount to anything." "You mustn't." "You'll fail." "You haven't got a chance." "You're all wrong." "It's no use." "It's not what you know, but who you know." "The world is going to the dogs." "What's the use, nobody cares." "It's no use trying so hard." "You're too old now." "Things are getting worse and worse." "Life is an endless grind." "Love is for the birds." "You just can't win." "Pretty soon you'll be bankrupt." "Watch out, you'll get the virus." "You can't trust a soul," etc.

Unless, as an adult, you use constructive autosuggestion, which is a reconditioning therapy, the impressions made on you in the past can cause behavior patterns that cause failure in your personal and social life. Autosuggestion is a means releasing you from the mass of negative verbal conditioning that might otherwise distort your life pattern, making the development of good habits difficult.

• You can counteract negative suggestions

Pick up the paper any day, and you can read dozens of items that could sow the seeds of futility, fear, worry, anxiety, and impending doom. If accepted by you, these thoughts of fear could cause you to lose the will for life. Knowing that you can reject all these negative suggestions by giving your subconscious mind constructive autosuggestions, you counteract all these destructive ideas.

Check regularly on the negative suggestions that people make to you. You do not have to be influenced by destructive heterosuggestion. All of us have suffered from it in our childhood and in our teens. If you look back, you can easily recall how parents, friends, relatives, teachers, and associates contributed in a campaign of negative suggestions. Study the things said to you, and you will discover much of it was in the form of propaganda. The purpose of much of what was said was to control you or instill fear into you.

This heterosuggestion process goes on in every home, office, factory, and club. You will find that many of these suggestions are for the purpose of making you think, feel, and act, as others want you to and in ways that are to their advantage.

• How suggestion killed a man

Here is an illustration of heterosuggestion: A relative of mine went to a crystal gazer in India who told him that he had a bad heart and predicted that he would die at the next new moon. He began to tell all members of his family about this prediction, and he arranged his will.

This powerful suggestion entered into his subconscious mind because he accepted it completely. My relative also told me that this crystal gazer was believed to have some strange occult powers, and he could do harm or good to a person. He died as predicted not knowing that he was the cause of his own death. I suppose many of us have heard similar stupid, ridiculous, superstitious stories.

Let us look at what happened in the light of our knowledge of the way the subconscious mind works. Whatever the conscious, reasoning mind of man believes; the subconscious mind will accept and act upon. My relative was happy, healthy, vigorous, and robust when he went to see the fortuneteller. She gave him a very negative suggestion, which he accepted. He became terrified, and constantly dwelt upon the fact that he was going to die at the next new moon. He proceeded to tell everyone about it, and he prepared for the end. The activity took place in his own mind, and his own thought was the cause. He brought about his own so-called death, or rather destruction of the physical body, by his fear and expectation of the end.

The woman who predicted his death had no more power than the stones and sticks in the field. Her suggestion had no power to create or bring about the end she suggested. If he had known the laws of his mind, he would have completely rejected the negative suggestion and refused to give her words any attention, knowing in his heart that he was governed and controlled by his own thought and feeling. Like tin arrows aimed at a battleship, her prophecy could have been completely neutralized and dissipated without hurting him.

The suggestions of others in themselves have absolutely no power whatever over you except the power that you give them through your own thoughts. You have to give your mental consent; you have to entertain the thought. Then, it becomes your thought, and you do the thinking. Remember, you have the capacity to choose. Choose life! Choose love! Choose health!

• The power of an assumed major premise

Your mind works like a syllogism. This means that whatever major premise your conscious mind assumes to be true determines the conclusion your subconscious mind comes to in regard to any particular question or problem in your mind. If your premise is true, the conclusion must be true as in the following example:

Every virtue is laudable; Kindness is a virtue; Therefore, kindness is laudable.

Another example is as follows:

All formed things change and pass away; The Pyramids of Egypt are formed things; Therefore, some day the Pyramids will pass away.

The first statement is referred to as the major premise, and the right conclusion must necessarily follow the right premise.

A college professor, who attended some of my science of mind lectures in May 1962, at Town Hall, New York, said to me, "Everything in my life is topsy-turvy, and I have lost health, wealth, and friends. Everything I touch turns out wrong."

I explained to him that he should establish a major premise in his thinking, that the infinite intelligence of his subconscious mind was guiding, directing, and prospering him spiritually, mentally, and materially. Then, his subconscious mind would automatically direct him wisely in his investments, decisions, and also heal his body and restore his mind to peace and tranquility.

This professor formulated an over-all picture of the way he wanted his life to be, and this was his major premise:

"Infinite intelligence leads and guides me in all my ways.

Perfect health is mine, and the Law of Harmony operates in my mind and body. Beauty, love, peace, and abundance are mine. The principle of right action and divine order govern my entire life. I know my major premise is based on the eternal truths of life, and I know, feel, and believe that my subconscious mind responds according to the nature of my conscious mind thinking."

He wrote me as follows: "I repeated the above statements slowly, quietly, and lovingly several times a day knowing that they were sinking deep down into my subconscious mind, and that results must follow. I am deeply grateful for the interview you gave me, and I would like to add that all departments of my life are changing for the better. It works!"

• The subconscious does not argue controversially

Your subconscious mind is all-wise and knows the answers to all questions. It does not argue with you or talk back to you. It does not say, "You must not impress me with that." For example, when you say, "I can't do this." "I am too old now." "I can't meet this obligation." "I was born on the wrong side of the tracks." "I don't know the right politician," you are impregnating your subconscious with these negative thoughts, and it responds accordingly. You are actually blocking your own good, thereby bringing lack, limitation, and frustration into your life.

When you set up obstacles, impediments, and delays in your conscious mind, you are denying the wisdom and intelligence resident in your subconscious mind. You are actually saying in effect that your subconscious mind cannot solve your problem. This leads to mental and emotional congestion, followed by sickness and neurotic tendencies.

To realize your desire and overcome your frustration, affirm boldly several times a day: "The infinite intelligence which gave me this desire leads, guides, and reveals to me the perfect plan for the unfolding of my desire. I know the deeper wisdom of my subconscious is now responding, and what I feel and claim within is expressed in the without. There is a balance, equilibrium, and equanimity."

If you say, "There is no way out; I am lost; there is no way out of this dilemma; I am stymied and blocked," you will get no answer or response from your subconscious mind. If you want the subconscious to work for you, give it the right request, and attain its co-operation. It is always working for you. It is controlling your heartbeat this minute and also your breathing. It heals a cut on your finger, and its tendency is lifeward, forever seeking to take care of you and preserve you. Your subconscious has a mind of its own, but it accepts your patterns of thought and imagery.

When you are seeking an answer to a problem, your subconscious will respond, but it expects you to come to a decision and to a true judgment in your conscious mind. You must acknowledge the answer is in your subconscious mind. However, if you say, "I don't think there is any way out; I am all mixed up and confused; why don't I get an answer?" you are neutralizing your prayer. Like the soldier marking time, you do not get anywhere.

Still the wheels of your mind, relax, let go, and quietly affirm: "My subconscious knows the answer. It is responding to me now. I give thanks because I know the infinite intelligence of my subconscious knows all things and is revealing the perfect answer to me now. My real conviction is now setting free the majesty and glory of my subconscious mind. I rejoice that it is so."

• Review of highlights

1. Think good, and good follows. Think evil, and evil follows. You are what you think all day long.

2. Your subconscious mind does not argue with you. It accepts what your conscious mind decrees. If you say, "I can't afford it," it may be true, but do not say it. Select a better thought, decree, "I'll buy it. I accept it in my mind."

3. You have the power to choose. Choose health and happiness. You can choose to be friendly, or you can choose to be unfriendly. Choose to be co-operative, joyous, friendly, lovable, and the whole world will respond. This is the best way to develop a wonderful personality.

4. Your conscious mind is the "watchman at the gate." Its chief function is to protect your subconscious mind from false impressions. Choose to believe that something good can happen and is happening now. Your greatest power is your capacity to choose. Choose happiness and abundance.

5. The suggestions and statements of others have no power to hurt you. The only power is the movement of your own thought. You can choose to reject the thoughts or statements of others and affirm the good. You have the power to choose how you will react.

6. Watch what you say. You have to account for every idle word. Never say, "I will fail; I will lose my job; I can't pay the rent." Your subconscious cannot take a joke. It brings all these things to pass.

7. Your mind is not evil. No force of nature is evil. It depends how you use the powers of nature. Use your mind to bless, heal, and inspire all people everywhere.

8. Never say, "I can't." Overcome that fear by substituting the following, "I can do all things through the power of my own subconscious mind."

9. Begin to think from the standpoint of the eternal truths and principles of life and not from the standpoint of fear, ignorance, and superstition. Do not let others do your thinking for you. Choose your own thoughts and make your own decisions.

10. You are the captain of your soul (subconscious mind) and the master of your fate. Remember, you have the capacity to choose. Choose life! Choose love! Choose health! Choose happiness!

11. Whatever your conscious mind assumes and believes to be true, your subconscious mind will accept and bring to pass. Believe in good fortune, divine guidance, right action, and all the blessings of life.

Chapter 3: The Miracle-Working Power of Your Subconscious

The power of your subconscious is enormous. It inspires you, it guides you, and it reveals to you names, facts, and scenes from the storehouse of memory. Your subconscious started your heartbeat, controls the circulation of your blood, and regulates your digestion, assimilation, and elimination. When you eat a piece of bread, your subconscious mind transmutes it into tissue, muscle, bone, and blood. This process is beyond the ken of the wisest man who walks the earth. Your subconscious mind controls all the vital processes and functions of your body and knows the answer to all problems.

Your subconscious mind never sleeps, never rests. It is always on the job. You can discover the miracle-working power of your subconscious by plainly stating to your subconscious prior to sleep that you wish a certain specific thing accomplished. You will be delighted to discover that forces within you will be released, leading to the desired result. Here, then, is a source of power and wisdom which places you in touch with omnipotence or the power that moves the world, guides the planets in their course, and causes the sun to shine.

Your subconscious mind is the source of your ideals, aspirations, and altruistic urges. It was through the subconscious mind that Shakespeare perceived great truths hidden from the average man of his day. Undoubtedly, it was the response of his subconscious mind that caused the Greek sculptor, Phidias, to portray beauty, order, symmetry, and proportion in marble and bronze. It enabled the Italian artist, Raphael, to paint Madonnas, and Ludwig van Beethoven to compose symphonies.

In 1955 I lectured at the Yoga Forest University, Rishikesh, India, and there I chatted with a visiting surgeon from Bombay. He told me about Dr. James Esdaille, a Scotch surgeon, who worked in Bengal before ether or other modern methods of anesthesia were discovered. Between 1843 and 1846, Dr. Es-daille performed about four hundred major operations of all kinds, such as amputations, removal of tumors and cancerous growths, as well as operations on the eye, ear, and throat. All operations were conducted under mental anesthesia only. This Indian doctor at Rishikesh informed me that the postoperative mortality rate of patients operated on by Dr. Esdaille was extremely low, probably two or three percent. Patients felt no pain, and there were no deaths during the operations.

Dr. Esdaille suggested to the subconscious minds of all his patients, who were in a hypnotic state, that no infection or septic condition would develop. You must remember that this was before Louis Pasteur, Joseph Lister, and others who pointed out the bacterial origin of disease and causes of infection due to unsterilized instruments and virulent organisms.

This Indian surgeon said that the reason for the low mortality rate and the general absence of infection, which was reduced to a minimum, was undoubtedly due to the suggestions of Dr. Esdaille to the subconscious minds of his patients. They responded according to the nature of his suggestion.

It is simply wonderful, when you conceive how a surgeon, over one hundred twenty years ago, discovered the miraculous wonder-working powers of the subconscious mind. Doesn't it cause you to be seized with a sort of mystic awe when you stop and think of the transcendental powers of your subconscious mind? Consider its extrasensory perceptions, such as its capacity for clairvoyance and clairaudience, its independence of time and space, its capacity to render you free from all pain and suffering, and its capacity to get the answer to all problems, be they what they may.

All these and many more reveal to you that there is a power and intelligence within you that far transcends your intellect, causing you to marvel at the wonders of it ail. All these experiences cause you to rejoice and believe in the miracle-working powers of your own subconscious mind.

• Your subconscious is your Book of Life

Whatever thoughts, beliefs, opinions, theories, or dogmas you write, engrave, or impress on your subconscious mind, you shall experience them as the objective manifestation of circumstances, conditions, and events. What you write on the inside, you will experience on the outside. You have two sides to your life, objective and subjective, visible and invisible, thought and its manifestation.

Your brain receives your thought, which is the organ of your conscious reasoning mind. When your conscious or objective mind accepts the thought completely, it is sent to the solar plexus, called the brain of your mind, where it becomes flesh and is made manifest in your experience.

As previously outlined, your subconscious cannot argue. It acts only from what you write on it. It accepts your verdict or the conclusions of your conscious mind as final. This is why you are always writing on the book of life, because your thoughts become your experiences. The American essayist, Ralph Waldo Emerson said, "Man is what he thinks all day long."

• What is impressed in the subconscious is expressed

William James, the father of American psychology, said that the power to move the world is in your subconscious mind. Your subconscious mind is one with infinite intelligence and boundless wisdom. It is fed by hidden springs, and is called the law of life. Whatever you impress upon your subconscious mind, the latter will move heaven and earth to bring it to pass. You must, therefore, impress it with right ideas and constructive thoughts.

The reason there is so much chaos and misery in the world is because people do not understand the interaction of their conscious and subconscious minds. When these two principles work in accord, in concord, in peace, and synchronously together, you will have heath, happiness, peace and joy. There is no sickness or discord when the conscious and subconscious work together harmoniously and peacefully.

The tomb of Hermes was opened with great expectancy and a sense of wonder because people believed that the greatest secret of the ages was contained therein. The secret was as within, so without; as above, so below.

In other words, whatever is impressed in your subconscious mind is expressed on the screen of space. This same truth was proclaimed by Moses, Isaiah and all the illumined seers of the ages. Whatever you feel as true subjectively is expressed as conditions, experiences, and events. Motion and emotion must balance. As in heaven [your own mind], so on earth [in your body and environment]. This is the great law of life.

You will find throughout all nature the law of action and reaction, of rest and motion. These two must balance, then there will be harmony and equilibrium. You are here to let the life principle flow through you rhythmically and harmoniously. The intake and the outgo must be equal. The impression and the expression must be equal. All your frustration is due to unfulfilled desire.

If you think negatively, destructively, and viciously, these thoughts generate destructive emotions which must be expressed and find an outlet. These emotions, being of a negative nature, are frequently expressed as ulcers, heart trouble, tension, and anxieties.

What is your idea or feeling about yourself now? Every part of your being expresses that idea. Your vitality, body, financial status, friends, and social status represent a perfect reflection of the idea you have of yourself. This is the real meaning of what is impressed in your subconscious mind, and which is expressed in all phases of your life.

We injure ourselves by the negative ideas, which we entertain. How often have you wounded yourself by getting angry, fearful, jealous, or vengeful? These are the poisons that enter your subconscious mind. You were not born with these negative attitudes. Feed your subconscious mind life-giving thoughts, and you will wipe out all the negative patterns lodged therein. As you continue to do this, all the past will be wiped out and remembered no more.

• The subconscious heals a malignancy of the skin

A personal healing will ever be the most convincing evidence of the healing power of the subconscious mind. Over forty years ago I resolved a malignancy of the skin through prayer. Medical therapy had failed to check the growth, and it was getting progressively worse.

A clergyman, with a deep psychological knowledge, explained to me the inner meaning of the 139th Psalm wherein it says, "In thy book all my members were written, which in continuance were fashioned, when as yet there was none of them." He explained that the term book meant my subconscious mind, which fashioned and molded all my organs from an invisible cell. He also pointed out that inasmuch as my subconscious mind made my body, it could also recreate it and heal it according to the perfect pattern within it.

This clergyman showed me his watch and said, "This had a maker, and the watchmaker had to have the idea first in mind before the watch became an objective reality, and if the watch was out of order, the watchmaker could fix it." My friend reminded me that the subconscious intelligence, which created my body, was like a watchmaker, and it also knew exactly how to heal, restore, and direct all the vital functions and processes of my body, but that I had to give it the perfect idea of health. This would act as cause, and the effect would be a healing.

I prayed in a very simple way as follows: "My body and all its organs were created by the infinite intelligence in my subconscious mind. It knows how to heal me. Its wisdom fashioned all my organs, tissues, muscles, and bones. This infinite healing presence within me is now transforming every atom of my being making me whole and perfect now. I give thanks for the healing I know is taking place now. Wonderful are the works of the creative intelligence within me."

I prayed aloud for about five minutes two or three times a day repeating the above simple prayer. In about three months my skin was whole and perfect.

As you can see, all I did was give life-giving patterns of wholeness, beauty, and perfection to my subconscious mind, thereby obliterating the negative images and patterns of thought lodged in my subconscious mind which were the cause of all my trouble. Nothing appears on your body except when the mental equivalent is first in your mind, and as you change your mind by drenching it with incessant affirmatives, you change your body.

This is the basis of all healing. ". . . Marvelous are thy works; and that my soul [subconscious mind] knoweth right well." Psalm 139:14.

• How the subconscious controls all functions of the body
While you are awake or sound asleep upon your bed, the ceaseless, tireless action of your subconscious mind controls all the vital functions of your body without the help of your conscious mind. For example, while you are asleep your heart continues to beat rhythmically, your lungs do not rest, and the process of inhalation and exhalation, whereby your blood absorbs fresh air, goes on just the same as when you are awake. Your subconscious controls your digestive processes and glandular secretions, as well as all the other mysterious operations of your body. The hair on your face continues to grow whether you are asleep or awake. Scientists tell us that the skin secretes much more perspiration during sleep than during the waking hours. Your eyes, ears, and other senses are active during sleep. For instance, many of our great scientists have received answers to perplexing problems while they were asleep. They saw the answers in a dream.

Oftentimes your conscious mind interferes with the normal rhythm of the heart, lungs, and functioning of the stomach and intestines by worry, anxiety, fear, and depression.

These patterns of thought interfere with the harmonious functioning of your subconscious mind. When mentally disturbed, the best procedure is to let go, relax, and still the wheels of your thought processes. Speak to your subconscious mind, telling it to take over in peace, harmony, and divine order. You will find that all the functions of your body will become normal again. Be sure to speak to your subconscious mind with authority and conviction, and it will conform to your command.

Your subconscious seeks to preserve your life and restore you to health at all costs. It causes you to love your children, which also illustrates an instinctive desire to preserve all life. Let us suppose you accidentally ate some bad food. Your subconscious mind would cause you to regurgitate it. If you inadvertently took some poison, your subconscious powers would proceed to neutralize it. If you completely entrusted yourself to its wonder-working power, you would be entirely restored to health.

• How to get the subconscious to work for you
The first thing to realize is that your subconscious mind is always working. It is active night and day, whether you act upon it or not. Your subconscious is the builder of your body, but you cannot consciously perceive or hear that inner silent process. Your business is with your conscious mind and not your subconscious mind. Just keep your conscious mind busy with the expectation of the best, and make sure the thoughts you habitually think are based on whatsoever things are lovely, true, just, and of good report. Begin now to take care of your conscious mind, knowing in your heart and soul that your subconscious mind is always expressing, reproducing, and manifesting according to your habitual thinking.

Remember, just as water takes the shape of the pipe it flows through, the life principle in you flows through you according to the nature of your thoughts. Claim that the healing presence in your subconscious is flowing through you as harmony, health, peace, joy, and abundance. Think of it as a living intelligence, a lovely companion on the way. Firmly believe it is continually flowing through you vivifying, inspiring, and prospering you. It will respond exactly this way. It is done unto you as you believe.

• Healing principle of the subconscious restores atrophied optic nerves

There is the well-known, duly authenticated case of Madame Bire of France, recorded in the archives of the medical department of Lourdes, France. She was blind; the optic nerves were atrophied and useless. She visited Lourdes and had what she termed a miraculous healing. Ruth Cranston, a Protestant young lady who investigated and wrote about healings at Lourdes in McCall's magazine, November, 1955, writes about Madame Bire as follows: "At Lourdes she regained her sight incredibly, with the optic nerves still lifeless and useless, as several doctors could testify after repeated examinations. A month later, upon re-examination, it was found that the seeing mechanism had been restored to normal. But at first, so far as medical examination could tell, she was seeing with 'dead eyes.'"

I have visited Lourdes several times where I, too, witnessed some healings, and of course, as we shall explain in the next chapter, there is no doubt that healings take place at many shrines throughout the world, Christian and non-Christian.

The waters of the shrine did not heal Madame Bire, to whom we just referred, but by her own subconscious mind, which responded to her belief. The healing principle within her subconscious mind responded to the nature of her thought. Belief is a thought in the subconscious mind. It means to accept something as true. The thought accepted executes itself automatically. Undoubtedly, Madame Bire went to the shrine with expectancy and great faith, knowing in her heart she would receive a healing. Her subconscious mind responded accordingly, releasing the ever-present healing forces. The subconscious mind, which created the eye, can certainly bring a dead nerve back to life. What the creative principle created, it can recreate. According to your belief is it done unto you.

• How to convey the idea of perfect health to your subconscious mind

A Protestant minister I knew in Johannesburg, South Africa, told me the method he used to convey the idea of perfect health to his subconscious mind. He had cancer of the lung. His technique, as given to me in his own handwriting, is exactly as follows: "Several times a day I would make certain that I was completely relaxed mentally and physically. I relaxed my body by speaking to it as follows, 'My feet are relaxed, my ankles are relaxed, my legs are relaxed, my abdominal muscles are relaxed, my heart and lungs are relaxed, my head is relaxed, my whole being is completely relaxed.' After about five minutes I would be in a sleepy drowsy state, and then I affirmed the following truth, 'the perfection of God is now being expressed through me. The idea of perfect health is now filling my subconscious mind. The image God has of me is a perfect image, and my subconscious mind recreates my body in perfect accordance with the perfect image held in the mind of God.'" This minister had a remarkable healing. This is a simple easy way of conveying the idea of perfect health to your subconscious mind.

Another wonderful way to convey the idea of health to your subconscious is through disciplined or scientific imagination. I told a man who was suffering from functional paralysis to make a vivid picture of himself walking around in his office, touching the desk, answering the telephone, and doing all the things he ordinarily would do if he were healed. I explained to him that this idea and mental picture of perfect health would be accepted by his subconscious mind.

He lived the role and actually felt himself back in the office. He knew that he was giving his subconscious mind something definite to work upon. His subconscious mind was the film upon which the picture was impressed. One day, after several weeks of frequent conditioning of the mind with this mental picture, the telephone rang by prearrangement and kept ringing while his wife and nurse were out. The telephone was about twelve feet away, but nevertheless he managed to answer it. He was healed at that hour. The healing power of his subconscious mind responded to his mental imagery, and a healing followed.

This man had a mental block, which prevented impulses from the brain reaching his legs; therefore, he said he could not walk. When he shifted his attention to the healing power within him, the power flowed through, his focused attention, enabling him to walk. Whatsoever ye shall ask in prayer, believing, ye shall receive.

• Ideas worth remembering

1. Your subconscious mind controls all the vital processes of your body and knows the answer to all problems.

2. Prior to sleep, turn over a specific request to your subconscious mind and prove its miracle-working power to yourself.

3. Whatever you impress on your subconscious mind is expressed on the screen of space as conditions, experiences, and events. Therefore, you should carefully watch all ideas and thoughts entertained in your conscious mind.

4. The law of action and reaction is universal. Your thought is action, and the reaction is the automatic response of your subconscious mind to your thought. Watch your thoughts!

5. All frustration is due to unfulfilled desires. If you dwell on obstacles, delays, and difficulties, your subconscious mind responds accordingly, and you are blocking your own good.

6. The Life Principle will flow through you rhythmically and harmoniously if you consciously affirm: "I believe that the subconscious power which gave me this desire is now fulfilling it through me." This dissolves all conflicts.

7. You can interfere with the normal rhythm of your heart, lungs, and other organs by worry, anxiety, and fear. Feed your subconscious with thoughts of harmony, health, and peace, and all the functions of your body will become normal again.

8. Keep your conscious mind busy with the expectation of the best, and your subconscious will faithfully reproduce your habitual thinking.

9. Imagine the happy ending or solution to your problem, feel the thrill of accomplishment, and what you imagine and feel will be accepted by your subconscious mind and bring it to pass.

Chapter 4: Mental Healings in Ancient Times

Down through the ages men of all nations have somehow instinctively believed that somewhere there resided a healing power which could restore to normal the functions and sensations of man's body. They believed that this strange power could be invoked under certain conditions, and that the alleviation of human suffering would follow. The history of all nations presents testimony in support of this belief.

In the early history of the world the power of secretly influencing men for good or evil, including the healing of the sick, was said to be possessed by the priests and holy men of all nations. Healing of the sick was supposed to be a power derived directly by them from God, and the procedures and processes of healing varied throughout the world. The healing processes took the form of supplications to God attended by various ceremonies, such as the laying on of hands, incantations, the application of amulets, talismans, rings, relics, and images.

For example, in the religions of antiquity priests in the ancient temples gave drugs to the patient and practiced hypnotic suggestions prior to the patient's sleep, telling him that the gods would visit him in his sleep and heal him. Many healings followed. Obviously, all this was the work of potent suggestions to the subconscious mind.

After the performance of certain mysterious rites, the devotees of Hecate would see the goddess during sleep, provided that before going to sleep they had prayed to her according to weird and fantastic instructions. They were told to mix lizards with resin, frankincense, and myrrh, and pound all this together in the open air under the crescent moon. Healings were reported in many cases following this grotesque procedure.

It is obvious that these strange procedures, as mentioned in the illustrations given, favored suggestion and acceptance by the subconscious mind of these people by making a powerful appeal to their imagination. Actually, in all these healings, the subconscious mind of the subject was the healer.

In all ages unofficial healers have obtained remarkable results in cases where authorized medical skill has failed. This gives cause for thought. How do these healers in all parts of the world effect their cures? The answer to all these healings is due to the blind belief of the sick person, which released the healing power resident in his subconscious mind. Many of the remedies and methods employed were rather strange and fantastic which fired the imagination of the patients, causing an aroused emotional state. This state of mind facilitated the suggestion of health, and was accepted both by the conscious and subconscious mind of the sick. This will be elaborated on further in the next chapter.

• Biblical accounts on the use of the subconscious powers

What things soever ye desire, when ye pray believe that ye receive them, and ye shall have them.

Note the difference in tenses. The inspired writer tells us to believe and accept as true the fact that our desire has already been accomplished and fulfilled, that it is already completed, and that its realization will follow as a thing in the future.

The success of this technique depends on the confident conviction that the thought, the idea, the picture is already a fact in mind. In order for anything to have substance in the realm of mind, it must be thought of as actually existing there.

Here in a few cryptic words is a concise and specific direction for making use of the creative power of thought by impressing upon the subconscious the particular thing, which you desire. Your thought, idea, plan, or purpose is as real on its own plane as your hand or your heart. In following the Biblical technique, you completely eliminate from your mind all consideration of conditions, circumstances, or anything, which might imply adverse contingencies. You are planting a seed (concept) in the mind, which, if you leave it undisturbed, will infallibly germinate into external fruition.

The prime condition is faith. Over and over again you read in the Bible, According to your faith is it done unto you. If you plant certain types of seeds in the ground, you have faith they will grow after their kind. This is the way of seeds, and trusting the laws of growth and agriculture, you know that the seeds will come forth after their kind. Faith as mentioned in the Bible is a way of thinking, an attitude of mind, an inner certitude, knowing that the idea you fully accept in your conscious mind will be embodied in your subconscious mind and made manifest. Faith is, in a sense, accepting as true what your reason and senses deny, i.e., a shutting out of the little, rational, analytical, conscious mind and embracing an attitude of complete reliance on the inner power of your subconscious mind.

• Miracles at various shrines throughout the world

It is an established fact that cures have taken place at various shrines throughout the world, such as in Japan, India, Europe, and America. I have visited several of the famous shrines in Japan. At the world famous shrine called Diabutsu is a gigantic divinity of bronze where Buddha is seated with folded hands, and the head is inclined in an attitude of profound contemplative ecstasy. It is 42 feet in height and is called the great Buddha. Here I saw young and old making offerings at its feet. Money, fruit, rice, and oranges were offered. Candles were lit, incense was burned, and prayers of petition recited.

The guide explained the chant of a young girl as she murmured a prayer, bowed low, and placed two oranges as an offering. She also lit a candle. He said she had lost her voice, and it was restored at the shrine. She was thanking Buddha for restoring her voice. She had the simple faith that Buddha would give her back her singing voice if she followed a certain ritual, fasted, and made certain offerings. All this helped to kindle faith and expectancy, resulting in a conditioning of her mind to the point of belief. Her subconscious mind responded to her belief.

To illustrate further the power of imagination and blind belief I will relate the case of a relative of mine who had tuberculosis. His lungs were badly diseased. His son decided to heal his father. He came home to Perth, Western Australia, where his father lived, and said to him that he had met a monk who had returned from one of the healing shrines in Europe. This monk sold him a piece of the true cross. He said that he gave the monk the equivalent of $500 for it.

This young man had actually picked up a splinter of wood from the sidewalk, went to the jeweler's, and had it set in a ring so that it looked real. He told his father that just touching the ring or the cross healed many. He inflamed and fired his father's imagination to the point that the old gentleman snatched the ring from him, placed it over his chest, prayed silently, and went to sleep. In the morning he was healed. All the clinic's tests proved negative.

You know, of course, it was not the splinter of wood from the sidewalk that healed him. It was his imagination aroused to an intense degree, plus the confident expectancy of a

33

perfect healing. Imagination was joined to faith or subjective feeling, and the union of the two brought about a healing. The father never learned of the trick that had been played upon him. If he had, he probably would have had a relapse. He remained completely cured and passed away fifteen years later at the age of 89.

• One universal healing principle

It is a well-known fact that all of the various schools of healing effect cures of the most wonderful character. The most obvious conclusion, which strikes your mind, is that there must be some underlying principle, which is common to them all, namely, the subconscious mind, and the one process of healing is faith.

It will now be in order to recall to your mind once more the following fundamental truths:

First that you possess mental functions which have been distinguished by designating one the conscious mind and the other the subconscious mind.

Secondly, your subconscious mind is constantly amenable to the power of suggestion. Furthermore, your subconscious mind has complete control of the functions, conditions, and sensations of your body.

I venture to believe that all the readers of this book are familiar with the fact that symptoms of almost any disease can be induced in hypnotic subjects by suggestion. For example, a subject in the hypnotic state can develop a high temperature, flushed face, or chills according to the nature of the suggestion given. By experiment, you can suggest to the person that he is paralyzed and cannot walk: it will be so. By illustration, you can hold a cup of cold water under the nose of the hypnotic subject and tell him, "This is full of pepper; smell it!" He will proceed to sneeze. What do you think caused him to sneeze, the water or the suggestion?

If a man says he is allergic to Timothy grass, you can place a synthetic flower or an empty glass in front of his nose, when he is in a hypnotic state, and tell him it is Timothy grass. He will portray the usual allergic symptoms. This indicates that the cause of the disease is in the mind. The healing of the disease can also take place mentally.

You realize that remarkable healings take place through osteopathy, chiropractic medicine, and naturopathy, as well as through all the various religious bodies throughout the world, but it is obvious that all of these healings are brought about through the subconscious mind—the only healer there is.

Notice how it heals a cut on your face caused by shaving. It knows exactly how to do it. The doctor dresses the wound and says, "Nature heals it!" Nature refers to natural law, the law of the subconscious mind, or self-preservation, which is the function of the subconscious mind. The instinct of self-preservation is the first law of nature. Your strongest instinct is the most potent of all autosuggestions.

• Widely different theories

It would be tedious and unprofitable to discuss to any great extent the numerous theories advanced by different religious sects and prayer therapy groups. There are a great number who claim that because their theory produces results it is, therefore, the correct one. This, as explained in this chapter, cannot be true.

You are aware that there are all types of healing. Franz Anton Mesmer, an Austrian physician (1734-1815) who practiced in Paris, discovered that by applying magnets to the diseased body, he could cure that disease miraculously. He also performed cures with various other pieces of glass and metals. He discontinued this form of healing and claimed that his cures were due to "animal magnetism," theorizing that this substance was projected from the healer to the patient.

His method of treating disease from then on was by hypnotism, which was called mesmerism in his day. Other physicians said that all his healings were due to suggestion and nothing else.

All of these groups, such as psychiatrists, psychologists, osteopaths, chiropractors, physicians, and all the churches are using the one universal power resident in the subconscious mind. Each may proclaim the healings are due to their theory. The process of all healing is a definite, positive, mental attitude, an inner attitude, or a way of thinking, called faith. Healing is due to a confident expectancy, which acts as a powerful suggestion to the subconscious mind releasing its healing potency.

One man does not heal by a different power than another. It is true he may have his own theory or method. There is only one process of healing and that is faith. There is only one healing power, namely, your subconscious mind. Select the theory and method you prefer. You can rest assured, if you have faith, you shall get results.

• Views of Paracelsus

Philippus Paracelsus, a famous Swiss alchemist and physician, who lived from 1493 to 1541, was a great healer in his day. He stated what is now an obvious scientific fact when he uttered these words, "Whether the object of your faith be real or false, you will nevertheless obtain the same effects. Thus, if I believed in Saint Peter's statue as I should have believed in Saint Peter himself, I shall obtain the same effects that I should have obtained from Saint Peter. But that is superstition. Faith, however, produces miracles; and whether it is true or false faith, it will always produce the same wonders."

The views of Paracelsus were also entertained in the sixteenth century by Pietro Pomponazzi, an Italian philosopher and contemporary of Paracelsus, who said, "We can easily conceive the marvelous effects which confidence and imagination can produce, particularly when both qualities are reciprocated between the subjects and the person who influences them. The cures attributed to the influence of certain relics are the effect of their imagination and confidence. Quacks and philosophers know that if the bones of any skeleton were put in place of the saint's bones, the sick would none the less experience beneficial effects, if they believed that they were veritable relics."

Then, if you believe in the bones of saints to heal, or if you believe in the healing power of certain waters, you will gel results because of the powerful suggestion given to your subconscious mind. It is the latter that does the healing.

• Bernheitn's experiments

Hippolyte Bernheim, professor of medicine at Nancy, France, 1910-1919, was the expounder of the fact that the suggestion of the physician to the patient was exerted through the subconscious mind.

Bernheim, in his Suggestive Therapeutics, page 197, tells a story of a man with paralysis of the tongue which had yielded to no form of treatment. His doctor told the patient that he had a new instrument with which he promised to heal him. He introduced a pocket thermometer into the patient's mouth. The patient imagined it to be the instrument, which was to save him. In a few moments he cried out joyfully that he could once more move his tongue freely.

"Among our cases," continues Bernheim, "facts of the same sort will be found. A young girl came into my office, having suffered from complete loss of speech for nearly four weeks. After making sure of the diagnosis, I told my students that loss of speech sometimes yielded instantly to electricity, which might act simply by its suggestive influence. I sent for the induction apparatus. I applied my hand over the larynx and moved a little, and said, 'Now you can speak aloud.' In an instant I made her saw 'a,' then 'b,' then 'Maria.' She continued to speak distinctly; the loss of voice had disappeared."

Here Bernheim is showing the power of faith and expectancy on the part of the patient, which acts as a powerful suggestion to the subconscious mind.

• Producing a blister by suggestion

Bernheim states that he produced a blister on the back of a patient's neck by applying a postage stamp and suggesting to the patient that it was a fly-plaster. This has been confirmed by the experiments and experiences of many doctors in many parts of the world, which leave no doubt that structural change, are a possible result of oral suggestion to patients.

• The cause of bloody stigmata

In Hudson's Law of Psychic Phenomena, page 153, he states, "Hemorrhages and bloody stigmata may be induced in certain subjects by means of suggestion.

"Dr. M. Bourru put a subject into the somnambulistic condition, and gave him the following suggestion: 'At four o'clock this afternoon, after the hypnosis, you will come into my office, sit down in the armchair, cross your arms upon your breast, and your nose will begin to bleed.' At the hour appointed the young man did as directed. Several drops of blood came from the left nostril.

"On another occasion the same investigator traced the patient's name on both his forearms with the dull point of an instrument. Then when the patient was in the somnambulistic condition, he said, 'At four o'clock this afternoon you will go to sleep, and your arms will bleed along the lines which I have traced, and your name will appear written on your arms in letters of blood.' He was watched at four o'clock and seen to fall asleep. On the left arm the letters stood out in bright relief, and in several places there were drops of blood. The letters were still visible three months afterward, although they had gradually grown faint."

These facts demonstrate at once the correctness of the two fundamental propositions previously stated, namely, the constant amenability of the subconscious mind to the power of suggestion and the perfect control, which the subconscious mind exercises, over the functions, sensations, and conditions of the body.

All the foregoing phenomena dramatize vividly abnormal conditions induced by suggestion, and are conclusive proof that as a man thinketh in his heart [subconscious mind] so is he.

• Healing points in review

1. Remind yourself frequently that the healing power is in your own subconscious mind.

2. Know that faith is like a seed planted in the ground; it grows after its kind. Plant the idea (seed) in your mind, water and fertilize it with expectancy, and it will manifest.

3. The idea you have for a book, new invention, or play is real in your mind. This is why you can believe you have it now. Believe in the reality of your idea, plan, or invention, and as you do, it will become manifest.

4. In praying for another, know that your silent inner knowing of wholeness, beauty, and perfection can change the negative patterns of the other's subconscious mind and bring about wonderful results.

5. The miraculous healings you hear about at various shrines are due to imagination and blind faith which act on the subconscious mind, releasing the healing power.

6. All disease originates in the mind. Nothing appears on the body unless there is a mental pattern corresponding to it.

7. The symptoms of almost any disease can be induced in you by hypnotic suggestion. This shows you the power of your thought.

8. There is only one process of healing and that is faith. There is only one healing power, namely, your subconscious mind.

9. Whether the object of your faith is real or false, you will get results. Your subconscious mind responds to the thought in your mind. Look upon faith as a thought in your mind, and that will suffice.

Chapter 5: Mental Healings in Modern Times

Everyone is definitely concerned with the healing of bodily conditions and human affairs. What is it that heals? Where is this healing power? These are questions asked by everyone. The answer is that this healing power is ha the subconscious mind of each person, and a changed mental attitude on the part of the sick person releases this healing power.

No mental or religious science practitioner, psychologist, psychiatrist, or medical doctor ever healed a patient. There is an old saying, "The doctor dresses the wound, but God heals it." The psychologist or psychiatrist proceeds to remove the mental blocks in the patient so that the healing principle may be released, restoring the patient to health. Likewise, the surgeon removes the physical block enabling the healing currents to function normally. No physician, surgeon, or mental science practitioner claims, "he healed the patient." The one healing power is called by many names—Nature, Life, God, Creative Intelligence, and Subconscious Power.

As previously outlined, there are many different methods used to remove the mental, emotional, and physical blocks which inhibit the flow of the healing life principle animating all of us. The healing principle resident in your subconscious mind can and will, if properly directed by you or some other person, heal your mind and body of all disease. This healing principle is operative in all men regardless of creed, color, or race. You do not have to belong to some particular church in order to use and participate in this healing process. Your subconscious will heal the burn or cut on your hand even though you profess to be an atheist or agnostic.

The modern mental therapeutic procedure is based on the truth that the infinite intelligence and power of your subconscious mind responds according to your faith. The mental science practitioner or minister follows the injunction of the Bible, i.e., he goes into his closet and shuts the door, which means he stills his mind, relaxes, lets go, and thinks of the infinite healing presence within him. He closes the door of his mind to all outside distractions as well as appearances, and then he quietly and knowingly turns over his request or desire to his subconscious mind, realizing that the intelligence of his mind will answer him according to his specific needs.

The most wonderful thing to know is this: Imagine the end desired and feel its reality; then the infinite life principle will respond to your conscious choice and your conscious request. This is the meaning of believe you have received, and you shall receive. This is what the modern mental scientist does when he practices prayer therapy.

• One process of healing

There is only one universal healing principle operating through everything—the cat, the dog, the tree, the grass, the wind, the earth—for everything is alive. This life principle operates through the animal, vegetable, and mineral kingdoms as instinct and the law of growth. Man is consciously aware of this life principle, and he can consciously direct it to bless himself in countless ways.

There are many different approaches, techniques, and methods in using the universal power, but there is only one process of healing, which is faith, for according to your faith is it done unto you.

• The law of belief

All religions of the world represent forms of belief, and these beliefs are explained in many ways. The law of life is belief. What do you believe about yourself, life, and the universe? It is done unto you, as you believe.

Belief is a thought in your mind, which causes the power of your subconscious to be distributed into all phases of your life according to your thinking habits. You must realize the Bible is not talking about your belief in some ritual, ceremony, form, institution, man, or formula. It is talking about belief itself. The belief of your mind is simply the thought of your mind. If thou canst believe, all things are possible to him that believeth.

It is foolish to believe in something to hurt or harm you. Remember, it is not the thing believed in that hurts or harms you, but the belief or thought in your mind, which creates the result. All your experiences, all your actions, and all the events and circumstances of your life are but the reflections and reactions to your own thought.

• Prayer therapy is the combined function of the conscious and subconscious mind scientifically directed

Prayer therapy is the synchronized, harmonious, and intelligent function of the conscious and subconscious levels of mind specifically directed for a definite purpose. In scientific prayer or prayer therapy, you must know what you are doing and why you are doing it. You trust the law of healing. Prayer therapy is sometimes referred to as mental treatment, and another term is scientific prayer.

In prayer therapy you consciously choose a certain idea, mental picture, or plan which you desire to experience. You realize your capacity to convey this idea or mental image to your subconscious by feeling the reality of the state assumed. As you remain faithful in your mental attitude, your prayer will be answered. Prayer therapy is a definite mental action for a definite specific purpose.

Let us suppose that you decide to heal a certain difficulty by prayer therapy. You are aware that your problem or sickness, whatever it may be, must be caused by negative thoughts charged with fear and lodged in your subconscious mind, and that if you can succeed in cleansing your mind of these thoughts, you will get a healing.

You, therefore, turn to the healing power within your own subconscious mind and remind yourself of its infinite power and intelligence and its capacity to heal all conditions. As you dwell on these truths, your fear will begin to dissolve, and the recollection of these truths also corrects the erroneous beliefs.

You give thanks for the healing that you know will come, and then you keep your mind off the difficulty until you feel guided, after an interval, to pray again. While you are praying, you absolutely refuse to give any power to the negative conditions or to admit for a second that the healing will not come. This attitude of mind brings about the harmonious union of the conscious and subconscious mind, which releases the healing power.

• Faith healing, what it means, and how blind faith works

What is popularly termed faith healing is not the faith mentioned in the Bible, which means knowledge of the interaction of the conscious and subconscious mind. A faith healer is one who heals without any real scientific understanding of the powers and forces involved. He may claim that he has a special gift of healing, and the sick person's blind belief in him or his powers may bring results.

The voodoo doctor in South Africa and other parts of the world may heal by incantations, or touching the so-called bones of saints, or anything else may heal a person, which cause the patients to honestly believe in the method or process.

Any method, which causes you to move from fear and worry to faith and expectancy, will heal. There are many persons, each of whom claims that because his personal theory produces results, it is, therefore, the correct one. This, as already explained in this chapter, cannot be true.

To illustrate how blind faith works: You will recall our discussion of the Swiss physician, Franz Anton Mesmer. In 1776 he claimed many cures when he stroked diseased bodies with artificial magnets. Later on he threw away his magnets and evolved the theory of animal magnetism. This he held to be a fluid, which pervades the universe, but is most active in the human organism.

He claimed that this magnetic fluid, which was going forth from him to his patients, healed them. People flocked to him, and many wonderful cures were affected.

Mesmer moved to Paris, and while there the Government appointed a commission composed of physicians and members of the Academy of Science, of which Benjamin Franklin was a member, to investigate his cures. The report admitted the leading facts claimed by Mesmer, but held that there was no evidence to prove the correctness of his magnetic fluid theory, and said the effects were due to the imagination of the patients.

Soon after this, Mesmer was driven into exile, and died in 1815. Shortly afterwards, Dr. Braid of Manchester undertook to show that magnetic fluid had nothing to do with the production of the healings of Dr. Mesmer. Dr. Braid discovered that patients could be thrown into hypnotic sleep by suggestion, during which many of the well-known phenomena ascribed to magnetism by Mesmer could be produced.

You can readily see that all these cures were undoubtedly brought about by the active imagination of the patients together with a powerful suggestion of health to their subconscious minds. All this could be termed blind faith, as there was no understanding in those days as to how the cures were brought about.

• Subjective faith and what it means

You will recall the proposition, which need not be repeated at length, that the subjective or subconscious mind of an individual is as amenable to the control of his own conscious or objective mind as it is by the suggestions of another. It follows that whatever may be your objective belief, if you will assume to have faith actively or passively, your subconscious mind will be controlled by the suggestion, and your desire will be fulfilled.

The faith required in mental healings is a purely subjective faith, and it is attainable upon the cessation of active opposition on the part of the objective or conscious mind.

 In the healing of the body it is, of course, desirable to secure the concurrent faith of both the conscious and subconscious mind. However, it is not always essential if you will enter into a state of passivity and receptivity by relaxing the mind and the body and getting into a sleepy state. In this drowsy state your passivity becomes receptive to subjective impression.

Recently, I was asked by a man, "How is it that I got a healing through a minister? I did not believe what he said when he told me that there is no such thing as disease and that matter does not exist."

This man at first thought his intelligence was being insulted, and he protested against such a palpable absurdity. The explanation is simple. He was quieted by soothing words and told to get into a perfectly passive condition, to say nothing, and think of nothing for the time being. His minister also became passive, and affirmed quietly, peacefully, and constantly for about one half hour that this man would have perfect health, peace, harmony, and wholeness. He felt immense relief and was restored to health.

It is easy to see that his subjective faith had been made manifest by his passivity under treatment, and the suggestions of perfect healthfulness by the minister were conveyed to his subconscious mind. The two subjective minds were then en rapport.

The minister was not handicapped by antagonistic autosuggestions of the patient arising from objective doubt of the power of the healer or the correctness of the theory. In this sleepy, drowsy state the conscious mind resistance is reduced to a minimum, and results followed. The subconscious mind of the patient being necessarily controlled by such suggestion exercised its functions in accordance therewith, and a healing followed.

• The meaning of absent treatment

Suppose you learned that your mother was sick in New York City and you lived in Los Angeles. Your mother would not be physically present where you are, but you could pray for her. It is the Father within which doeth the work.

The creative law of mind (subconscious mind) serves you and will do the work. Its response to you is automatic. Your treatment is for the purpose of inducing an inner realization of health and harmony in your mentality. This inner realization, acting through the subconscious mind, operates through your mother's subconscious mind as there is but one creative mind. Your thoughts of health, vitality, and perfection operate through the one universal subjective mind, and set a law in motion on the subjective side of life, which manifests through her body as a healing.

In the mind principle there is no time or space. It is the same mind that operates through your mother no matter where she may be. In reality there is no absent treatment as opposed to present treatment for the universal mind is omnipresent. You do not try to send out thoughts or hold a thought. Your treat-ment is a conscious movement of thought, and as you become conscious of the qualities of health, well-being, and relaxation, these qualities will be resurrected in the experience of your mother, and results will follow.

The following is a perfect example of what is called absent treatment. Recently, a listener of our radio program in Los Angeles prayed as follows for her mother in New York who had a coronary thrombosis: "The healing presence is right where my mother is. Her bodily condition is but a reflection of her thought-life like shadows cast on the screen. I know that in order to change the images on the screen I must change the projection reel. My mind is the projection reel, and I now project in my own mind the image of wholeness, harmony, and perfect health for my mother. The infinite healing presence, which created my mother's body and all her organs is now saturating every atom of her being, and a river of peace, flows through every cell of her body. The doctors are divinely guided and directed, and whoever touches my mother is guided to do the right thing. I know that disease has no ultimate reality; if it had, no one could be healed. I now align

41

myself with the infinite principle of love and life, and I know and decree that harmony, health, and peace are now being expressed in my mother's body."

She prayed in the above manner several times daily, and her mother had a most remarkable recovery after a few days, much to the amazement of her specialist. He complimented her on her great faith in the power of God.

The conclusion arrived at in the daughter's mind set the creative law of mind in motion on the subjective side of life, which manifested itself through her mother's body as perfect health and harmony. What the daughter felt as true about her mother was simultaneously resurrected in the experience of her mother.

• Releasing the kinetic action of the subconscious mind

A psychologist friend of mine told me that one of his lungs was infected. X rays and analysis showed the presence of tuberculosis. At night before going to sleep he would quietly affirm, "Every cell, nerve, tissue, and muscle of my lungs are now being made whole, pure, and perfect. My whole body is being restored to health and harmony."

These are not his exact words, but they represent the essence of what he affirmed. A complete healing followed in about a month's time. Subsequent X rays showed a perfect healing.

I wanted to know his method, so I asked him why he repeated the words prior to sleep. Here is his reply, "The kinetic action of the subconscious mind continues throughout your sleep-time period. Hence, give the subconscious mind something good to work on as you drop off into slumber." This was a very wise answer. In thinking of harmony and perfect health, he never mentioned his trouble by name.

I strongly suggest that you cease talking about your ailments or giving them a name. The only sap from which they draw life is your attention and fear of them. Like the above-mentioned psychologist, become a mental surgeon. Then your troubles will be cut off, like dead branches are pruned from a tree.

If you are constantly naming your aches and symptoms, you inhibit the kinetic action, which means the release of the healing power and energy of your subconscious mind. Furthermore, by the law of your own mind, these imaginings tend to take shape, as the thing I greatly feared. Fill your mind with the great truths of life and walk forward in the light of love.

• Summary of your aids to health

1. Find out what it is that heals you. Realize that correct directions given to your subconscious mind will heal your mind and body.

2. Develop a definite plan for turning over your requests or desires to your subconscious mind.

3. Imagine the end desired and feel its reality. Follow it through, and you will get definite results.

4. Decide what belief is. Know that belief is a thought in your mind, and what you think you create.

5. It is foolish to believe in sickness and something to hurt or to harm you. Believe in perfect health, prosperity, peace, wealth, and divine guidance.

6. Great and noble thoughts upon which you habitually dwell become great acts.

7. Apply the power of prayer therapy in your life. Choose a certain plan, idea, or mental picture. Mentally and emotionally unite with that idea, and as you remain faithful to your mental attitude, your prayer will be answered.

8. Always remember, if you really want the power to heal, you can have it through faith, which means knowledge of the working of your conscious and subconscious mind. Faith comes with understanding.

9. Blind faith means that a person may get results in healing without any scientific understanding of the powers and forces involved.

10. Learn to pray for your loved ones who may be ill. Quiet your mind, and your thoughts of health, vitality, and perfection operating through the one universal subjective mind will be felt and resurrected in the mind of your loved one.

Chapter 6: Practical Techniques in Mental Healings

An engineer has a technique and a process for building a bridge or an engine. Like the engineer, your mind also has a technique for governing, controlling, and directing your life. You must realize that methods and techniques are primary.

In building the Golden Gate Bridge, the chief engineer understood mathematical principles, stresses and strains. Secondly, he had a picture of the ideal bridge across the bay. The third step was his application of tried and proven methods by which the principles were implemented until the bridge took form and we drive on it. There also are techniques and methods by which your prayers are answered. If your prayer is answered, there is a way in which it is answered, and this is a scientific way. Nothing happens by chance. This is a world of law and order. In this chapter you will find practical techniques for the unfolding and nurture of your spiritual life. Your prayers must not remain up in the air like a balloon. They must go somewhere and accomplish something in your life.

When we come to analyze prayer we discover there are many different approaches and methods. We will not consider in this book the formal, ritual prayers used in religious services. These have important place in group worship. We are immediately concerned with the methods of personal prayer as it is applied in your daily life and as it is used to help others.

Prayer is the formulation of an idea concerning something we wish to accomplish. Prayer is the soul's sincere desire. Your desire is your prayer. It comes out of your deepest needs and it reveals the things you want in life. Blessed are they that hunger and thirst after righteousness: for they shall be filled. That is really prayer, life's hunger and thirst for peace, harmony, health, joy, and all the other blessings of life.

• The passing-over technique for impregnating the subconscious

This consists essentially in inducing the subconscious mind to take over your request as handed it by the conscious mind. This passing over is best accomplished in the reverie-like state. Know that in your deeper mind are Infinite Intelligence and Infinite Power. Just calmly think over what you want; see it coming into fuller fruition from this moment forward. Be like the little girl who had a very bad cough and a sore throat. She declared firmly and repeatedly, "It is passing away now. It is passing away now." It passed away in about an hour. Use this technique with complete simplicity and naïveté.

• Your subconscious will accept your blueprint

If you were building a new home for yourself and family, you know that you would be intensely interested in regard to the blueprint for your home; you would see to it that the builders conformed to the blueprint. You would watch the material and select only the best wood, steel, in fact, the best of everything. What about your mental home and your mental blueprint for happiness and abundance? All your experiences and everything that enters into your life depend upon the nature of the mental building blocks, which you use in the construction of your mental home.

If your blueprint is full of mental patterns of fear, worry, anxiety, or lack, and if you are despondent, doubtful, and cynical, then the texture of the mental material you are weaving into your mind will come forth as more toil, care, tension, anxiety, and limitation of all kinds.

The most fundamental and the most far-reaching activity in life is that which you build into your mentality every waking hour. Your word is silent and invisible; nevertheless, it is real.

You are building your mental home all the time, and your thought and mental imagery represent your blueprint. Hour by hour, moment by moment, you can build radiant health, success, and happiness by the thoughts you think, the ideas which you harbor, the beliefs that you accept, and the scenes that you rehearse in the hidden studio of your mind. This stately mansion, upon the construction of which you are perpetually engaged, is your personality, your identity in this plane, your whole life story on this earth.

Get a new blueprint; build silently by realizing peace, harmony, joy, and good will in the present moment. By dwelling upon these things and claiming them, your subconscious will accept your blueprint and bring all these things to pass. By their fruits ye shall know them.

• The science and art of true prayer

The term "science" means knowledge, which is coordinated, arranged, and systematized. Let us think of the science and art of true prayer as it deals with the fundamental principles of life and the techniques and processes by which they can be demonstrated in your life, as well as in the life of every human being when he applies them faithfully. The art is your technique or process, and the science behind it is the definite response of creative mind to your mental picture or thought.

Ask, and it shall be given you; seek, and ye shall find; knock, and it shall be opened unto you.

Here you are told you shall receive that for which you ask. It shall be opened to you when you knock, and you shall find that for which you are searching. This teaching implies the definiteness of mental and spiritual laws. There is always a direct response from the Infinite Intelligence of your subconscious mind to your conscious thinking. If you ask for bread, you will not receive a stone. You must ask believing, if you are to receive. Your mind moves from the thought to the thing. Unless there is first an image in the mind, it cannot move, for there would be nothing for it to move toward. Your prayer, which is your mental act must be accepted as an image in your mind before the power from your subconscious will play upon it and make it productive. You must reach a point of acceptance in your mind, an unqualified and undisputed state of agreement.

This contemplation should be accompanied by a feeling of joy and restfulness in foreseeing the certain accomplishment of your desire. The sound basis for the art and science of true prayer is your knowledge and complete confidence that the movement of your conscious mind will gain a definite response from your subconscious mind, which is one with boundless wisdom and infinite power. By following this procedure, your prayers will be answered.

• The visualization technique

The easiest and most obvious way to formulate an idea is to visualize it, to see it in your mind's eye as vividly as if it were alive. You can see with the naked eye only what already exists in the external world; in a similar way, that which you can visualize in your mind's eye already exists in the invisible realms of your mind. Any picture, which you have in your mind, is the substance of things hoped for and the evidence of things not seen. What you form in your imagination is as real as any part of your body. The idea and the thought are real and will one day appear in your objective world if you are faithful to your mental image.

This process of thinking forms impressions in your mind; these impressions in turn become manifested as facts and experiences in your life. The builder visualizes the type of building he wants; he sees it as he desires it to be completed. His imagery and thought-processes become a plastic mold from which the building will emerge—a beautiful or an ugly one, a skyscraper or a very low one. His mental imagery is projected as it is drawn on paper. Eventually, the contractor and his workers gather the essential materials, and the building progresses until it stands finished, conforming perfectly to the mental patterns of the architect.

I use the visualization technique prior to speaking from the platform. I quiet the wheels of my mind in order that I may present to the subconscious mind my images of thought. Then, I picture the entire auditorium and the seats filled with men and women, and each one of them illumined and inspired by the infinite healing presence within each one. I see them as radiant, happy, and free.

Having first built up the idea in my imagination, I quietly sustain it there as a mental picture while I imagine I hear men and women saying, "I am healed," "I feel wonderful," "I've had an instantaneous healing," "I'm transformed." I keep this up for about ten minutes or more, knowing and feeling that each person's mind and body are saturated with love, wholeness, beauty, and perfection. My awareness grows to the point where in my mind I can actually hear the voices of the multitude proclaiming their health and happiness; then I release the whole picture and go onto the platform. Almost every Sunday some people stop and say that their prayers were answered.

• Mental movie method

The Chinese say, "A picture is worth a thousand words." William James, the father of American psychology, stressed the fact that the subconscious mind will bring to pass any picture held in the mind and backed by faith. Act as though I am, and I will be.

A number of years ago I was in the Middle West lecturing in several states, and I desired to have a permanent location in the general area from which I could serve those who desired help. I traveled far, but the desire did not leave my mind. One evening, while in a hotel in Spokane, Washington, I relaxed completely on a couch, immobilized my attention, and in a quiet, passive manner imagined that I was talking to a large audience, saying in effect, "I am glad to be here; I have prayed for the ideal opportunity." I saw in my mind's eye the imaginary audience, and I felt the reality of it all. I played the role of the actor, dramatized this mental movie, and felt satisfied that this picture was being conveyed to my subconscious mind, which would bring it to pass in its own way. The next morning, on awakening, I felt a great sense of peace and satisfaction, and in a few days' time I received a telegram asking me to take over an organization in the Midwest, which I did, and I enjoyed it immensely for several years.

The method outlined here appeals to many who have described it as "the mental movie method." I have received numerous letters from people who listen to my radio talks and weekly public lectures, telling me of the wonderful results they get using this technique in the sale of their property. I suggest to those who have homes or property for sale that they satisfy themselves in their own mind that their price is right. Then, I claim that the Infinite Intelligence is attracting to them the buyer who really wants to have the property and who will love it and prosper in it. After having done this I suggest that they quiet their mind, relax, let go, and get into a drowsy, sleepy state, which reduces all mental effort to a minimum. Then, they are to picture the check in their hands, rejoice in the check, give thanks for the check, and go off to sleep feeling the naturalness of the whole mental movie created in their own mind. They must act as though it were an objective reality, and the subconscious mind will take it as an impression, and through the deeper currents of the mind the buyer and the seller are brought together. A mental picture held in the mind, backed by faith, will come to pass.

• The Baudoin technique

Charles Baudoin was a professor at the Rousseau Institute in France. He was a brilliant psychotherapist and a research director of the New Nancy School of Healing, who in 1910 taught that the best way to impress the subconscious mind was to enter into a drowsy, sleepy state, or a state akin to sleep in which all effort was reduced to a minimum. Then in a quiet, passive, receptive way, by reflection, he would convey the idea to the subconscious. The following is his formula: "A very simple way of securing this (impregnation of the subconscious mind) is to condense the idea which is to be the object of suggestion, to sum it up in a brief phrase which can be readily graven on the memory, and to repeat it over and over again as a lullaby."

Some years ago, a young lady in Los Angeles was engaged in a prolonged bitter family lawsuit over a will. Her husband had bequeathed his entire estate to her, and his sons and daughters by a previous marriage were bitterly fighting to break the will. The Baudoin technique was outlined to her, and this is what she did: She relaxed her body in an armchair, entered into the sleepy state and, as suggested, condensed the idea of her need into a phrase consisting of six words easily graven on the memory. "It is finished in Divine Order." The significance to her of these words meant that Infinite Intelligence operating through the laws of her subconscious mind would bring about a harmonious adjustment through the principle of harmony. She continued this procedure every night for about ten nights. After she got into a sleepy state, she would affirm slowly, quietly, and feelingly the statement: "It is finished in Divine Order," over and over again, feeling a sense of inner peace and an all-pervading tranquility; then she went off into her deep, normal sleep.

On the morning of the eleventh day, following the use of the above technique, she awakened with a sense of well-being, a conviction that it was finished. Her attorney called her the same day, saying that the opposing attorney and his clients were willing to settle. A harmonious agreement was reached, and litigation was discontinued.

• The sleeping technique

By entering into a sleepy, drowsy state, effort is reduced to a minimum. The conscious mind is submerged to a great extent when in a sleepy state. The reason for this is that the highest degree of outcropping of the subconscious occurs prior to sleep and just after we awaken. In this state the negative thoughts, which tend to neutralize your desire and so prevent acceptance by your subconscious mind, are no longer present.

Suppose you want to get rid of a destructive habit. Assume a comfortable posture, relax your body, and be still. Get into a sleepy state, and in that sleepy state, say quietly, over and over again as a lullaby, "I am completely free from this habit; harmony and peace of mind reign supreme." Repeat the above slowly, quietly, and lovingly for five or ten minute's night and morning. Each time you repeat the words the emotional value becomes greater. When the urge comes to repeat the negative habit, repeat the above formula out loud by yourself. By this means you induce the subconscious to accept the idea, and a healing follows.

• The "thank-you" technique

In the Bible, Paul recommends that we make known our requests with praise and thanksgiving. Some extraordinary results follow this simple method of prayer. The thankful heart is always close to the creative forces of the universe, causing countless blessings to flow toward it by the law of reciprocal relationship, based on a cosmic law of action and reaction.

For instance, a father promises his son a car for graduation; the boy has not yet received the car, but he is very thankful and happy, and is as joyous as though he had actually received the car. He knows his father will fulfill his promise, and he is full of gratitude and joy even though he has not yet received the car, objectively speaking. He has, however, received it with joy and thankfulness in his mind.

I shall illustrate how Mr. Broke applied this technique with excellent results. He said, "Bills are piling up, I am out of work, I have three children and no money. What shall I do?" Regularly every night and morning, for a period of about three weeks, he repeated the words, "Thank you, Father, for my wealth," in a relaxed, peaceful manner until the feeling or mood of thankfulness dominated his mind. He imagined he was addressing the infinite power and intelligence within him knowing, of course, that he could not see the creative intelligence or infinite mind. He was seeing with the inner eye of spiritual perception, realizing that his thought-image of wealth was the first cause, relative to the money, position, and food he needed. His thought feeling was the substance of wealth untrammeled by antecedent conditions of any kind. By repeating, "Thank you, Father," over and over again, his mind and heart were lifted up to the point of acceptance, and when fear, thoughts of lack, poverty, and distress came into his mind, he would say, "Thank you, Father," as often as necessary. He knew that as he kept up the thankful attitude he would recondition his mind to the idea of wealth, which is what happened.

The sequel to his prayer is very interesting. After praying in the above-mentioned manner, he met a former employer of his on the street whom he had not seen for twenty years. The man offered him a very lucrative position and advanced him $500 on a temporary loan. Today, Mr. Broke is vice-president of the company for which he works. His recent remark to me was, "I shall never forget the wonders of 'Thank you, Father.' It has worked wonders for me."

• The affirmative method

The effectiveness of an affirmation is determined largely by your understanding of the truth and the meaning back of the words, "In praying use not vain repetition." Therefore, the power of your affirmation lies in the intelligent application of definite and specific positives. For example, a boy adds three and three and puts down seven on the blackboard. The teacher affirms with mathematical certainty that three and three are six; therefore, the boy changes his figures accordingly. The teacher's statement did not make three and three equal six because the latter was already a mathematical truth. The mathematical truth caused the boy to rearrange the figures on the blackboard. It is abnormal to be sick; it is normal to be healthy. Health is the truth of your being. When you affirm health, harmony, and peace for yourself or another, and when you realize these are universal principles of your own being, you will rearrange the negative patterns of your subconscious mind based on your faith and understanding of that which you affirm.

The result of the affirmative process of prayer depends on your conforming to the principles of life, regardless of appearances. Consider for a moment that there is a principle of mathematics and none of error; there is a principle of truth but none of dishonesty. There is a principle of intelligence but none of ignorance; there is a principle of harmony and none of discord. There is a principle of health but none of disease, and there is a principle of abundance but none of poverty.

The affirmative method was chosen by the author for use on his sister who was to be operated on for the removal of gallstones in a hospital in England. The condition described was based on the diagnosis of hospital tests and the usual X-ray procedures. She asked me to pray for her. We were separated geographically about 6,500 miles, but there is no time or space in the mind principle. Infinite mind or intelligence is present in its entirety at every point simultaneously. I withdrew all thought from the contemplation of symptoms and from the corporeal personality altogether. I affirmed as follows: "This prayer is for my sister Catherine. She is relaxed and at peace, poised, balanced, serene, and calm. The healing intelligence of her subconscious mind, which created her body, is now transforming every cell, nerve, tissue, muscle, and bone of her being according to the perfect pattern of all organs lodged in her subconscious mind. Silently, quietly, all distorted thought patterns in her subconscious mind are removed and dissolved, and the vitality, wholeness, and beauty of the life principle are made manifest in every atom of her being. She is now open and receptive to the healing currents, which are flowing through her like a river, restoring her to perfect health, harmony, and peace. All distortions and ugly images are now washed away by the infinite ocean of love and peace flowing through her, and it is so."

I affirmed the above several times a day, and at the end of two weeks my sister had an examination, which showed a remarkable healing, and the X ray proved negative.

To affirm is to state that it is so, and as you maintain this attitude of mind as true, regardless of all evidence to the contrary, you will receive an answer to your prayer. Your thought can only affirm, for even if you deny something, you are actually affirming the presence of what you deny. Repeating an affirmation, knowing what you are saying and why you are saying it, leads the mind to that state of consciousness where it accepts that which you state as true. Keep on affirming the truths of life until you get the subconscious reaction, which satisfies.

• The argumentative method

This method is just what the word implies. It stems from the procedure of Dr. Phineas Parkhurst Quimby of Maine. Dr. Quimby, a pioneer in mental and spiritual healing, lived and practiced in Belfast, Maine, about one hundred years ago. A book called The Quimby Manuscripts, published in 1921 by Thomas Y. Crowell Company, New York City, and edited by Horatio Dresser, is available in your library. This book gives newspaper accounts of this man's remarkable results in prayer treatment of the sick. Quimby duplicated many of the healing miracles recorded in the Bible. In brief, the argumentative method employed according to Quimby consists of spiritual reasoning where you convince the patient and yourself that his sickness is due to his false belief, groundless fears, and negative patterns lodged in his subconscious mind. You reason it out clearly in your mind and convince your patient that the disease or ailment is due only to a distorted, twisted pattern of thought, which has taken form in his body. This wrong belief in some external power and external causes has now externalized itself as sickness, and can be changed by changing the thought patterns.

You explain to the sick person that the basis of all healing is a change of belief. You also point out that the subconscious mind created the body and all its organs; therefore, it knows how to heal it, can heal it, and is doing so now as you speak. You argue in the courtroom of your mind that the disease is a shadow of the mind based on disease-soaked, morbid thought-imagery. You continue to build up all the evidence you can muster on behalf of the healing power within, which created all the organs in the first place, and which has a perfect pattern of every cell, nerve, and tissue within it. Then, you render a verdict in the courthouse of your mind in favor of yourself or your patient. You liberate the sick one by faith and spiritual understanding. Your mental and spiritual evidence is overwhelming; they're being but one mind, what you feel as true will be resurrected in the experience of the patient. This procedure is essentially the argumentative method used by Dr. Quimby of Maine from 1849 to 1869.

• The absolute method is like modern sound wave therapy

Many people throughout the world practice this form of prayer treatment with wonderful results. The person using the absolute method mentions the name of the patient, such as John Jones, then quietly and silently thinks of God and His qualities and attributes, such as, God is all bliss, boundless love, infinite intelligence, all-powerful, boundless wisdom, absolute harmony, indescribable beauty, and perfection. As he quietly thinks along these lines he is lifted up in consciousness into a new spiritual wave length, at which times he feels the infinite ocean of God's love is now dissolving everything unlike itself in the mind and body of John Jones for whom he is praying. He feels all the power and love of God are now focused on John Jones, and whatever is bothering or vexing him is now completely neutralized in the presence of the infinite ocean of life and love.

The absolute method of prayer might be likened to the sound wave or sonic therapy recently shown me by a distinguished physician in Los Angeles. He has an ultra sound wave machine, which oscillates at a tremendous speed and sends sound waves to any area of the body to which it is directed. These sound waves can be controlled, and he told me of achieving remarkable results in dissolving arthritic calcareous deposits, as well as the healing and removal of other disturbing conditions.

To the degree that we rise in consciousness by contemplating qualities and attributes of God, do we generate spiritual electronic waves of harmony, health, and peace. Many remarkable healings follow this technique of prayer.

• A cripple walks

Dr. Phineas Parkhurst Quimby, of whom we spoke previously in this chapter, used the absolute method in the latter years of his healing career. He was really the father of psychosomatic medicine and the first psychoanalyst. He had the capacity to diagnose clairvoyantly the cause of the patient's trouble, pains, and aches.

The following is a condensed account of the healing of a cripple as recorded in Quimby's Manuscripts:

Quimby was called on to visit a woman who was lame, aged, and bedridden. He states that her ailment was due to the fact that she was imprisoned by a creed so small and contracted that she could not stand upright and move about. She was living in the tomb of fear and ignorance; furthermore, she was taking the Bible literally, and it frightened her. "In this tomb," Quimby said, "was the presence and power of God trying to burst the bands, break through the bonds, and rise from the dead." When she would ask others for an explanation of some passage of the Bible, the answer would be a stone; then she would hunger for the bread of life. Dr. Quimby diagnosed her case as a mind cloudy and stagnated, due to excitation and fear, caused by the inability to see clearly the meaning of the passage of the Bible, which she had been reading. This showed itself in the body by her heavy and sluggish feeling, which would terminate as paralysis.

Quimby traveled in his mind and contemplated the divine ideal; i.e., the vitality, intelligence, harmony, and power of God functioning in the sick person. This is why he said to the woman, "Therefore, where I go you cannot come, for you are in your narrow, restricted belief, and I am in health." This prayer and explanation produced an instantaneous sensation, and a change came over her mind. She walked without her crutches! Quimby said it was one of the most singular of all his healings. She was, as it were, dead to error, and to bring her to life or truth was to raise her from the dead. He also explained to her that the truth, which she accepted, was the angel or idea, which rolled away the stone of fear, ignorance, and superstition, thereby, releasing the healing power of God, which made her whole.

• The decree method

Power goes into our word according to the feeling and faith behind it. When we realize the power that moves the world is moving on our behalf and is backing up our word, our confidence and assurance grow. You do not try and add power to power; therefore, there must be no mental striving, coercion, force, or mental wrestling.

A young girl used the decree method on a young man who was constantly phoning her, pressing her for dates, and meeting her at her place of business; she found it very difficult to get rid of him. She decreed as follows: "I release.........unto God. He is in his true place at all times. I am free, and he is free. I now decree that my words go forth into infinite mind and it brings it to pass. It is so." She said he vanished and she has never seen him since, adding, "It was as though the ground swallowed him up."

Thou shalt decree a thing, and it shall be established unto thee: and the light shall shine upon thy ways. JOB 22:28.

• Serve yourself with scientific truth

1. Be a mental engineer and use tried and proven techniques in building a grander and greater life.

2. Your desire is your prayer. Picture the fulfillment of your desire now and feel its reality, and you will experience the joy of the answered prayer.

3. Desire to accomplish things the easy way—with the sure aid of mental science.

4. You can build radiant health, success, and happiness by the thoughts you think in the hidden studio of your mind.

5. Experiment scientifically until you personally prove that there is always a direct response from the infinite intelligence of your subconscious mind to your conscious thinking.

6. Feel the joy and restfulness in foreseeing the certain accomplishment of your desire. Any mental picture, which you have in your mind, is the substance of things hoped for and the evidence of things not seen.

7. A mental picture is worth a thousand words. Your subconscious will bring to pass any picture held in the mind backed by faith.

8. Avoid all effort or mental coercion in prayer. Get into a sleepy, drowsy state and lull yourself to sleep feeling and knowing that your prayer is answered.

9. Remember that the thankful heart is always close to the riches of the universe.

10. To affirm is to state that it is so, and as you maintain this attitude of mind as true, regardless of all evidence to the contrary, you will receive an answer to your prayer.

11. Generate electronic waves of harmony, health, and peace by thinking of the love and the glory of God.

12. What you decree and feel as true will come to pass. Decree harmony, health, peace, and abundance.

Chapter 7: The Tendency of the Subconscious Is Lifeward

Over 90 percent of your mental life is subconscious, so men and women who fail to make use of this marvelous power live within very narrow limits.

Your subconscious processes are always lifeward and constructive. Your subconscious is the builder of your body and maintains all its vital functions. It is on the job 24 hours a day and never sleeps. It is always trying to help and preserve you from harm.

Your subconscious mind is in touch with infinite life and boundless wisdom, and its impulses and ideas are always lifeward. The great aspirations, inspirations, and visions for a grander and nobler life, spring from the subconscious. Your profoundest convictions are those you cannot argue about rationally because they do not come from your conscious mind; they come from your subconscious mind. Your subconscious speaks to you in intuitions, impulses, hunches, intimations, urges, and ideas, and it is always telling you to rise, transcend, grow, advance, adventure, and move forward to greater heights. The urge to love, to save the lives of others comes from the depths of your subconscious. For example, during the great San Francisco earthquake and fire of April 18, 1906, invalids and cripples who had been confined to bed for long periods of time, rose up and performed some of the most amazing feats of bravery and endurance. The intense desire welled up within them to save others at all costs, and their subconscious responded accordingly.

Great artists, musicians, poets, speakers, and writers tune in with their subconscious powers and become animated and inspired. For example, Robert Louis Stevenson, before he went to sleep, used to charge his subconscious with the task of evolving stories for him while he slept. He was accustomed to ask his subconscious to give him a good, marketable thriller when his bank account was low. Stevenson said the intelligence of his deeper mind gave him the story piece by piece, like a serial. This shows how your subconscious will speak lofty and wise sayings through you, which your conscious mind knows nothing about.

Mark Twain confided to the world on many occasions that he never worked in his life. All his humor and all his great writings were due to the fact that he tapped the inexhaustible reservoir of his subconscious mind.

• How the body portrays the workings of the mind

The interaction of your conscious and subconscious mind requires a similar interaction between the corresponding system of nerves. The cerebrospinal system is the organ of the conscious mind, and the sympathetic system is the organ of the subconscious mind. The cerebrospinal system is the channel through which you receive conscious perception by means of your five physical senses and exercise control over the movement of your body. This system has its nerves in the brain, and it is the channel of your volitional and conscious mental action.

The sympathetic system, sometimes referred to as the involuntary nervous system, has its center in a ganglionic mass at the back of the stomach known as the solar plexus, and is sometimes spoken of as the abdominal brain. It is the channel of that mental action which unconsciously supports the vital functions of the body.

The two systems may work separately or synchronously. Judge Thomas Troward says[1], "The vaguest nerve passes out of the cerebral region as a portion of the voluntary system, and through it we control the vocal organs; then it passes onward to the thorax sending out branches to the heart and lungs; finally, passing through the diaphragm, it loses the outer coating which distinguishes the nerves of the voluntary system and becomes identified with those of the sympathetic system, so forming a connecting link between the two and making the man physically a single entity.

"Similarly different areas of the brain indicate their connection with the objective and subjective activities of the mind respectively, and speaking in a general way we may assign the frontal portion of the brain to the former and the posterior portion to the latter, while the intermediate portion partakes of the character of both."

A rather simple way of looking at the mental and physical interaction is to realize that your conscious mind grasps an idea, which induces a corresponding vibration in your voluntary system of nerves. This in turn causes a similar current to be generated in your involuntary system of nerves, thus handling the idea over to your subconscious mind, which is the creative medium. This is how your thoughts become things.

Every thought entertained by your conscious mind and accepted as true is sent by your brain to your solar plexus, the brain of your subconscious mind, to be made into your flesh, and to be brought forth into your world as a reality.

• There is an intelligence which takes care of the body

When you study the cellular system and the structure of the organs, such as eyes, ears, heart, liver, bladder, etc., you learn they consist of groups of cells which form a group intelligence whereby they function together and are able to take orders and carry them out in deductive function at the suggestion of the master mind (conscious mind).

A careful study of the single-celled organism shows you what goes on in your complex body. Though the mono-cellular organism has no organs, it still gives evidence of mind action and reaction performing the basic functions of movement, ali-mentation, assimilation, and elimination.

Many say there is an intelligence, which will take care of your body if you let it alone. That is true, but the difficulty is that the conscious mind always interferes with its five-sense evidence based on outer appearances, leading to the sway of false beliefs, fears, and mere opinion. When fear, false beliefs, and negative patterns are made to register in your subconscious mind through psychological, emotional conditioning, there is no other course open to the subconscious mind except to act on the blueprint specifications offered it.

• The subconscious mind works continually for the common good

The subjective self within you works continuously for the general good, reflecting an innate principle of harmony behind all things. Your subconscious mind has its own will, and it is a very real something in itself. It acts night and day whether you act upon it or not. It is the builder of your body, but you cannot see, hear, or feel it building, as all this is a silent process. Your subconscious has a life of its own which is always moving toward

---

[1] The Edinburgh Lectures on Mental Science (New York: Robert McBride & Co.).

54

harmony, health, and peace. This is the divine norm within it seeking expression through you at all times.

• How man interferes with the innate principle of harmony

To think correctly, scientifically, we must know the "Truth." To know the truth is to be in harmony with the infinite intelligence and power of your subconscious mind, which is always moving lifeward.

Every thought or action, which is not harmonious, whether through ignorance or design, will result in discord and limitation of all kinds.

Scientists inform us that you build a new body every eleven months; so you are really only eleven months old from a physical standpoint. If you build defects back into your body by thoughts of fear, anger, jealousy, and ill will, you have no one to blame but yourself.

You are the sum total of your own thoughts. You can keep from entertaining negative thought and imagery. The way to get rid of darkness is with light; the way to overcome cold is with heat; the way to overcome the negative thought is to substitute the good thought. Affirm the good, and the bad will vanish.

• Why it's normal to be healthy, vital, and strong—it's abnormal to be sick

The average child born into the world is perfectly healthy with all its organs functioning perfectly. This is the normal state, and we should remain healthy, vital, and strong. The instinct of self-preservation is the strongest instinct of your nature, and it constitutes a most potent, ever-present, and constantly operative truth, inherent in your nature. It is, therefore, obvious that all your thoughts, ideas, and beliefs must operate with greater potentiality when they are in harmony with the innate life-principle in you, which is forever seeking to preserve and protect you along all lines. It follows from this that normal conditions can be restored with greater ease and certainty than abnormal conditions can be induced.

It is abnormal to be sick; it simply means you are going against the stream of life and thinking negatively. The law of life is the law of growth; all nature testifies to the operation of this law by silently, constantly expressing itself in the law of growth. Where there is growth and expression, there must be life; where there is life there must be harmony, and where there is harmony, there is perfect health.

If your thought is in harmony with the creative principle of your subconscious mind, you are in tune with the innate principle of harmony. If you entertain thoughts which are not in accordance with the principle of harmony, these thoughts cling to you, harass you, worry you, and finally bring about disease, and if persisted in, possibly death.

In the healing of disease, you must increase the inflow and distribution of the vital forces of your subconscious mind throughout your system. This can be done by eliminating thoughts of fear, worry, anxiety, jealousy, hatred, and every other destructive thought which tends to tear down and destroy your nerves and glands—body tissue which controls the elimination of all waste material.

• Pott's disease cured

In the Nautilus magazine of March, 1917, there appears an article about a boy suffering from Pott's disease, or tuberculosis of the spine, who had a remarkable healing. His name was Frederick Elias Andrews of Indianapolis, now minister of Unity School of Christianity, Kansas City, Missouri. His physician pronounced him incurable. He began to pray, and from a crooked, twisted cripple going about on hands and knees, he became a strong, straight, well-formed man. He created his own affirmation, mentally absorbing the qualities he needed.

He affirmed over and over again many times a day, "I am whole, perfect, strong, powerful, loving, harmonious, and happy." He persevered and said that this prayer was the last utterance on his lips at night and the first in the morning. He prayed for others also by sending out thoughts of love and health. This attitude of mind and way of prayer returned to him multiplied many times. His faith and perseverance paid off with big dividends. When thoughts of fear, anger, jealousy, or envy drew his attention, he would immediately start his counteracting force of affirmation going in his mind. His subconscious mind responded according to the nature of his habitual thinking.

• How faith in your subconscious powers makes you whole

A young man, who came to my lectures on the healing power of the subconscious mind, had severe eye trouble, which his doctor said necessitated an operation. He said to himself, "My subconscious made my eyes, and it can heal me."

Each night, as he went to sleep, he entered into a drowsy, meditative state, the condition akin to sleep. His attention was immobilized and focused on the eye doctor. He imagined the doctor was in front of him, and he plainly heard, or imagined he heard, the doctor saying to him, "A miracle has happened!" He heard this over and over again every night for perhaps five minutes or so before going to sleep. At the end of three weeks he again went to the ophthalmologist who had previously examined his eyes, and the physician said to this man, "This is a miracle!" What happened? This man impressed his subconscious mind using the doctor as an instrument or a means of convincing it or conveying the idea. Through repetition, faith, and expectancy he impregnated his subconscious mind. His subconscious mind made his eye; within it was the perfect pattern, and immediately it proceeded to heal the eye. This is another example of how faith in the healing power of your subconscious can make you whole.

Pointers to review

1. Your subconscious is the builder of your body and is on the job 24 hours a day. You interfere with its life-giving patterns by negative thinking.

2. Charge your subconscious with the task of evolving an answer to any problem, prior to sleep and it will answer you.

3. Watch your thoughts. Every thought accepted as true is sent by your brain to your solar plexus—your abdominal brain—and is brought into your world as a reality.

4. Know that you can remake yourself by giving a new blueprint to your subconscious mind.

5. The tendency of your subconscious is always lifeward. Your job is with your conscious mind. Feed your subconscious mind with premises, which are true. Your subconscious is always reproducing according to your habitual mental patterns.

6. You build a new body every eleven months. Change your body by changing your thoughts and keeping them changed.

7. It is normal to be healthy. It is abnormal to be ill. There is within the innate principle of harmony.

8. Thoughts of jealousy, fear, worry, and anxiety tear down and destroy your nerves and glands bringing about mental and physical diseases of all kinds.

9. What you affirm consciously and feel as true will be made manifest in your mind, body and affairs. Affirm the good and enter into the joy of living.

Chapter 8: How to Get the Results You Want

The principle reasons for failure are: Lack of confidence and too much effort. Many people block answers to their prayers by failing to fully comprehend the workings of their subconscious mind. When you know how your mind functions, you gain a measure of confidence. You must remember whenever your subconscious mind accepts an idea; it immediately begins to execute it. It uses all its mighty resources to that end and mobilizes all the mental and spiritual laws of your deeper mind. This law is true for good or bad ideas. Consequently, if you use it negatively, it brings trouble, failure, and confusion. When you use it constructively, it brings guidance, freedom, and peace of mind.

The right answer is inevitable when your thoughts are positive, constructive, and loving. From this it is perfectly obvious that the only thing you have to do in order to overcome failure is to get your subconscious to accept your idea or request by feeling its reality now, and the law of your mind will do the rest. Turn over your request with faith and confidence, and your subconscious will take over and answer for you.

You will always fail to get results by trying to use mental coercion—your subconscious mind does not respond to coercion, it responds to your faith or conscious mind acceptance.

Your failure to get results may also arise from such statements as: "Things are getting worse." "I will never get an answer." "I see no way out." "It is hopeless." "I don't know what to do." "I'm all mixed up." When you use such statements, you get no response or co-operation from your subconscious mind. Like a soldier marking time, you neither go forward nor backward; in other words, you don't get anywhere.

If you get into a taxi and give half dozen different directions to the driver in five minutes, he would become hopelessly confused and probably would refuse to take you anywhere. It is the same when working with your subconscious mind. There must be a clear-cut idea in your mind. You must arrive at the definite decision that there is a way out, a solution to the vexing problem in sickness. Only the infinite intelligence within your subconscious knows the answer. When you come to that clear-cut conclusion in your conscious mind, your mind is then made up, and according to your belief is it done unto you.

• Easy does it

A house owner once remonstrated with a furnace repairman for charging two hundred dollars for fixing the boiler. The mechanic said, "I charged five cents for the missing bolt and one hundred ninety-nine dollars and ninety-five cents for knowing what was wrong." Similarly, your subconscious mind is the master mechanic, the all-wise one, who knows ways and means of healing any organ of your body, as well as your affairs. Decree health, and your subconscious will establish it, but relaxation is the key. "Easy does it." Do not be concerned with details and means, but know the end result. Get the feel of the happy solution to your problem whether it is health, finances, or employment. Remember how you felt after you had recovered from a severe state of illness. Bear in mind that your feeling is the touchstone of all subconscious demonstration. Your new idea must be felt subjectively in a finished state, not the future, but as coming about now.

• Infer no opponent, use imagination and not will power

In using your subconscious mind you infer no opponent, you use no will power. You imagine the end and the freedom state. You will find your intellect trying to get in the way, but persist in maintaining a simple, childlike, miracle-making faith. Picture yourself without the ailment or problem. Imagine the emotional accompaniment of the freedom state you crave. Cut out all red tape from the process. The simple way is the best.

• How disciplined imagination works wonders

A wonderful way to get a response from your subconscious mind is through disciplined or scientific imagination. As previously pointed out, your subconscious mind is the builder of the body and controls all its vital functions.

The Bible says, whatsoever ye shall ask in prayer, believing, ye shall receive. To believe is to accept something as true, or to live in the state of being it. As you sustain this mood, you shall experience the joy of the answered prayer!

• The three steps to success in prayer

The usual procedure is as follows:

1. Take a look at the problem.

2. Turn to the solution or way out known only to the subconscious mind.

3. Rest in a sense of deep conviction that it is done.

Do not weaken your prayer by saying, "I wish I might be healed." "I hope so." Your feeling about the work to be done is "the boss." Harmony is yours. Know that health is yours. Become intelligent by becoming a vehicle for the infinite healing power of the subconscious mind. Pass on the idea of health in your subconscious mind to the point of conviction; then relax. Get yourself off your hands. Say to the condition and circumstance, "This, too, shall pass." Through relaxation you impress your subconscious mind enabling the kinetic energy behind the idea to take over and bring it into concrete realization.

• The law of reversed effort and why you get the opposite of what you pray for

Coué, the famous psychologist from France who visited America about forty years ago, defined the law of reversed effort as follows: "When your desires and imagination are in conflict, your imagination invariably gains the day."

If, for example, you were asked to walk a plank on the floor, you would do so without question. Now suppose the same plank were placed twenty feet up in the air between two walls, would you walk it? Your desire to walk it would be counter-acted by your imagination or fear of falling. Your dominant idea, which would be the picture of falling, would conquer. Your desire, will, or effort to walk on the plank would be reversed, and the dominant idea of failure would be reinforced.

Mental effort is invariably self-defeated, eventuating always in the opposite of what is desired. The suggestions of powerlessness to overcome the condition dominate the mind; your subconscious is always controlled by the dominant idea. Your subconscious will accept the stronger of two contradictory propositions. The effortless way is the better.

If you say, "I want a healing, but I can't get it;" "I try so hard;" "I force myself to pray;" "I use all the will power I have," you must realize that your error lies in your effort. Never try to compel the subconscious mind to accept your idea by exercising will power. Such attempts are doomed to failure, and you get the opposite of what you prayed for.

The following is a rather common experience. Students, when taking examinations and reading through their papers, find that all their knowledge has suddenly deserted them. Their minds become appalling blanks, and they are unable to recall one relevant thought. The more they grit their teeth and summon the powers of the will, the further the answers seem to flee. But, when they have left the examination room and the mental pressure relaxes, the answers they were seeking flow tantalizingly back into their minds. Trying to force themselves to remember was the cause of their failure. This is an example of the law of reversed effort whereby you get the opposite of what you asked or prayed for.

• The conflict of desire and imagination must be reconciled
To use mental force is to presuppose that there is opposition. When your mind is concentrated on the means to overcome a problem, it is no longer concerned with the obstacle.

When there is no longer any quarrel in either part of your mind, your prayer will be answered. The two agreeing may also be represented as you and your desire, your thought and feeling, your idea and emotion, your desire and imagination.

You avoid all conflict between your desires and imagination by entering into a drowsy, sleepy state which brings all effort to a minimum. The conscious mind is submerged to a great extent when in a sleepy state. The best time to impregnate your subconscious is prior to sleep. The reason for this is that the highest degree of outcropping of the subconscious occurs prior to sleep and just after we awaken. In this state the negative thoughts and imagery, which tend to neutralize your desire and so prevent acceptance by your subconscious mind no longer present themselves. When you imagine the reality of the fulfilled desire and feel the thrill of accomplishment, your subconscious brings about the realization of your desire.

A great many people solve all their dilemmas and problems by the play of their controlled, directed, and disciplined imagination, knowing that whatever they imagine and feel as true will and must come to pass.

The following will clearly illustrate how a young girl overcame the conflict between her desire and her imagination. She desired a harmonious solution to her legal problem, yet her mental imagery was constantly on failure, loss, bankruptcy, and poverty. It was a complicated lawsuit and there was one postponement after another with no solution in sight.

At my suggestion, she got into a sleepy, drowsy state each night prior to sleep, and she began to imagine the happy ending, feeling it to the best of her ability. She knew that the image in her mind had to agree with her heart's desire. Prior to sleep she began to dramatize as vividly as possible her lawyer having an animated discussion with her regarding the outcome.

She would ask him questions, and he would answer her appropriately. He would say to her over and over again, "There has been a perfect, harmonious solution. The case has been settled out of court." During the day when fear thoughts came into her mind, she would run her mental movie with gestures, voice, and sound equipment. She could easily imagine the sound of his voice, smile, and mannerism. She ran this mental picture so often; it became a subjective pattern, a regular train track. At the end of a few weeks her attorney called her and confirmed objectively what she had been imagining and feeling as true subjectively.

This is really what the Psalmist meant when he wrote, Let the words of my mouth [your thoughts, mental images, good] and the meditations of my heart [your feeling, nature, emotion] be acceptable in thy sight, O Lord [the law of your subconscious mind], my strength, and my redeemer [the power and wisdom of your subconscious mind can redeem you from sickness, bondage, and misery]. PSALM 19:14.

• Ideas worth recalling

1. Mental coercion or too much effort shows anxiety and fear, which block your answer. Easy does it.

2. When your mind is relaxed and you accept an idea, your subconscious goes to work to execute the idea.

3. Think and plan independently of traditional methods. Know that there is always an answer and a solution to every problem.

4. Do not be overly concerned with the beating of your heart, with the breathing of your lungs, or the functions of any part of your anatomy. Lean heavily upon your subconscious and proclaim frequently that Divine right action is taking place.

5. The feeling of health produces health; the feeling of wealth produces wealth. How do you feel?

6. Imagination is your most powerful faculty. Imagine what is lovely and of good report. You are what you imagine yourself to be.

7. You avoid conflict between your conscious and subconscious in the sleepy state. Imagine the fulfillment of your desire over and over again prior to sleep. Sleep in peace and wake in joy.

Chapter 9: How to Use the Power of Your Subconscious for Wealth

If you are having financial difficulties, if you are trying to make ends meet, it means you have not convinced your subconscious mind that you will always have plenty and some to spare. You know men and women who work a few hours a week and make fabulous sums of money. They do not strive or slave hard. Do not believe the story that the only way you can become wealthy is by the sweat of your brow and hard labor. It is not so; the effortless way of life is the best. Do the thing you love to do, and do it for the joy and thrill of it.

I know an executive in Los Angeles who receives a salary of $75,000 yearly. Last year he went on a nine-month cruise seeing the world and its beauty spots. He said to me that he had succeeded in convincing his subconscious mind that he is worth that much money. He told me that many men in his organization getting about one hundred dollars a week knew more about the business than he did, and could manage it better, but they had no ambition, no creative ideas, and were not interested in the wonders of their subconscious mind.

• Wealth is of the mind

Wealth is simply a subconscious conviction on the part of the individual. You will not become a millionaire by saying, "I am a millionaire, I am a millionaire." You will grow into a wealth consciousness by building into your mentality the idea of wealth and abundance.

• Your invisible means of support

The trouble with most people is that they have no invisible means of support. When business falls away, the stock market drops, or they lose their investments, they seem helpless. The reason for such insecurity is that they do not know how to tap the subconscious mind. They are unacquainted with the inexhaustible storehouse within.

A man with a poverty type mind finds himself in poverty-stricken conditions. Another man with a mind filled with ideas of wealth is surrounded with everything he needs. It was never intended that man should lead a life of indigence. You can have wealth, everything you need, and plenty to spare. Your words have power to cleanse your mind of wrong ideas and to instill right ideas in their place.

• The ideal method for building a wealth consciousness

Perhaps you are saying as you read this chapter, "I need wealth and success." This is what you do: Repeat for about five minutes to yourself three or four times a day, "Wealth— Success." These words have tremendous power. They represent the inner power of the subconscious mind. Anchor your mind on this substantial power within you; then conditions and circumstances corresponding to their nature and quality will be manifested in your life. You are not saying, "I am wealthy," you are dwelling on real powers within you. There is no conflict in the mind when you say, "Wealth."

Furthermore, the feeling of wealth will well up within you as you dwell on the idea of wealth.

The feeling of wealth produces wealth; keep this in mind at all times. Your subconscious mind is like a bank, a sort of universal financial institution. It magnifies whatever you deposit or impress upon it whether it is the idea of wealth or of poverty. Choose wealth.

• Why your affirmations for wealth fail

I have talked to many people during the past thirty-five years whose usual complaint is, "I have said for weeks and months, 'I am wealthy, I am prosperous,' and nothing has happened." I discovered that when they said, "I am prosperous, I am wealthy," they felt within that they were lying to themselves.

One man told me, "I have affirmed that I am prosperous until I am tired. Things are now worse. I knew when I made the statement that it was obviously not true." His statements were rejected by the conscious mind, and the very opposite of what he outwardly affirmed and claimed was made manifest.

Your affirmation succeeds best when it is specific and when it does not produce a mental conflict or argument; hence the statements made by this man made matters worse because they suggested his lack. Your subconscious accepts what you really feel to be true, not just idle words or statements. The dominant idea or belief is always accepted by the subconscious mind.

• How to avoid mental conflict

The following is the ideal way to overcome this conflict for those who have this difficulty. Make this practical statement frequently, particularly prior to sleep: "By day and by night I am being prospered in all of my interests." This affirmation will not arouse any argument because it does not contradict your subconscious mind's impression of financial lack.

I suggested to one businessman whose sales and finances were very low and who was greatly worried, that he sit down in his office, become quiet, and repeat this statement over and over again: "My sales are improving every day." This statement engaged the cooperation of the conscious and subconscious mind; results followed.

• Don't sign blank checks

You sign blank checks when you make such statements as, "There is not enough to go around." "There is a shortage." "I will lose the house because of the mortgage," etc. If you are full of fear about the future, you are also writing a blank check and attracting negative conditions to you. Your subconscious mind takes your fear and negative statement as your request and proceeds in its own way to bring obstacles, delays, lack, and limitation into your life.

• Your subconscious gives you compound interest

To him that hath the feeling of wealth, more wealth shall be added; to him that hath the feeling of lack, more lack shall be added. Your subconscious multiplies and magnifies

63

whatever you deposit in it. Every morning as you awaken deposit thoughts of prosperity, success, wealth, and peace. Dwell upon these concepts. Busy your mind with them as often as possible. These constructive thoughts will find their way as deposits in your subconscious mind, and bring forth abundance and prosperity.

• Why nothing happened
I can hear you saying, "Oh, I did that and nothing happened." You did not get results because you indulged in fear thoughts perhaps ten minutes later and neutralized the good you had affirmed. When you place a seed in the ground, you do not dig it up. You let it take root and grow.

Suppose, for example, you are going to say, "I shall not be able to make that payment." Before you get further than, "I shall—" stop the sentence and dwell on a constructive statement, such as, "By day and by night I am prospered in all my ways."

• True source of wealth
Your subconscious mind is never short of ideas. There are within it an infinite number of ideas ready to flow into your conscious mind and appear as cash in your pocketbook in countless ways. This process will continue to go on in your mind regardless of whether the stock market goes up or down, or whether the pound sterling or dollar drops in value. Your wealth is never truly dependent on bonds, stocks, or money in the bank; these are really only symbols necessary and useful, of course, but only symbols.

The point I wish to emphasize is that if you convince your subconscious mind that wealth is yours, and that it is always circulating in your life, you will always and inevitably have it, regardless of the form it takes.

• Trying to make ends meet and the real cause
There are people who claim that they are always trying to make ends meet. They seem to have a great struggle to meet their obligations. Have you listened to their conversation? In many instances their conversation runs along this vein. They are constantly condemning those who have succeeded in life and who have raised their heads above the crowd. Perhaps they are saying, "Oh, that fellow has a racket; he is ruthless; he is a crook." This is why they lack; they are condemning the thing they desire and want. The reason they speak critically of their more prosperous associates is because they are envious and covetous of the others prosperity. The quickest way to cause wealth to take wings and fly away is to criticize and condemn others who have more wealth than you.

• A common stumbling block to wealth
There is one emotion, which is the cause of the lack of wealth in the lives of many. Most people learn this the hard way. It is envy. For example, if you see a competitor depositing large sums of money in the bank, and you have only a meager amount to deposit, does it make you envious? The way to overcome this emotion is to say to yourself, "Isn't it wonderful! I rejoice in that man's prosperity. I wish for him greater and greater wealth."

To entertain envious thoughts is devastating because it places you in a very negative position; therefore, wealth flows from you instead of to you. If you are ever annoyed or irritated by the prosperity or great wealth of another, claim immediately that you truly wish for him greater wealth in every possible way. This will neutralize the negative thoughts in your mind and cause an ever-greater measure of wealth to flow to you by the law of your own subconscious mind.

• Rubbing out a great mental block to wealth

If you are worried and critical about someone whom you claim is making money dishonestly, cease worrying about him. You know such a person is using the law of mind negatively; the law of mind takes care of him. Be careful not to criticize him for the reasons previously indicated. Remember: The block or obstacle to wealth is in your own mind. You can now destroy that mental block. This you may do by getting on mental good terms with everyone.

• Sleep and grow rich

As you go to sleep at night, practice the following technique. Repeat the word, "Wealth," quietly, easily, and feelingly. Do this over and over again, just like a lullaby. Lull yourself to sleep with the one word, "Wealth." You should be amazed at the result. Wealth should flow to you in avalanches of abundance. This is another example of the magic power of your subconscious mind.

• Serve yourself with the powers of your mind

1. Decide to be wealthy the easy way, with the infallible aid of your subconscious mind.

2. Trying to accumulate wealth by the sweat of your brow and hard labor is one way to become the richest man in the graveyard. You do not have to strive or slave hard.

3. Wealth is a subconscious conviction. Build into your mentality the idea of wealth.

4. The trouble with most people is that they have no invisible means of support.

5. Repeat the word, "Wealth," to yourself slowly and quietly for about five minutes prior to sleep and your subconscious will bring wealth to pass in your experience.

6. The feeling of wealth produces wealth. Keep this in mind at all times.

7. Your conscious and subconscious mind must agree. Your subconscious accepts what you really feel to be true. The dominant idea is always accepted by your subconscious mind. The dominant idea should be wealth, not poverty.

8. You can overcome any mental conflict regarding wealth by affirming frequently, "By day and by night I am being prospered in all of my interests."

9. Increase your sales by repeating this statement over and over again, "My sales are improving every day; I am advancing, progressing, and getting wealthier every day."

10. Stop writing blank checks, such as, "There is not enough to go around," or "There is a shortage," etc. Such statements magnify and multiply your loss.

11. Deposit thoughts of prosperity, wealth, and success in your subconscious mind, and the latter will give you compound interest.

12. What you consciously affirm, you must not mentally deny a few moments later. This will neutralize the good you have affirmed.

13. Your true source of wealth consists of the ideas in your mind. You can have an idea worth millions of dollars. Your subconscious will give you the idea you seek.

14. Envy and jealousy are stumbling blocks to the flow of wealth. Rejoice in the prosperity of others.

15. The block to wealth is in your own mind. Destroy that block now by getting on good mental terms with everyone.

Chapter 10: Your Right to Be Rich

It is your right to be rich. You are here to lead the abundant life and be happy, radiant, and free. You should, therefore, have all the money you need to lead a full, happy, and prosperous life.

You are here to grow, expand, and unfold spiritually, mentally, and materially. You have the inalienable right to fully develop and express yourself along all lines. You should surround yourself with beauty and luxury.

Why be satisfied with just enough to go around when you can enjoy the riches of your subconscious mind? In this chapter you can learn to make friends with money, and you should always have a surplus. Your desire to be rich is a desire for a fuller, happier, more wonderful life. It is a cosmic urge. It is not only good, but also very good.

• Money is a symbol

Money is a symbol of exchange. It means to you not only freedom from want, but beauty, luxury, abundance, and refinement. It is merely a symbol of the economic health of the nation. When your blood is circulating freely in your body, you are healthy. When money is circulating freely in your life, you are economically healthy. When people begin to hoard money, to put it away in tin boxes, and become charged with fear, there is economic illness. Money has taken many forms as a medium of exchange down through the centuries, such as, salt, beads, and trinkets of various kinds. In early times a man's wealth was determined by the number of sheep and oxen he had. Now we use currency, and other negotiable instruments, as it is much more convenient to write a check than carry some sheep around with you to pay bills.

• How to walk the royal road to riches

Knowledge of the powers of your subconscious mind is the means to the royal road to riches of all kinds—spiritual, mental, or financial. The student of the laws of mind believes and knows definitely that regardless of economic situations, stock market fluctuation, depression, strikes, war, other conditions or circumstances, he will always be amply supplied, regardless of what form money takes. The reason for this is that he has conveyed the idea of wealth to his subconscious mind, and it keeps him supplied wherever he may be. He has convinced himself in his mind that money is forever flowing freely in his life and that there is always a wonderful surplus. Should there be a financial collapse of government tomorrow and all the man's present holdings become valueless, as the German marks did after the First World War, he would still attract wealth and be cared for, regardless of the form the new currency took.

• Why you do not have more money

As you read this chapter, you are probably saying, "I am worthy of a higher salary than I am receiving." I believe most people are inadequately compensated. One of the causes many people does not have more money is that they are silently or openly condemning it. They refer to money as "filthy lucre" or "the love of money is the root of all evil." Another reason they do not prosper is that they have a sneaky subconscious feeling there is some virtue in poverty. This subconscious pattern may be due to early childhood training, superstition, or it could be based on a false interpretation of scriptures.

• Money and a balanced life

One time a man said to me, "I am broke. I do not like money. It is the root of all evil." These statements represent a confused neurotic mind. Love of money to the exclusion of everything else will cause you to become lopsided and unbalanced. You are here to use your power or authority wisely. Some men crave power others crave money. If you set your heart on money exclusively and say, "Money is all I want; I am going to give all my attention to amassing money; nothing else matters," you can get money and attain a fortune, but you have forgotten that you are here to lead a balanced life. You must also satisfy the hunger for peace of mind, harmony, love, joy, and perfect health.

By making money your sole aim, you simply made a wrong choice. You thought that was all you wanted, but you found after all your efforts that it was not only the money you needed. You also desired true expression of your hidden talents, true place in life, beauty, and the joy of contributing to the welfare and success of others. By learning the laws of your subconscious mind, you could have a million dollars or many millions, if you wanted them, and still have peace of mind, harmony, perfect health, and perfect expression.

• Poverty is a mental disease

There is no virtue in poverty; it is a disease like any other mental disease. If you were physically ill, you would think there was something wrong with you. You would seek help and do something about the condition at once. Likewise, if you do not have money constantly circulating in your life, there is something radically wrong with you.

The urge of the life principle in you is toward growth, expansion, and the life more abundant. You are not here to live in a hovel, dress in rags, and go hungry. You should be happy, prosperous, and successful.

• Why you must never criticize money

Cleanse your mind of all weird and superstitious beliefs about money. Do not ever regard money as evil or filthy. If you do, you cause it to take wings and fly away from you. Remember that you lose what you condemn. You cannot attract what you criticize.

• Getting the right attitude toward money

Here is a simple technique you may use to multiply money in your experience. Use the following statements several times a day, "I like money, I love it, I use it wisely, constructively, and judiciously. Money is constantly circulating in my life. I release it with joy, and it returns to me multiplied in a wonderful way. It is good and very good. Money flows to me in avalanches of abundance. I use it for good only, and I am grateful for my good and for the riches of my mind."

• How the scientific thinker looks at money

Suppose, for example, you found gold, silver, lead, copper, or iron in the ground. Would you pronounce these things evil? All evil comes from man's darkened understanding, from his ignorance, from his false interpretation of life, and from his misuse of his subconscious mind. Uranium, lead, or some other metal could have been used as a medium of exchange. We use paper bills, checks, nickel, and silver surely these are not evil. Physicists and chemists know today that the only difference between one metal and another is the number and rate of motion of electrons revolving around a central nucleus. They can now change one metal into another through a bombardment of the atoms in the powerful cyclotron. Gold under certain conditions becomes mercury. I believe that our modern scientists in the near future will be able to make gold, silver, and other metals synthetically in the chemical laboratory. The cost may be prohibitive now, but it can be done. I cannot imagine any intelligent person seeing anything evil in electrons, neutrons, protons, and isotopes.

The piece of paper in your pocket is composed of atoms and molecules with their electrons and protons arranged differently. Their number and rate of motion are different. That is the only way the paper differs from the silver in your pocket.

• How to attract the money you need

Many years ago I met a young boy in Australia who wanted to become a physician and surgeon, but he had no money. I explained to him how a seed deposited in the soil attracts to itself everything necessary for its unfolding, and that all he had to do was to take a lesson from the seed and deposit the required idea in his subconscious mind. For expenses this young, brilliant boy used to clean out doctors' offices, wash windows, and do odd repair jobs. He told me that every night, as he went to sleep, he used to picture in his mind's eye a medical diploma on a wall with his name on it in big, bold letters. He used to clean and shine the framed diplomas in the medical building where he worked. It was not hard for him to engrave the image of a diploma in his mind and develop it there. Definite results followed as he persisted with his mental picture every night for about four months.

The sequel of this story was very interesting. One of the doctors took a great liking to this young boy and after training him in the art of sterilizing instruments, giving hypodermic injections, and other miscellaneous first-aid work, he employed him as a technical assistant in his office. The doctor later sent him to medical school at his own expense. Today, this young man is a prominent medical doctor in Montreal, Canada. He discovered the law of attraction by using his subconscious mind the right way. He operated an age-old law, which says, "Having seen the end, you have willed the means to the realization of the end." The end in this case was to become a medical doctor.

This young man was able to imagine, see, and feel the reality of being a doctor. He lived with that idea, sustained it, nourished it, and loved it until through his imagination it penetrated the layers of his subconscious mind and became a conviction, thereby attracting to him everything necessary for the fulfillment of his dream.

• Why some men do not get a raise in pay

If you are working in a large organization and you are silently thinking of and resenting the fact you are underpaid, that you are not appreciated, and that you deserve more money and greater recognition, you are subconsciously severing your ties with that organization. You are setting a law in motion, and the superintendent or manager will say to you, "We have to let you go." Actually, you dismissed yourself. The manager was simply the instrument through which your own negative mental state was confirmed. It was an example of the law of action and reaction. The action was your thought, and the reaction was the response of your subconscious mind.

• Obstacles and impediments on the pathway to riches

I am sure you have heard men say, "That fellow has a racket." "He is a racketeer." "He is getting money dishonestly." "He is a faker." "I knew him when he had nothing." "He is a crook, a thief, and a swindler."

If you analyze the man who talks like that, you discover he is usually in want or suffering from some financial or physical illness. Perhaps his former college friends went up the ladder of success and excelled him. Now he is bitter and envious of their progress. In many instances this is the cause of his downfall. Thinking negatively of these classmates and condemning their wealth causes the wealth and prosperity he is praying for to vanish and flee away. He is condemning the thing he is praying for.

He is praying two ways. On the one hand he is saying, "Wealth is flowing to me now," and in the next breath, silently or audibly, he is saying, "I resent that fellow's wealth." Always make it a special point to rejoice in the wealth of the other person.

• Protect your investments

If you are seeking wisdom regarding investments, or if you are worried about your stocks or bonds, quietly claim, "Infinite intelligence governs and watches over all my financial transactions, and whatsoever I do shall prosper." Do this frequently and you will find that your investments will be wise; moreover, you will be protected from loss, as you will be prompted to sell your securities or holdings before any loss accrues to you.

• You cannot get something for nothing

In large stores the management employs store detectives to prevent people from stealing. They catch a number of people every day trying to get something for nothing. All such people are living in the mental atmosphere of lack and limitation and are stealing from themselves peace, harmony, faith, honesty, integrity, good will, and confidence. Furthermore, they are attracting to themselves all manner of loss, such as, loss of character, prestige, social status, and peace of mind. These people lack faith in the source of supply and the understanding of how their minds work. If they would mentally call on the powers of their subconscious mind and claim that they are guided to their true expression, they would find work and constant supply. Then by honesty, integrity, and perseverance, they would become a credit to themselves and to society at large.

• Your constant supply of money

Recognizing the powers of your subconscious mind and the creative power of your thought or mental image is the way to opulence, freedom, and constant supply. Accept the abundant life in your own mind. Your mental acceptance and expectancy of wealth has its own mathematics and mechanics of expression. As you enter into the mood of opulence, all things necessary for the abundant life will come to pass.

Let this be your daily affirmation; write it in your heart, "I am one with the infinite riches of my subconscious mind. It is my right to be rich, happy, and successful. Money flows to me freely, copiously, and endlessly. I am forever conscious of my true worth. I give of my talents freely, and I am wonderfully blessed financially. It is wonderful!"

• Step up this way to riches

1. Be bold enough to claim that it is your right to be rich and your deeper mind will honor your claim.

2. You don't want just enough to go around. You want all the money you need to do all the things you want to do and when you want to do them. Get acquainted with the riches of your subconscious mind.

3. When money is circulating freely in your life, you are economically healthy. Look at money like the tide and you will always have plenty of it. The ebb and flow of the tide is constant. When the tide is out, you are absolutely sure that it will return.

4. Knowing the laws of your subconscious mind, you will always be supplied regardless of what form money takes.

5. One reason many people simply make ends meet and never have enough money is that they condemn money. What you condemn takes wings and flies away.

6. Do not make a god of money. It is only a symbol. Remember that the real riches are in your mind. You are here to lead a balanced life—this includes acquiring all the money you need.

7. Don't make money your sole aim. Claim wealth, happiness, peace, true expression, and love, and personally radiate love and good will to all. Then your subconscious mind will give you compound interest in all these fields of expression.

8. There is no virtue in poverty. It is a disease of the mind, and you should heal yourself of this mental conflict or malady at once.

9. You are not here to live in a hovel, to dress in rags, or to go hungry. You are here to lead the life more abundant.

10. Never use the terms "filthy lucre" or "I despise money." You lose what you criticize. There is nothing good or bad, but thinking of it in either light makes it so.

11. Repeat frequently, "I like money. I use it wisely, constructively, and judiciously. I release it with joy, and it returns a thousand fold."

12. Money is not evil any more so than copper, lead, tin, or iron which you may find in the ground. All evil is due to ignorance and misuse of the mind's powers.

13. To picture the end result in your mind causes your subconscious to respond and fulfill your mental picture.

14. Stop trying to get something for nothing. There is no such thing as a free lunch. You must give to receive. You must give mental attention to your goals, ideals, and

enterprises, and your deeper mind will back you up. The key to wealth is application of the laws of the subconscious mind by impregnating it with the idea of wealth.

Chapter 11: Your Subconscious Mind as a Partner in Success

Success means successful living. A long period of peace, joy, and happiness on this plane may be termed success. The real things of life, such as peace, harmony, integrity, security, and happiness are intangible. They come from the Deep Self of man. Meditating on these qualities builds these treasures of heaven in our subconscious.

• The three steps to success

Let us discuss three steps to success: The first step to success is to find out the thing you love to do, then do it. Success is in loving your work. Although, if a man is a psychiatrist, it is not adequate for him to get a diploma and place it on the wall; he must keep up with the times, attend conventions, and continue studying the mind and its workings. The successful psychiatrist visits clinics and reads the latest scientific articles. In other words, he is informed in the most advanced methods of alleviating human suffering. The successful psychiatrist or doctor must have the interest of his patients at heart.

Someone may say, "How can I put the first step into operation? I do not know what I should do." In such a case, pray for guidance as follows: "The infinite intelligence of my subconscious mind reveals to me my true place in life." Repeat this prayer quietly, positively, and lovingly to your deeper mind. As you persist with faith and confidence, the answer will come to you as a feeling, a hunch, or a tendency in a certain direction. It will come to you clearly and in peace, and as an inner silent awareness.

The second step to success is to specialize in some particular branch of work and know more about it than anyone else. For example, if a young man chooses chemistry as his profession, he should concentrate on one of the many branches in this field. He should give all of his time and attention to his chosen specialty. He should become sufficiently enthusiastic to try to know all there is available about his field; if possible, he should know more than anyone else. The young man should become ardently interested in his work and should desire to serve the world.

He that is greatest among you, let him become your servant. There is a great contrast in this attitude of mind in com-parison to that of the man who only wants to makes a living or just "get by." "Getting by" is not true success. Man's motive must be greater, nobler, and more altruistic. He must serve others, thereby casting his bread upon the waters.

The third step is the most important one. You must be sure that the thing you want to do does not redound to your success only. Your desire must not be selfish; it must benefit humanity. The path of a complete circuit must be formed. In other words, your idea must go forth with the purpose of blessing or serving the world. It will then come back to you pressed down, shaken together, and running over. If it is to benefit yourself exclusively, the circle or complete circuit is not formed, and you may experience a short circuit in your life which may consist of limitation or sickness.

• The measure of true success

Some people may say, "But Mr. James made a fortune in selling fraudulent oil stock." A man may seem to succeed for a while, but the money he obtained by fraud usually takes wings and flies away. When we rob from another, we rob from ourselves, because we are in a mood of lack and limitation, which may manifest itself in our body, home life, and affairs. What we think and feel, we create. We create what we believe. Even though a man may have accumulated a fortune fraudulently, he is not successful. There is no success without peace of mind. What good is man's accumulated wealth if he cannot sleep nights, is sick, or has a guilt complex?

I knew a man in London who told me of his exploits. He had been a professional pickpocket and had amassed a large amount of money. He had a summer home in France and lived in a royal fashion in England. His story was that he was in constant dread of being arrested by Scotland Yard. He had many inner disorders, which were undoubtedly caused by his constant fear and deep-seated guilt complex. He knew he had done wrong. This deep sense of guilt attracted all kinds of trouble to him. Subsequently, he voluntarily surrendered to the police and served a prison sentence. After his release from prison, he sought psychological and spiritual counsel and became transformed. He went to work and became an honest, law-abiding citizen. He found what he loved to do and was happy. A successful person loves his work and expresses himself fully. Success is contingent upon a higher ideal than the mere accumulation of riches. The man of success is the man who possesses great psychological and spiritual understanding. Many of the great industrialists today depend upon the correct use of their subconscious minds for their success.

There was an article published some years ago about Flagler, an oil magnate. He admitted that the secret of his success was his ability to see a project in its completion. For instance, in his case, he closed his eyes, imagined a big oil industry, saw trains running on tracks, heard whistles blowing, and saw smoke. Having seen and felt the fulfillment of his prayer, his subconscious mind brought about its realization. If you imagine an objective clearly, you will be provided with the necessities, in ways you know not of, through the wonder-working power of your subconscious mind.

In considering the three steps to success you must never forget the underlying power of the creative forces of your subconscious mind. This is the energy in back of all steps in any plan of success. Your thought is creative. Thought fused with feeling becomes a subjective faith or belief, and according to your belief is it done unto you.

Knowledge of a mighty force in you, which is capable of bringing to pass all your desires, gives you confidence and a sense of peace. Whatever your field of action may be, you should learn the laws of your subconscious mind. When you know how to apply the powers of your mind, and when you are expressing yourself fully and giving of your talents to others, you are on the sure path to true success. If you are about God's business, or any part of it, God, by His very nature, is for you, so who can be against you? With this understanding there is no power in heaven or on earth to withhold success from you.

• How he made his dream come true

A movie actor told me that he had very little education, but he had a dream as a boy of becoming a successful movie actor. Out in the field mowing hay, driving the cows home, or even when milking them he said, "I would constantly imagine I saw my name in big lights at a large theatre. I kept this up for years until finally I ran away from home. I got extra jobs in the motion-picture field, and the day finally came when I saw my name in great, big lights as I did when I was a boy!" Then he added, "I know the power of sustained imagination to bring success."

• His dream pharmacy became a reality

Thirty years ago I knew a young pharmacist who was receiving forty dollars a week plus commission on sales. "After twenty-five years," he said to me, "I will get a pension and retire."

I said to this young man, "Why don't you own your own store? Get out of this place. Raise your sights! Have a dream for your children. Maybe your son wants to be a doctor; perhaps your daughter desires to be a great musician."

His answer was that he had no money! He began to awaken to the fact that whatever he could conceive as true, he could give conception.

The first step toward his goal was his awakening to the powers of his subconscious mind, which I briefly elaborated on for his benefit. His second step was his realization that if he could succeed in conveying an idea to his subconscious mind, the latter would somehow bring it to pass.

He began to imagine that he was in his own store. He mentally arranged the bottles, dispensed prescriptions, and imagined several clerks in the store waiting on customers. He also visualized a big bank balance. Mentally he worked in that imaginary store. Like a good actor he lived the role. Act as though I am, and I will be. This pharmacist put himself whole-heartedly into the act, living, moving, and acting on the assumption that he owned the store.

The sequel was interesting. He was discharged from his position. He found new employment with a large chain store, became manager, and later on, district manager. He saved enough money in four years to provide a down payment on a drugstore of his own. He called it his "Dream Pharmacy."

"It was," he said, "exactly the store I saw in my imagination." He became a recognized success in his chosen field, and was happy doing what he loved to do.

• Using the subconscious mind in business

Some years ago I gave a lecture to a group of businessmen on the powers of imagination and the subconscious mind. In this lecture I pointed out how Goethe used his imagination wisely when confronted with difficulties and predicaments.

His biographers point out that he was accustomed to fill many hours quietly holding imaginary conversations. It is well known that his custom was to imagine one of his friends before him in a chair answering him in the right way. In other words, if he were concerned over any problems, he imagined his friend giving him the right or appropriate answer, accompanied with the usual gestures and tonal qualities of the voice, and he made the entire imaginary scene as real and as vivid as possible.

One of the men present at this lecture was a young stockbroker. He proceeded to adopt the technique of Goethe. He began to have mental, imaginary conversations with a multi-millionaire banker friend of his who used to congratulate him on his wise and sound judgment, and compliment him on his purchase of the right stocks. He used to dramatize this imaginary conversation until he had psychologically fixed it as a form of belief in his mind.

This broker's inner talking and controlled imagination certainly agreed with his aim, which was to make sound investments for his clients. His main purpose in life was to make money for his clients and to see them prosper financially by his wise counsel. He is still using his subconscious mind in his business, and he is a brilliant success in his field of endeavor.

• Boy of sixteen years turns failure into success

A young boy who was attending high school said to me, "I am getting very poor grades. My memory is failing. I do not know what is the matter." I discovered that the only thing wrong with this boy was his attitude, which was one of indifference and resentment toward some of his teachers and fellow students. I taught him how to use his subconscious mind, and how to succeed in his studies.

He began to affirm certain truths several times a day, particularly at night prior to sleep, and also in the morning after awakening. These are the best times to impregnate the subconscious mind.

He affirmed as follows: "I realize that my subconscious mind is a storehouse of memory. It retains everything I read and hear from my teachers. I have a perfect memory, and the infinite intelligence in my subconscious mind constantly reveals to me everything I need to know at all my examinations, whether written or oral. I radiate love and good will to all my teachers and fellow students. I sincerely wish for them success and all good things."

This young man is now enjoying a greater freedom than he has ever known. He is now receiving all "A's." He constantly imagines the teachers and his mother congratulating him on his success in his studies.

• How to become successful in buying and selling

In buying and selling, remember that your conscious mind is the starter and your subconscious mind is the motor. You must start the motor to enable it to perform its work. Your conscious mind is the dynamo that awakens the power of your subconscious mind.

The first step in conveying your clarified desire, idea, or image to the deeper mind is to relax, immobilize the attention, get still, and be quiet. This quiet, relaxed, and peaceful attitude of mind prevents extraneous matter and false ideas from interfering with your mental absorption of your ideal. Furthermore, in the quiet, passive, and receptive attitude of mind, effort is reduced to a minimum.

The second step is to begin to imagine the reality of that which you desire. For example, you may wish to buy a home, and in your relaxed state of mind affirm as follows: "The infinite intelligence of my subconscious mind is all-wise. It reveals to me now the ideal home, which is central, ideal, is in a lovely environment, meets with all my requirements, and is commensurate with my income. I am now turning this request over to my subconscious mind, and I know it responds according to the nature of my request. I release this request with absolute faith and confidence in the same way that a farmer deposits a seed in the ground, trusting implicitly in the laws of growth."

The answer to your prayer may come through an advertisement in the paper, through a friend, or you may be guided directly to a particular home, which is exactly what you are seeking. There are many ways by which your prayer may be answered. The principal knowledge, in which you may place your confidence, is that the answer always comes, provided you trust the working of your deeper mind.

You may wish to sell a home, land, or any kind of property. In private consultation with real estate brokers I have told them of the way I sold my own home on Orlando Avenue in Los Angeles. Many of them have applied the technique I used with remarkable and speedy results. I placed a sign which read, "For sale by owner" in the garden in front of my home. The day after I said to myself as I was going to sleep, "Supposing you sold your house, what would you do?"

I answered my own question and I said, "I would take that sign down and throw it into the garage." In my imagination I took hold of the sign, pulled it up from the ground, placed it on my shoulder, went to the garage, threw it on the floor, and said jokingly to the sign, "I don't need you any more!" I felt the inner satisfaction of it all, realizing it was finished.

The next day a man gave me a deposit of $1,000 and said to me, "Take your sign down. We will go into escrow now."

Immediately I pulled the sign up and took it to the garage. The outer action conformed to the inner. There is nothing new about this. As within, so without, meaning according to the image impressed on your subconscious mind, so it is on the objective screen of your life. The outside mirrors the inside. External action follows internal action.

Here is another very popular method used in selling homes, land, or any kind of property. Affirm slowly, quietly, and feelingly as follows: "Infinite intelligence attracts to me the buyer for this home who wants it and who prospers in it. This buyer is being sent to me by the creative intelligence of my subconscious mind, which makes no mistakes. This buyer may look at many other homes, but mine is the only one he wants and will buy, because he is guided by the infinite intelligence within him. I know the buyer is right, the time is right, and the price is right. Everything about it is right. The deeper currents of my subconscious mind are now in operation bringing both of us together in divine order. I know that it is so."

Remember always, that what you are seeking is also seeking you, and whenever you want to sell a home or property of any kind, there is always someone who wants what you have to offer By using the powers of your subconscious mind correctly, you free your mind of all sense of competition and anxiety in buying and selling.

• How she succeeded in getting what she wanted

There is a young lady who regularly comes to my lectures and classes. She had to change buses three times; it took her one and a half hours each time to come to the lectures. In one lecture I explained how a young man who needed a car in his work received one.

She went home and experimented as outlined in my lecture. Here is her letter in part, narrating her application of my method, and published by her permission:

Dear Dr. Murphy:

76

This is how I received a Cadillac car—I wanted one to come to the lectures regularly. In my imagination I went through the identical process I would go through if I were actually driving a car. I went to the showroom, and the salesman took me for a ride in one. I also drove it several blocks. I claimed the Cadillac car as my own over and over again.

I kept the mental picture of getting into the car, driving it, feeling the upholstery, etc., consistently for over two weeks. Last week I drove to your lectures in a Cadillac. My uncle in Inglewood passed away, and left me his Cadillac and his entire estate.

• A success technique employed by many outstanding executives and businessmen

There are many prominent businessmen who quietly use the abstract term, "success," over and over many times a day until they reach a conviction that success is theirs. They know that the idea of success contains all the essential elements of success. Likewise, you can begin now to repeat the word, "success," to yourself with faith and conviction. Your subconscious mind will accept it as true of you, and you will be under a subconscious compulsion to succeed.

You are compelled to express your subjective beliefs, impressions, and convictions. What does success imply to you? You want, undoubtedly, to be successful in your home life and in your relationship with others. You wish to be outstanding in your chosen work or profession. You wish to possess a beautiful home, and all the money you need to live comfortably and happily. You want to be successful in your prayer life and in your contact with the powers of your subconscious mind.

You are a businessman also because you are in the business of living. Become a successful businessman by imagining yourself doing what you long to do, and possessing the things you long to possess. Become imaginative; mentally participate in the reality of the successful state. Make a habit of it. Go to sleep feeling successful every night, and perfectly satisfied, and you will eventually succeed in implanting the idea of success in your subconscious mind. Believe you were born to succeed, and wonders will happen as you pray!

• Profitable pointers

1. Success means successful living. When you are peaceful, happy, joyous, and doing what you love to do, you are successful.

2. Find out what you love to do, and then do it. If you don't know your true expression, ask for guidance, and the lead will come.

3. Specialize in your particular field and try to know more about it than anyone else.

4. A successful man is not selfish. His main desire in life is to serve humanity.

5. There is no true success without peace of mind.

6. A successful man possesses great psychological and spiritual understanding.

7. If you imagine an objective clearly, you will be provided with the necessities through the wonder-working power of your subconscious mind.

8. Your thought fused with feeling becomes a subjective belief, and according to your belief is it done unto you.

9. The power of sustained imagination draws forth the miracle-working powers of your subconscious mind.

10. If you are seeking promotion in your work, imagine your employer, supervisor, or loved one congratulating you on your promotion. Make the picture vivid and real. Hear the voice, see the gestures, and feel the reality of it all. Continue to do this frequently, and through frequent occupancy of your mind, you will experience the joy of the answered prayer.

11. Your subconscious mind is a storehouse of memory. For a perfect memory, affirm frequently: "The infinite intelligence of my subconscious mind reveals to me everything I need to know at all times, everywhere."

12. If you wish to sell a home or property of any kind, affirm slowly, quietly, and feelingly as follows: "Infinite intelligence attracts to me the buyer for this house or property, who wants it, and who prospers in it." Sustain this awareness, and the deeper currents of your subconscious mind will bring it to pass.

13. The idea of success contains all the elements of success. Repeat the word, "success," to yourself frequently with faith and conviction, and you will be under a subconscious compulsion to succeed.

Chapter 12: Scientists Use the Subconscious Mind

Many scientists realize the true importance of the subconscious mind. Edison, Marconi, Kettering, Poincarè, Einstein, and many others have used the subconscious mind. It has given them the insight and the "know-how" for all their great achievements in modern science and industry. Research has shown that the ability to bring into action the subconscious power has determined the success of all the great scientific and research workers.

An instance of how a famous chemist, Friedrich von Stradonitz, used his subconscious mind to solve his problem is as follows: He had been working laboriously for a long time trying to rearrange the six carbon and the six hydrogen atoms of the benzine formula, and he was constantly perplexed and unable to solve the matter. Tired and exhausted, he turned the request over completely to his subconscious mind. Shortly afterward, as he was about to board a London bus, his subconscious presented his conscious mind with a sudden flash of a snake biting its own tail and turning around like a pinwheel. This answer, from his subconscious mind, gave him the long-sought answer of the circular rearrangement of the atoms that is known as the benzine ring.

• How a distinguished scientist brought forth his inventions

Nikola Tesla was a brilliant electrical scientist who brought forth the most amazing innovations. When an idea for a new invention came into his mind, he would build it up in his imagination, knowing that his subconscious mind would reconstruct and reveal to his conscious mind all the parts needed for its manufacture in concrete form. Through quietly contemplating every possible improvement, he spent no time in correcting defects, and was able to give the technicians the perfect product of his mind.

He said, "Invariably, my device works as I imagined it should. In twenty years there has not been a single exception."

• How a famous naturalist solved his problem

Professor Agassiz, a distinguished American naturalist, discovered the indefatigable activities of his subconscious mind while he slept. His widow in her biography of her famous husband has reported the following.

"He had been for two weeks striving to decipher the somewhat obscure impression of a fossil fish on the stone slab in which it was preserved. Weary and perplexed, he put his work aside at last, and tried to dismiss it from his mind. Shortly after, he waked one night persuaded that while asleep he had seen his fish with all the missing features perfectly restored. But when he tried to hold and make fast the image it escaped him. Nevertheless, he went early to the Jardin des Plantes, thinking that on looking anew at the impression he should see something, which would put him on the track of his vision. In vain—the blurred record was as black as ever. The next night he saw the fish again, but with no more satisfactory result. When he awoke it disappeared from his memory as before. Hoping that the same experience might be repeated, on the third night he placed a pencil and paper beside his bed before going to sleep.

"Accordingly, toward morning the fish reappeared in his dream, confusedly at first, but at last with such distinctness that he had no longer any doubt as to its zoological characters. Still half dreaming, in perfect darkness, he traced these characters on the sheet of paper at the bedside. In the morning he was surprised to see in his nocturnal sketch features, which he thought it impossible the fossil itself should reveal. He hastened to the Jardin des Plantes, and, with his drawing as a guide, succeeded in chiseling away the surface of the stone under which portions of the fish proved to be hidden. When wholly exposed it corresponded with his dream and his drawing, and he succeeded in classifying it with ease."

• An outstanding physician solved the problem of diabetes

Some years ago I received a clipping from a magazine describing the origin of the discovery of insulin. This is the essence of the article as I recall it.

About forty years ago or more, Dr. Frederick Banting, a brilliant Canadian physician and surgeon, was concentrating his attention on the ravages of diabetes. At that time medical science offered no effective method of arresting the disease. Dr. Banting spent considerable time experimenting and studying the international literature on the subject. One night he was exhausted and fell asleep. While asleep, his subconscious mind instructed him to extract the residue from the degenerated pancreatic duct of dogs. This was the origin of insulin which has helped millions of people.

You will note that Dr. Banting had been consciously dwelling on the problem for some time seeking a solution, a way out, and his subconscious responded accordingly.

It does not follow that you will always get an answer overnight. The answer may not come for some time. Do not be discouraged. Keep on turning the problem over every night to the subconscious mind prior to sleep, as if you had never done it before.

One of the reasons for the delay may be that you look upon it as a major problem. You may believe it will take a long time to solve it.

Your subconscious mind is timeless and spaceless. Go to sleep believing you have the answer now. Do not postulate the answer in the future. Have an abiding faith in the outcome. Become convinced now as you read this book that there is an answer and a perfect solution for you.

• How a famous scientist and physicist escaped from a Russian concentration camp

Dr. Lothar von Blenk-Schmidt, a member of the Rocket Society and an outstanding research electronic engineer, gives the following condensed summary of how he used his subconscious mind to free himself from certain death at the hands of brutal guards in a Russian prison camp coal mine. He states as follows:

"I was a prisoner of war in a coal mine in Russia, and I saw men dying all around me in that prison compound. We were watched over by brutal guards, arrogant officers, and sharp, fast-thinking commissars. After a short medical checkup, a quota of coal was assigned to each person. My quota was three hundred pounds per day. In case any man did not fill his quota, his small food ration was cut down, and in a short time he was resting in the cemetery.

"I started concentrating on my escape. I knew that my subconscious mind would somehow find a way. My home in Germany was destroyed, my family wiped out; all my friends and former associates were either killed in the war or were in concentration camps.

"I said to my subconscious mind, 'I want to go to Los Angeles, and you will find the way.' I had seen pictures of Los Angeles and I remembered some of the boulevards very well as well as some of the buildings.

"Every day and night I would imagine I was walking down Wilshire Boulevard with an American girl whom I met in Berlin prior to the war (she is now my wife). In my imagination we would visit the stores, ride buses, and eat in the restaurants. Every night I made it a special point to drive my imaginary American automobile up and down the boulevards of Los Angeles. I made all this vivid and real. These pictures in my mind were as real and as natural to me as one of the trees outside the prison camp.

"Every morning the chief guard would count the prisoners as they were lined up. He would call out 'one, two, three,' etc., and when seventeen was called out, which was my number in sequence, I stepped aside. In the meantime, the guard was called away for a minute or so, and on his return he started by mistake on the next man as number seventeen. When the crew returned in the evening, the number of men was the same, and I was not missed, and the discovery would take a long time.

"I walked out of the camp undetected and kept walking for twenty-four hours, resting in a deserted town the next day. I was able to live by fishing and killing some wild life. I found coal trains going to Poland and traveled on them by night, until finally I reached Poland. With the help of friends, I made my way to Lucerne, Switzerland.

"One evening at the Palace Hotel, Lucerne, I had a talk with a man and his wife from the United States of America. This man asked me if I would care to be a guest at his home in Santa Monica, California. I accepted, and when I arrived in Los Angeles, I found that their chauffeur drove me along Wilshire Boulevard and many other boulevards, which I had imagined, so vividly in the long months in the Russian coalmines. I recognized the buildings, which I had seen in my mind so often. It actually seemed as if I had been in Los Angeles before. I had reached my goal.

"I will never cease to marvel at the wonders of the subconscious mind. Truly, it has ways we know not of."

• How archaeologists and paleontologists reconstruct ancient scenes

These scientists know that their subconscious mind has a memory of everything that has ever transpired. As they study the ancient ruins and fossils, through their imaginative perception, their subconscious mind aids them in reconstructing the ancient scenes. The dead past becomes alive and audible once more. Looking at these ancient temples and studying the pottery, statuary, tools, and household utensils of these ancient times, the scientist tells us of an age when there was no language. Communication was done by grunts, groans, and signs.

The keen concentration and disciplined imagination of the scientist awakens the latent powers of his subconscious mind enabling him to clothe the ancient temples with roofs, and surround them with gardens, pools, and fountains. The fossil remains are clothed with eyes, sinews, and muscles, and they again walk and talk. The past becomes the living present, and we find that in mind there is no time or space. Through disciplined, controlled, and directed imagination, you can be a companion of the most scientific and inspired thinkers of all time.

• How to receive guidance from your subconscious

When you have what you term "a difficult decision" to make, or when you fail to see the solution to your problem, begin at once to think constructively about it. If you are fearful and worried, you are not really thinking. True thinking is free from fear.

Here is a simple technique you can use to receive guidance on any subject: Quiet the mind and still the body. Tell the body to relax; it has to obey you. It has no volition, initiative, or self-conscious intelligence. Your body is an emotional disk, which records your beliefs and impressions. Mobilize your attention; focus your thought on the solution to your problem. Try to solve it with your conscious mind. Think how happy you would be about the perfect solution. Sense the feeling you would have if the perfect answer were yours now. Let your mind play with this mood in a relaxed way; then drop off to sleep. When you awaken, and you do not have the answer, get busy about something else. Probably, when you are preoccupied with something else, the answer will come into your mind like toast pops out of a toaster.

In receiving guidance from the subconscious mind, the simple way is the best. This is an illustration: I once lost a valuable ring, which was an heirloom. I looked everywhere for it and could not locate it. At night I talked to the subconscious in the same manner that I would talk to anyone. I said to it prior to dropping off to sleep, "You know all things; you know where that ring is, and you now reveal to me where it is."

In the morning I awoke suddenly with the words ringing in my ear, "Ask Robert!"

I thought it very strange that I should ask Robert, a young boy about nine years of age; however, I followed the inner voice of intuition.

Robert said, "Oh, yes, I picked it up in the yard while I was playing with the boys. I placed it on the desk in my room. I did not think it worth anything, so I did not say anything about it."

The subconscious mind will always answer you if you trust it.

• His subconscious revealed the location of his father's will

A young man who attends my lectures had this experience. His father died and apparently left no will. However, this man's sister told him that their father had confided to her that a will had been executed which was fair to all. Every attempt to locate the will failed.

Prior to sleep he talked to his deeper mind as follows: "I now turn this request over the subconscious mind. It knows just where that will is, and reveals it to me." Then he condensed his request down to one word, "Answer," repeating it over and over again as a lullaby. He lulled himself to sleep with the word, "Answer."

The next morning this young man had an overpowering hunch to go to a certain bank in Los Angeles where he found a safe deposit vault registered in the name of his father, the contents of which solved all his problems.

Your thought, as you go to sleep, arouses the powerful latency which is within you. For example, let us suppose you are wondering whether to sell your home, buy a certain stock, sever partnership, move to New York or stay in Los Angeles, dissolve the present contract or take a new one. Do this: Sit quietly in your armchair or at the desk in your office. Remember that there is a universal law of action and reaction. The action is your thought. The reaction is the response from your subconscious mind. The subconscious mind is reactive and reflexive; this is its nature. It rebounds, rewards, and repays. It is the law of correspondence. It responds by corresponding. As you contemplate right action, you will automatically experience a reaction or response in yourself, which represents the guidance or answer of your subconscious mind.

In seeking guidance, you simply think quietly about right action, which means that you are using the infinite intelligence resident in the subconscious mind to the point where it begins to use you. From there on, your course of action is directed and controlled by the subjective wisdom within you, which is all wise and omnipotent. Your decision will be right. There will only be right action because you are under a subjective compulsion to do the right thing. I use the word compulsion because the law of the subconscious is compulsion.

• The secret of guidance

The secret of guidance or right action is to mentally devote yourself to the right answer, until you find its response in you. The response is a feeling, an inner awareness, and an overpowering hunch whereby you know that you know. You have used the power to the point where it begins to use you. You cannot possibly fail or make one false step while operating under the subjective wisdom within you. You will find that all your ways are pleasantness and all your paths are peace.

Ideas worth recalling

1. Remember that the subconscious mind has determined the success and wonderful achievements of all great scientific workers.

2. By giving your conscious attention and devotion to the solution of a perplexing problem, your subconscious mind gathers all the necessary information and presents it ful-blown to the conscious mind.

3. If you are wondering about the answer to a problem, try to solve it objectively. Get all the information you can from research and also from others. If no answer comes, turn it over to your subconscious mind prior to sleep, and the answer always comes. It never fails.

4. You do not always get the answer overnight. Keep on turning your request over to your subconscious until the daybreaks and the shadows flee away.

5. You delay the answer by thinking it will take a long time or that it is a major problem. Your subconscious has no problem it knows only the answer.

6. Believe that you have the answer now. Feel the joy of the answer and the way you would feel if you had the perfect answer. Your subconscious will respond to your feeling.

7. Any mental picture, backed by faith and perseverance, will come to pass through the miracle-working power of your subconscious. Trust it, believe in its power, and wonders will happen as you pray.

8. Your subconscious is the storehouse of memory, and within your subconscious are recorded all your experiences since childhood.

9. Scientists meditating on ancient scrolls, temples, fossils, etc., are able to reconstruct scenes of the past and make them alive today. Their subconscious mind comes to their aid.

10. Turn over your request for a solution to your subconscious prior to sleep. Trust it and believe in it, and the answer will come. It knows all and sees all, but you must not doubt or question its powers.

11. The action is your thought, and the reaction is the response of your subconscious mind. If your thoughts are wise, your actions and decisions will be wise.

12. Guidance comes as a feeling, an inner awareness, an overpowering hunch whereby you know that you know. It is an inner sense of touch. Follow it.

Chapter 13: Your Subconscious and the Wonders of Sleep

You spend about eight out of every twenty-four hours, or one-third of your entire life, in sleep. This is an inexorable law of life. This also applies to the animal and vegetable kingdoms. Sleep is a divine law, and many answers to our problems come to us when we are sound asleep upon the bed.

Many people have advocated the theory that you get tired during the day, that you go to sleep to rest the body, and that a reparative process takes place while you sleep. Nothing rests in sleep. Your heart, lungs, and all your vital organs func-tion while you are asleep. If you eat prior to sleep, the food is digested and assimilated; also, your skin secretes perspiration, and your nails and hair continue to grow.

Your subconscious mind never rests or sleeps. It is always active, controlling all your vital forces. The healing process takes place more rapidly while you are asleep as there is no interference from your conscious mind. Remarkable answers are given to you while you are asleep.

• Why we sleep

Dr. John Bigelow, a famous research authority on sleep, demonstrated that at night while asleep you receive impressions showing that the nerves of the eyes, ears, nose, and taste buds are active during sleep, and also that the nerves of your brain are quite active. He says that the main reason we sleep is because:

"The nobler part of the soul is united by abstraction to our higher nature and becomes a participant in the wisdom and foreknowledge of the gods."

Dr. Bigelow states also, "The results of my studies have not only strengthened my convictions that the supposed exemption from customary toils and activities was not the final purpose of sleep, but have also made clearer to my mind the conviction that no part of a man's life deserves to be considered more indispensable to its symmetrical and perfect spiritual development than the while he is separated from the phenomenal world in sleep."

• Prayer, a form of sleep

Your conscious mind gets involved with vexations, strife, and contentions of the day, and it is very necessary to withdraw periodically from sense evidence and the objective world, and commune silently with the inner wisdom of your subconscious mind. By claiming guidance, strength, and greater intelligence in all phases of your life, you will be enabled to overcome all difficulties and solve your daily problems.

This regular withdrawal from sense evidence and the noise and confusion of everyday living is also a form of sleep, i.e., you become asleep to the world of the senses and alive to the wisdom and power of your subconscious mind.

• Startling effects of sleep deprivation

Lack of sleep can cause you to become irritable, moody, and depressed. Dr. George Stevenson of the National Association for Mental Health says, "I believe it can safely be said that all human beings need a minimum of six hours' sleep to be healthy. Most people need more. Those who think they can get along on less are fooling themselves."

Medical research scholars, investigating sleep processes and deprivation of sleep, point out that severe insomnia has preceded psychotic breakdown in some instances. Remember, you are spiritually recharged during sleep, and adequate sleep is essential to produce joy and vitality in life.

• You need more sleep

Robert O'Brien, in an article, "Maybe You Need More Sleep," in an issue of The Reader's Digest, reports the following experiment on sleep:

"For the last three years experiments have been in progress at Walter Reed Army Institute of Research in Washington, D.C. Subjects—more than one hundred military and civilian volunteers—have been kept awake for as long as four days. Thousands of tests have measured the effects on their behavior and personality. Results of these tests have given scientists astonishingly new insights into the mysteries of sleep.

"They now know that the tired brain apparently craves sleep so hungrily that it will sacrifice anything to get it. After only a few hours of sleep loss, fleeting stolen naps called 'lapses,' or micro-sleep, occurred at the rate of three or four an hour. As in real sleep, eyelids drooped, heartbeat slowed. Each lapse lasted just a fraction of a second. Sometimes the lapses were periods of blankness; sometimes they were filled with images, wisps of dreams. As hours of sleep loss mounted, the lapses took place more often and lasted longer, perhaps two or three seconds. Even if the subjects had been piloting an airliner in a thunderstorm, they still couldn't have resisted micro-sleeps for those few priceless seconds. And it can happen to you, as many who have fallen asleep at the wheel of a car can testify.

"Another startling effect of sleep deprivation was its attack on human memory and perception. Many sleep-deprived subjects were unable to retain information long enough to relate it to the task they were supposed to perform. They were totally befuddled in situations requiring them to hold several factors in mind and act on them, as a pilot must when he skillfully integrates wind direction, air speed, altitude, and glide path to make a safe landing."

• Sleep brings counsel

A young lady in Los Angeles who listens to my morning radio talks told me that she had been offered a lucrative position in New York City at twice her present salary. She was wondering whether to accept or not and prayed prior to sleep as follows: "The creative intelligence of my subconscious mind knows what is best for me. Its tendency is always lifeward, and it reveals to me the right decision, which blesses all concerned. I give thanks for the answer which I know will come to me."

She repeated this simple prayer over and over again as a lullaby prior to sleep, and in the morning she had a persistent feeling that she should not accept the offer. She rejected the offer and subsequent events verified her inward sense of knowing, because the company went bankrupt in a few months following their offer of employment to her.

The conscious mind may be correct on the facts objectively known, but the intuitive faculty of her subconscious mind saw the failure of the concern in question, and prompted her accordingly.

• Saved from certain disaster

I will illustrate how the wisdom of your subconscious mind can instruct you and protect you relative to your request for right action as you go to sleep.

Many years ago, before the Second World War, I was offered a very lucrative assignment in the Orient, and I prayed for guidance and the right decision as follows: "Infinite intelligence within me knows all things, and the right decision is revealed to me in divine order. I will recognize the answer when it comes."

I repeated this simple prayer over and over again as a lullaby prior to sleep, and in a dream came the vivid realization of things to come three years hence. An old friend appeared in the dream and said, "Read these headlines—do not go!" The headlines of the newspaper, which appeared in the dream, related to war and the attack on Pearl Harbor.

Occasionally, the writer dreams literally. The aforementioned dream was undoubtedly a dramatization of the subconscious mind which projected a person whom I trusted and respected. To some a warning may come in the form of a mother who appears in a dream. She tells the person not to go here or there, and the reason for the warning. Your subconscious mind is all-wise. It knows all things. Oftentimes it will speak to you only in a voice that your conscious mind will immediately accept as true. Sometimes your subconscious will warn you in a voice which sounds like that of your mother or some loved one which may cause you to stop on the street, and you find, if you had gone another foot, a falling object from a window might have struck you on the head.

My subconscious mind is one with the universal subconscious, and it knew the Japanese were planning a war, and it also knew when the war would start.

Dr. Rhine, director of the Department of Psychology at Duke University, has gathered together a vast amount of evidence showing that a great number of people all over the world see events before they happen, and in many instances are, therefore, able to avoid the tragic event which was foreseen vividly in a dream.

The dream which I had showed clearly the headlines in The New York Times about three years prior to the tragedy of Pearl Harbor. In consequence of this dream, I immediately cancelled the trip as I felt a subconscious compulsion to do so. Three years later the Second World War proved the truth of the inner voice of intuition.

• Your future is in your subconscious mind

Remember that the future, the result of your habitual thinking, is already in your mind except when you change it through prayer. The future of a country, likewise, is in the collective subconscious of the people of that nation. There is nothing strange in the dream I had wherein I saw the headlines of the New York newspapers long before the war began. The war had already taken place in mind, and all the plans of attack were already engraved on that great recording instrument, the subconscious mind or collective unconscious of the universal mind. Tomorrow's events are in your subconscious mind, so are next week's and next month's, and they may be seen by a highly psychic or clairvoyant person.

No disaster or tragedy can happen to you if you decide to pray. Nothing is predetermined or foreordained. Your mental attitude, i.e., the way you think, feel, and believe determines your destiny. You can, through scientific prayer, which is explained in a previous chapter, mold, fashion, and create your own future. Whatsoever a man soweth, that shall he also reap.

• A cat nap nets him $15,000

One of my students mailed me a newspaper clipping three or four years ago about a man called Ray Hammerstrom, a roller at the steel works in Pittsburgh operated by Jones and Laughlin Steel Corporation. He received $15,000 for his dream.

According to the article, the engineers could not fix a faulty switch in a newly installed bar mill which controlled the delivery of straight bars to the cooling beds. The engineers worked on the switch about eleven or twelve times to no avail.

Hammerstrom thought a lot about the problem and tried to figure out a new design, which might work. Nothing worked. One afternoon he lay down for a nap, and prior to sleep he began to think about the answer to the switch problem. He had a dream in which a perfect design for the switch was portrayed. When he awoke, he sketched his new design according to the outline of his dream.

This visionary catnap won Hammerstrom a check for $15,000; the largest award the firm ever gave an employee for a new idea.

• How a famous professor solved his problem in sleep

Dr. H. V. Helprecht, Professor of Assyrian at the Uni-versity of Pennsylvania, wrote as follows: "One Saturday evening . . . I had been wearying myself, in the vain attempt to decipher two small fragments of agate which were supposed to belong to the finger rings of some Babylonians.

"About midnight, weary and exhausted, I went to bed and dreamed the following remarkable dream: A tall, thin priest of Nippur, about forty years of age, led me to the treasure chamber of the temple . . . a small, low-ceilinged room without windows, while scraps of agate and lapis-lazuli lay scattered on the floor. Here he addressed me as follows: 'The two fragments which you have published separately on pages 22 and 26 belong together, are not finger rings . . .. The first two rings served as earrings for the statue of the god; the two fragments (you have) . . . are the portions of them. If you will put them together you will have confirmation of my words.' . . . I awoke at once . . . I examined the fragments . . . and to my astonishment found the dream verified. The problem was then at last solved."

This demonstrates clearly the creative manifestation of his subconscious mind, which knew the answer to all his problems.

• How the subconscious worked for a famous writer while he slept

Robert Louis Stevenson in one of his books, Across the Plains, devotes a whole chapter to dreams. He was a vivid dreamer and had the persistent habit of giving specific instructions to his subconscious every night prior to sleep. He would request his subconscious to evolve stories for him while he slept. For example, if Stevenson's funds were at low ebb, his command to his subconscious would be something like this: "Give me a good thrilling novel which will be marketable and profitable." His subconscious responded magnificently.

Stevenson says, "These little brownies [the intelligences and powers of his subconscious] can tell me a story piece by piece, like a serial, and keep me, its supposed creator, all the while in total ignorance of where they aim." And he added: "That part of my work which is done when I am up and about [while he is consciously aware and awake] is by no means necessarily mine, since all goes to show that the brownies have a hand in it even then."

• Sleep in peace and wake in joy

To those who suffer from insomnia, you will find the following prayer very effective. Repeat it slowly, quietly, and lovingly prior to sleep: "My toes are relaxed, my ankles are relaxed, my abdominal muscles are relaxed, my heart and lungs are relaxed, my hands and arms are relaxed, my neck is relaxed, my brain is relaxed, my face is relaxed, my eyes are relaxed, my whole mind and body are relaxed. I fully and freely forgive everyone, and I sincerely wish for them harmony, health, peace, and all the blessings of me. I am at peace; I am poised, serene, and calm. I rest in security and in peace. A great stillness steals over me, and a great calm quiets my whole being as I realize the Divine Presence within me. I know that the realization of life and love heals me. I wrap myself in the mantle of love and fall asleep filled with good will for all. Throughout the night peace remains with me, and in the morning I shall be filled with life and love. A circle of love is drawn around me. I will fear no evil, for Thou art with me. I sleep in peace, I wake in joy, and in Him I live, move, and have my being"

• Summary of your aids to the wonders of sleep

1. If you are worried that you will not wake up on time, suggest to your subconscious mind prior to sleep the exact time you wish to arise, and it will awaken you. It needs no clock. Do the same thing with all problems. There is nothing too hard for your subconscious.

2. Your subconscious never sleeps. It is always on the job. It controls all your vital functions. Forgive yourself and everyone else before you go to sleep, and healing will take place much more rapidly.

3. Guidance is given you while you are asleep, sometimes in a dream. The healing currents are also released, and in the morning you feel refreshed and rejuvenated.

4. When troubled by the vexations and strife of the day, still the wheels of your mind and think about the wisdom and intelligence lodged in your subconscious mind, which is ready to respond to you. This will give you peace, strength, and confidence.

5. Sleep is essential for peace of mind and health of body. Lack of sleep can cause irritation, depression, and mental disorders. You need eight hours' sleep.

6. Medical research scholars point out that insomnia precedes psychotic breakdowns.

7. You are spiritually recharged during sleep. Adequate sleep is essential for joy and vitality in life.

8. Your tired brain craves sleep so hungrily that it will sacrifice anything to get it. Many who have fallen asleep at the wheel of an automobile can testify to this.

9. Many sleep-deprived people have poor memories and lack proper coordination. They become befuddled, confused, and disorientated.

10. Sleep brings counsel. Prior to sleep, claim that the infinite intelligence of your subconscious mind is guiding and di-recting you. Then, watch for the lead, which comes, perhaps on awakening.

11. Trust your subconscious completely. Know that its tendency is always lifeward. Occasionally, your subconscious answers you in a very vivid dream and a vision in the night. You can be forewarned in a dream in the same way as the author of this book was warned.

12. Your future is in your mind now, based on your habitual thinking and beliefs. Claim infinite intelligence leads and guides you and that all good is yours, and your future will be wonderful. Believe it and accept it. Expect the best, and invariably the best will come to you.

13. If you are writing a novel, play, or book, or are working on an invention, speak to your subconscious mind at night and claim boldly that its wisdom, intelligence, and power are guiding, directing, and revealing to you the ideal play, novel, book, or revealing the perfect solution whatever it may be. Wonders will happen as you pray this way.

Chapter 14: Your Subconscious Mind and Marital Problems

Ignorance of the functions and powers of the mind is the cause of all marital trouble. Each using the law of mind correctly can solve friction between husband and wife. By praying together they stay together. The contemplation of divine ideals, the study of the laws of life, the mutual agreement on a common purpose and plan, and the enjoyment of personal freedom bring about that harmonious marriage, that wedded bliss, that sense of oneness where the two become one.

The best time to prevent divorce is before marriage. It is not wrong to try to get out of a very bad situation. But, why get into the bad situation in the first place? Would it not be better to give attention to the real cause of marital problems, in other words, to really get at the root of the matter involved?

As with all other problems of men and women, the problems of divorce, separation, annulment, and endless litigation are directly traceable to lack of knowledge of the working and interrelationship of the conscious and subconscious mind.

• The meaning of marriage

Marriage to be real must first be on a spiritual basis. It must be of the heart, and the heart is the chalice of love. Honesty, sincerity, kindness, and integrity are also forms of love. Each partner should be perfectly honest and sincere with the other. It is not a true marriage when a man marries a woman for her money, social position, or to lift his ego, because this indicates a lack of sincerity, honesty, and true love. Such a marriage is a farce, a sham, and a masquerade.

When a woman says, "I am tired working; I want to get married because I want security," her premise is false. She is not using the laws of mind correctly. Her security depends upon her knowledge of the interaction of the conscious and subconscious mind and its application.

For example, a woman will never lack for wealth or health if she applies the techniques outlined in the respective chapters of this book. Her wealth can come to her independent of her husband, father, or anyone else. A woman is not dependent on her husband for health, peace, joy, inspiration, guidance, love, wealth, security, happiness, or anything in the world. Her security and peace of mind come from her knowledge of the inner powers within her and from the constant use of the laws of her own mind in a constructive fashion.

• How to attract the ideal husband

You are now acquainted with the way your subconscious mind works. You know that whatever you impress upon it will be experienced in your world. Begin now to impress your subconscious mind with the qualities and characteristics you desire in a man.

The following is an excellent technique: Sit down at night in your armchair, close your eyes, let go, relax the body, become very quiet, passive, and receptive. Talk to your subconscious mind and say to it, "I am now attracting a man into my experience who is honest, sincere, loyal, faithful, peaceful, happy, and prosperous. These qualities, which I admire, are sinking down into my subconscious mind now. As I dwell upon these characteristics, they become a part of me and are embodied subconsciously.

"I know there is an irresistible law of attraction and that I attract to me a man according to my subconscious belief. I attract that which I feel to be true in my subconscious mind.

"I know I can contribute to his peace and happiness. He loves my ideals, and I love his ideals. He does not want to make me over; neither do I want to make him over. There is mutual love, freedom, and respect."

Practice this process of impregnating your subconscious mind. Then, you will have the joy of attracting to you a man possessing the qualities and characteristics you mentally dwelt upon. Your subconscious intelligence will open up a pathway, whereby both of you will meet, according to the irresistible and changeless flow of your own subconscious mind. Have a keen desire to give the best that is in you of love, devotion, and co-operation. Be receptive to this gift of love, which you have given to your subconscious mind.

• How to attract the ideal wife

Affirm as follows: "I now attract the right woman who is in complete accord with me. This is a spiritual union because it is divine love functioning through the personality of someone with whom I blend perfectly. I know I can give to this woman love, light, peace, and joy. I feel and believe I can make this woman's life full, complete, and wonderful.

"I now decree that she possesses the following qualities and attributes: She is spiritual, loyal, faithful, and true. She is harmonious, peaceful, and happy. We are irresistibly attracted to each other. Only that which belongs to love, truth, and beauty can enter my experience. I accept my ideal companion now."

As you think quietly and with interest on the qualities and attributes, which you admire in the companion you seek, you will build the mental equivalent into your mentality. Then, the deeper currents of your subconscious mind will bring both of you together in divine order.

• No need for third mistake

Recently a teacher said to me, "I have had three husbands and all three have been passive, submissive, and dependent on me to make all decisions and govern everything. Why do I attract such type men?"

I asked her whether she had known that her second husband was the effeminate type, and she replied, "Of course not. Had I known, I would not have married him." Apparently she had not learned anything from the first mistake. The trouble was with her personality make-up. She was very masculine, domineering, and unconsciously wanted someone who would be submissive and passive so that she could play the dominant role. All this was unconscious motivation, and her subconscious picture attracted to her what she subjectively wanted. She had to learn to break the pattern by adopting the right prayer process.

• How she broke the negative pattern

The above-mentioned woman learned a simple truth. When you believe you can have the type of man you idealize, it is done unto you, as you believe. The following is the specific prayer she used to break the old subconscious pattern and attract to her the ideal mate: "I am building into my mentality the type of man I deeply desire. The man I attract for a husband is strong, powerful, loving, very masculine, successful, honest, loyal, and faithful. He finds love and happiness with me. I love to follow where he leads.

"I know he wants me, and I want him. I am honest, sincere, loving, and kind. I have wonderful gifts to offer him. They are good will, a joyous heart, and a healthy body. He offers me the same. It is mutual. I give and I receive. Divine intelligence knows where this man is, and the deeper wisdom of my subconscious mind is now bringing both of us together in its own way, and we recognize each other immediately. I release this request to my subconscious mind, which knows how to bring my request to pass. I give thanks for the perfect answer."

She prayed in the above manner night and morning, affirming these truths and knowing that through frequent occupation of the mind she would reach the mental equivalent of that which she sought.

• The answer to her prayer

Several months went by. She had a great number of dates and social engagements, none of which was agreeable to her. When she was about to question, waiver, doubt, and vacillate, she reminded herself that the infinite intelligence was bringing it to pass in its own way and that there was nothing to be concerned about. Her final decree in her divorce proceedings was granted which brought her a great sense of release and mental freedom.

Shortly afterward she went to work as a receptionist in a doctor's office. She told me that the minute she saw the physician she knew he was the man she was praying about. Apparently he knew it, too, because he proposed to her the first week she was in the office, and their subsequent marriage was ideally happy. This physician was not the passive or submissive type, but was a real man, a former football player, an outstanding athlete, and was a deeply spiritual man though he was completely devoid of any sectarian or denominational affiliation.

She got what she prayed for because she claimed it mentally until she reached the point of saturation. In other words, she mentally and emotionally united with her idea, and it became a part of her in the same way that an apple becomes a part of her blood stream.

• Should I get a divorce?

Divorce is an individual problem. It cannot be generalized. In some cases, of course, there never should have been a marriage. In some cases, divorce is not the solution, no more so than marriage is the solution for a lonely man. Divorce may be right for one person and wrong for another. A divorced woman may be far more sincere and noble than many of her married sisters who perhaps are living a lie.

For example, I once talked with a woman whose husband was a dope fiend, an ex-convict, a wife-beater, and a non-provider. She had been told it was wrong to get a divorce. I explained to her that marriage is of the heart. If two hearts blend harmoniously, lovingly, and sincerely, that is the ideal marriage. The pure action of the heart is love.

Following this explanation she knew what to do. She knew in her heart that there is no divine law which compelled her to be browbeaten, intimidated, and beaten because someone said, "I pronounce you man and wife."

If you are in doubt as to what to do, ask for guidance, knowing that there is always an answer, and you will receive it. Follow the lead that comes to you in the silence of your soul. It speaks to you in peace.

• Drifting into divorce

Recently a young couple, married for only a few months, was seeking a divorce. I discovered that the young man had a constant fear that his wife would leave him. He expected rejection, and he believed that she would be unfaithful. These thoughts haunted his mind, and became an obsession with him. His mental attitude was one of separation and suspicion. She felt unresponsive to him; it was his own feeling or atmosphere of loss and separation operating through them. This brought about a condition or action in accordance with the mental pattern behind it. There is a law of action and reaction, or cause and effect. The thought is the action, and the response of the subconscious mind is the reaction.

His wife left home and asked for a divorce, which is what he feared and believed she would do.

• Divorce begins in the mind

Divorce takes place first in the mind; the legal proceedings follow after. These two young people were full of resentment, fear, suspicion, and anger. These attitudes weaken, exhaust, and debilitate the whole being. They learned that hate divides and that love unites. They began to realize what they had been doing with their minds. Neither one of them knew the law of mental action, nor they were misusing their minds and bringing on chaos and misery. These two people went back together at my suggestion and experimented with prayer therapy.

They began to radiate love, peace, and good will to each other. Each one practiced radiating harmony, health, peace, and love to the other, and they alternated in the reading of the Psalms every night. Their marriage is growing more beautiful every day.

• The nagging wife

Many times the reason the wife nags is because she gets no attention. Oftentimes, it is a craving for love and affection. Give your wife attention, and show your appreciation. Praise and exalt all her many good points. There is also the nagging type of woman who wants to make the man conform to her particular pattern. This is about the quickest way in the world to get rid of a man.

The wife and the husband must cease being scavengers— always looking at the petty faults or errors in each other. Let each give attention and praise for the constructive and wonderful qualities in the other.

• The brooding husband

If a man begins to brood, grows morbid against his wife because of the things she said or did, he is, psychologically speaking, committing adultery. One of the meanings of adultery is idolatry, i.e., giving attention to or uniting mentally with that which is negative and destructive. When a man is silently resenting his wife and is full of hostility toward her, he is unfaithful. He is not faithful to his marriage vows, which are to love, cherish, and honor her all the days of his life.

The man who is brooding, bitter, and resentful can swallow his sharp remarks, abate his anger, and he can go to great lengths to be considerate, kind, and courteous. He can deftly skirt the differences. Through praise and mental effort, he can get out of the habit of antagonism. Then, he will be able to get along better, not only with his wife, but with business associates also. Assume the harmonious state, and eventually you will find peace and harmony.

• The great mistake

A great mistake is to discuss your marital problems or difficulties with neighbors and relatives. Suppose, for example, a wife says to the neighbor, "John never gives me any money. He treats my mother abominably, drinks to excess, and is constantly abusive and insulting."

Now, this wife is degrading and belittling her husband in the eyes of all the neighbors and relatives. He no longer appears as the ideal husband to them. Never discuss your marital problems with anyone except a trained counselor. Why cause numer-ous people to think negatively of your marriage? Moreover, as you discuss and dwell upon these shortcomings of your husband, you are actually creating these states within yourself. Who is thinking and feeling it? You are! As you think and feel, so are you.

Relatives will usually give you the wrong advice. It is usually biased and prejudiced because it is not given in an impersonal way. Any advice you receive which violates the golden rule, which is a cosmic law, is not good or sound.

It is well to remember that no two human beings ever lived beneath the same roof without clashes of temperament, periods of hurts and strain. Never display the unhappy side of your marriage to your friends. Keep your quarrels to yourself. Refrain from criticism and condemnation of your partner.

• Don't try to make your wife over

A husband must not try to make his wife over into a second edition of himself. The tactless attempt to change her in many ways is foreign to her nature. These attempts are always foolish, and many times result in dissolution of the marriage. These attempts to alter her destroy her pride and self-esteem, and arouse a spirit of contrariness and resentment that proves fatal to the marriage bond.

Adjustments are needed, of course, but if you have a good look inside your own mind, and study your character and behavior, you will find so many shortcomings, they will keep you busy the rest of your Me. If you say, "I will make him over into what I want," you are looking for trouble and the divorce court. You are asking for misery. You will have to learn the hard way that there is no one to change but yourself.

• Pray together and stay together through steps in prayer

The first step: Never carry over from one day to another accumulated irritations arising from little disappointments. Be sure to forgive each other for any sharpness before you retire at night. The moment you awaken in the morning, claim infinite intelligence is guiding you in all your ways. Send out loving thoughts of peace, harmony, and love to your marriage partner, to all members of the family, and to the whole world.

The second step: Say grace at breakfast. Give thanks for the wonderful food, for your abundance, and for all your blessings. Make sure that no problems, worries, or arguments shall enter into the table conversation; the same applies at dinnertime. Say to your wife or husband, "I appreciate all you are doing, and I radiate love and good will to you all day long."

The third step: The husband and wife should alternate in praying each night. Do not take your marriage partner for granted. Show your appreciation and love. Think appreciation and good will, rather than condemnation, criticism, and nagging. The way to build a peaceful home and a happy marriage is to use a foundation of love, beauty, harmony, mutual respect, faith in God, and all things good. Read the 23rd, 27th, and 91st Psalms, and other great texts of the Bible before going to sleep. As you practice these truths, your marriage will grow more and more blessed through the years.

Pointers to review

1. Ignorance of mental and spiritual laws is the cause of all marital unhappiness. By praying scientifically together, you stay together.

2. The best time to prevent divorce is before marriage. If you learn how to pray in the right way, you will attract the right mate for you.

3. Marriage is the union of a man and woman who are bound together by love. Their hearts beat as one, and they move onward, upward, and Godward.

4. Marriage does not bequeath happiness. People find happiness by dwelling on the eternal truths of God and the spiritual values of life. Then, the man and woman can contribute to each other's happiness and joy.

5. You attract the right mate by dwelling on the qualities and characteristics you admire in a woman or a man, and then your subconscious mind will bring you together in divine order.

6. You must build into your mentality the mental equivalent of what you want in a marriage partner. If you want to attract an honest, sincere, and loving partner in life, you must be honest, sincere, and loving yourself.

7. You do not have to repeat mistakes in marriage. When you really believe you can have the type man or woman you idealize, it is done unto you, as you believe. To believe is to accept something as true. Accept your ideal companion now mentally.

8. Do not wonder how, why, or where you will meet the mate you are praying for. Trust implicitly the wisdom of your subconscious mind. It has the "know-how," and you don't have to assist it.

9. You are mentally divorced when you indulge in peeves, grudges, ill will, and hostility toward your marriage partner. You are mentally dwelling with error in the bed of your mind. Adhere to your marriage vows, "I promise to cherish, love, and honor him (or her) all the days of my life."

10. Cease projecting fear patterns to your marriage partner. Project love, peace, harmony, and good will, and your marriage will grow more beautiful and more wonderful through the years.

11. Radiate love, peace, and good will to each other. These vibrations are picked up by the subconscious mind resulting in mutual trust, affection, and respect.

12. A nagging wife is usually seeking attention and appreciation. She is craving for love and affection. Praise and exalt her many good points. Show her that you love her and appreciate her.

13. A man who loves his wife does not do anything unloving or unkind in word, manner, or action. Love is what love does.

14. In marital problems, always seek expert advice. You would not go to a carpenter to pull a tooth; neither should you discuss your marriage problems with relatives or friends. You should go to a trained person for counsel.

15. Never try to make your wife or husband over. These attempts are always foolish and tend to destroy the pride and self-esteem of the other. Moreover, it arouses a spirit of resentment that proves fatal to the marriage bond. Cease trying to make the other a second edition of yourself.

16. Pray together and you will stay together. Scientific prayer solves all problems. Mentally picture your wife as she ought to be, joyous, happy, healthy, and beautiful. See your husband, as he ought to be, strong, powerful, loving, harmonious, and kind. Maintain this mental picture, and you will experience the marriage made in heaven, which is harmony and peace.

Chapter 15: Your Subconscious Mind and Your Happiness

William James, father of American psychology, said that the greatest discovery of the nineteenth century was not in the realm of physical science. The greatest discovery was the power of the subconscious touched by faith. In every human being is that limitless reservoir of power, which can overcome any problem in the world.

True and lasting happiness will come into your life the day you get the clear realization that you can overcome any weakness—the day you realize that your subconscious can solve your problems, heal your body, and prosper you beyond your fondest dream.

You might have felt very happy when your child was born, when you got married, when you graduated from college, or when you won a great victory or a prize. You might have been very happy when you became engaged to the loveliest girl or the most handsome man. You could go on and list innumerable experiences, which have made you happy. However, no matter how marvelous these experiences are, they do not give real lasting happiness—they are transitory.

The Book of Proverbs gives the answer: Whosoever trusteth in the Lord, happy is he. When you trust in the Lord (the power and wisdom of your subconscious mind) to lead, guide, govern, and direct all your ways, you will become poised, serene, and relaxed. As you radiate love, peace, and good will to all, you are really building a superstructure of happiness for all the days of your life.

• You must choose happiness

Happiness is a state of mind. There is a phrase in the Bible which says, Choose ye this day whom ye will serve. You have the freedom to choose happiness. This may seem extraordinarily simple, and it is. Perhaps this is why people stumble over the way to happiness; they do not see the simplicity of the key to happiness. The great things of life are simple, dynamic, and creative. They produce well-being and happiness.

St. Paul reveals to you how you can think your way into a life of dynamic power and happiness in these words: Finally, brethren, whatsoever things are true, whatsoever things are honest, whatsoever things are just, whatsoever things are pure, whatsoever things are lovely, whatsoever things are of good report; if there be any virtue, and if there be any praise, think on these things. PHIL. 4:8.

• How to choose happiness

Begin now to choose happiness. This is how you do it: When you open your eyes in the morning, say to yourself, "Divine order takes charge of my life today and every day. All things work together for good for me today. This is a new and wonderful day for me. There will never be another day like this one. I am divinely guided all day long, and whatever I do will prosper. Divine love surrounds me, enfolds me, and enwraps me, and I go forth in peace. Whenever my attention wanders away from that which is good and constructive, I will immediately bring it back to the contemplation of that which is lovely and of good report. I am a spiritual and mental magnet attracting to myself all things, which bless and prosper me. I am going to be a wonderful success in all my undertakings today. I am definitely going to be happy all day long."

Start each day in this manner: then you will be choosing happiness, and you will be a radiant joyous person.

• He made it a habit to be happy

A number of years ago, I stayed for about a week in a farmer's house in Connemarra on the west coast of Ireland. He seemed to be always singing and whistling and was full of humor.

I asked him the secret of his happiness, and his reply was: "It is a habit of mine to be happy. Every morning when I awaken and every night before I go to sleep, I bless my family, the crops, the cattle, and I thank God for the wonderful harvest."

This farmer had made a practice of this for over forty years. As you know, thoughts repeated regularly and systematically sink into the subconscious mind and become habitual. He discovered that happiness is a habit.

• You must desire to be happy

There is one very important point about being happy. You must sincerely desire to be happy. There are people who have been depressed, dejected, and unhappy so long that was they suddenly made happy by some wonderful, good, joyous news, they would actually be like the woman who said to me, "It is wrong to be so happy!" They have been so accustomed to the old mental patterns that they do not feel at home being happy! They long for the former, depressed, unhappy state.

I knew a woman in England who had rheumatism for many years. She would pat herself on the knee and say, "My rheumatism is bad today. I cannot go out. My rheumatism keeps me miserable."

This dear elderly lady got a lot of attention from her son, daughter, and the neighbors. She really wanted her rheumatism. She enjoyed her "misery" as she called it. This woman did not really want to be happy.

I suggested a curative procedure to her. I wrote down some biblical verses and told her that if she gave attention to these truths, her mental attitude would undoubtedly change and would result in her faith and confidence in being restored to health. She was not interested. There seems to be a peculiar, mental, morbid streak in many people, whereby they seem to enjoy being miserable and sad.

• Why choose unhappiness?

Many people choose unhappiness by entertaining these ideas: "Today is a black day; everything is going to go wrong."

"I am not going to succeed." "Everyone is against me." "Business is bad, and it is going to get worse." "I'm always late." "I never get the breaks." "He can, but I can't." If you have this attitude of mind the first thing in the morning, you will attract all these experiences to you, and you will be very unhappy.

Begin to realize that the world you live in is determined largely by what goes on in your mind. Marcus Aurelius, the great Roman philosopher and sage, said, "A man's life is what his thoughts make of it." Emerson, America's foremost philosopher, said, "A man is what he thinks all day long." The thoughts you habitually entertain in your mind have the tendency to actualize themselves in physical conditions.

Make certain you do not indulge in negative thoughts, defeatist thoughts, or unkind, depressing thoughts. Recall frequently to your mind that you can experience nothing outside your own mentality.

• If I had a million dollars, I would be happy

I have visited many men in mental institutions who were millionaires, but they insisted they were penniless and destitute. They were incarcerated because of psychotic, paranoid, and manic-depressive tendencies. Wealth in and of itself will not make you happy. On the other hand, it is not a deterrent to happiness. Today, there are many people trying to buy happiness through the purchase of radios, television sets, automobiles, a home in the country, a private yacht, and a swimming pool, but happiness cannot be purchased or procured in that way.

The kingdom of happiness is in your thought and feeling. Too many people have the idea that it takes something artificial to produce happiness. Some say, "If I were elected mayor, made president of the organization, promoted to general manager of the corporation, I would be happy."

The truth is that happiness is a mental and spiritual state. None of these positions mentioned will necessarily bequeath happiness. Your strength, joy, and happiness consist in finding out the law of divine order and right action lodged in your subconscious mind and by applying these principles in all phases of your life.

• He found happiness to be the harvest of a quiet mind

Lecturing in San Francisco some years ago, I interviewed a man who was very unhappy and dejected over the way his business was going. He was the general manager. His heart was filled with resentment toward the vice president and the president of the organization. He claimed that they opposed him. Because of this internal strife, business was declining; he was receiving no dividends or stock bonuses.

This is how he solved his business problem: The first thing in the morning he affirmed quietly as follows, "All those working in our corporation are honest, sincere, co-operative, faithful, and full of good will to all. They are mental and spiritual links in the chain of this corporation's growth, welfare, and prosperity. I radiate love, peace, and good will in my thoughts, words, and deeds to my two associates and to all those in the company. The president and the vice president of our company are divinely guided in all their undertakings. The infinite intelligence of my subconscious mind makes all decisions through me. There is only right action in all our business transactions and in our relationship with each other. I send the messengers of peace, love, and good will before me to the office. Peace and harmony reign supreme in the minds and hearts of all those in the company including myself. I now go forth into a new day, full of faith, confidence, and trust."

This business executive repeated the above meditation slowly three times in the morning, feeling the truth of what he affirmed. When fearful or angry thoughts came into his mind during the day, he would say to himself, "Peace, harmony, and poise govern my mind at all times."

As he continued disciplining his mind in this manner, all the harmful thoughts ceased to come, and peace came into his mind. He reaped the harvest.

Subsequently, he wrote me to the effect that at the end of about two weeks of reordering his mind, the president and the vice president called him into the office, praised his operations and his new constructive ideas, and remarked how fortunate they were in having him as general manager. He was very happy in discovering that man finds happiness within himself.

• The block or stump is not really there

I read a newspaper article some years ago, which told about a horse that had shied when he came to a stump on the road. Subsequently, every time the horse came to that same stump, he shied. The farmer dug the stump out, burned it, and leveled the old road. Yet, for twenty-five years, every time the horse passed the place where the former stump was, he shied. The horse was shying at the memory of a stump.

There is no block to your happiness save in your own thought life and mental imagery. Is fear or worry holding you back? Fear is a thought in your mind. You can dig it up this very moment by supplanting it with faith in success, achievement, and victory over all problems.

I knew a man who failed in business. He said to me, "I made mistakes. I've learned a lot. I am going back into business, and I will be a tremendous success." He faced up to that stump in his mind. He did not whine or complain, but he tore up the stump of failure, and through believing in his inner powers to back him up, he banished all fear thoughts and old depressions. Believe in yourself, and you will succeed and be happy.

• The happiest people

The happiest man is he who constantly brings forth and practices what is best in him. Happiness and virtue complement each other. The best are not only the happiest, but the happiest are usually the best in the art of living life successfully. God is the highest and best in you. Express more of God's love, light, truth, and beauty, and you will become one of the happiest persons in the world today.

Epictetus, the Greek stoic philosopher, said, "There is but one way to tranquility of mind and happiness; let this, therefore, be always ready at hand with thee, both when thou wakest early in the morning, and all the day long, and when thou goest late to sleep, to account no external things thine own, but commit all these to God."

Ideas worth recalling

1. William James said that the greatest discovery of the 19th century was the power of the subconscious mind touched by faith.

2. There is tremendous power within you. Happiness will come to you when you acquire a sublime confidence in this power. Then, you will make your dreams come true.

3. You can rise victorious over any defeat and realize the cherished desires of your heart through the marvelous power of your subconscious mind. This is the meaning of whosoever trusteth in the Lord [spiritual laws of the subconscious mind], happy is he.

4. You must choose happiness. Happiness is a habit. It is a good habit to ponder often on Whatsoever things are true, whatsoever things are honest, whatsoever things are just, whatsoever things are pure, whatsoever things are lovely, whatsoever things are of good report; if there be any virtue, and if there be any praise, think on these things.

5. When you open your eyes in the morning, say to yourself, I choose happiness today. I choose success today. I choose right action today. I choose love and good will for all today. I choose peace today. Pour life, love, and interest into this affirmation, and you have chosen happiness.

6. Give thanks for all your blessings several times a day. Furthermore, pray for the peace, happiness, and prosperity of all members of your family, your associates, and all people everywhere.

7. You must sincerely desire to be happy. Nothing is accomplished without desire. Desire is a wish with wings of imagination and faith. Imagine the fulfillment of your desire, and feel its reality, and it will come to pass. Happiness comes in answered prayer.

8. By constantly dwelling on thoughts of fear, worry, anger, hate, and failure, you will become very depressed and unhappy. Remember, your life is what your thoughts make of it.

9. You cannot buy happiness with all the money in the world. Some millionaires are very happy, some are very unhappy. Many people with very little worldly goods are very happy, and some are very unhappy. Some married people are happy, and some very unhappy. Some single people are happy, and some are very unhappy. The kingdom of happiness is in your thought and feeling.

10. Happiness is the harvest of a quiet mind. Anchor your thoughts on peace, poise, security, and divine guidance, and your mind will be productive of happiness.

11. There is no block to your happiness. External things are not causative; these are effects, not cause. Take your cue from the only creative principle within you. Your thought is cause, and a new cause produces a new effect. Choose happiness.

12. The happiest man is he who brings forth the highest and the best in him. God is the highest and the best in him, for the kingdom of God is within.

Chapter 16: Your Subconscious Mind and Harmonious Human Relations

In studying this book, you learn that your subconscious mind is a recording machine, which faithfully reproduces whatever you impress upon it. This is one of the reasons for the application of the Golden Rule in human relations.

"All things whatsoever ye would that men should do unto you, do ye even so to them". This quotation has outer and inner meanings. You are interested in its inner meaning from the standpoint of your subconscious mind, which is: As you would that men should think about you, think you about them in like manner. As you would that men should feel about you, feel you also about them in like manner. As you would want men to act toward you, act you toward them in like manner.

For example, you may be polite and courteous to someone in your office, but when his back is turned, you are very critical and resentful toward him in your mind. Such negative thoughts are highly destructive to you. It is like taking poison. You are actually taking mental poisons, which rob you of vitality, enthusiasm, strength, guidance, and good will. These negative thoughts and emotions sink down into your subconscious, and cause all kinds of difficulties and maladies in your life.

• The master key to happy relationships with others

Judge not, that ye be not judged. For with what judgment ye judge, ye shall be judged: and with what measure ye mete, it shall be measured to you again.

A study of these quotations and the application of the inner truths therein contained represent the real key to harmonious relations. To judge is to think, to arrive at a mental verdict or conclusion in your mind. The thought you have about the other person is your thought, because you are thinking it. Your thoughts are creative, therefore, you actually create in your own experience what you think and feel about the other person. It is also true that the suggestion you give to another, you give to yourself because your mind is the creative medium.

This is why it is said: For with what judgment ye judge, ye shall be judged. When you know this law and the way your subconscious mind works, you are careful to think, feel, and act rights toward the other. These verses teach you about the emancipation of man and reveal to you the solution to your individual problems.

• And with what measure ye mete, it shall be measured to you again

The good you do for others comes back to you in like measure; and the evil you do returns to you by the law of your own mind. If a man cheats and deceives another, he is actually cheating and deceiving himself. His sense of guilt and mood of loss inevitably will attract loss to him in some way, at some time. His subconscious records his mental act and reacts according to the mental intention or motivation.

Your subconscious mind is impersonal and unchanging, neither considering persons nor respecting religious affiliations or institutions of any kind. It is neither compassionate nor vindictive. The way you think, feel, and act toward others returns at last upon yourself.

• The daily headlines made him sick

Begin now to observe yourself. Observe your reactions to people, conditions, and circumstances. How do you respond to the events and news of the day? It makes no difference if all the other people were wrong and you alone were right. If the news disturbs you, it is your evil because your negative emotions robbed you of peace and harmony.

A woman wrote me about her husband, saying that he goes into a rage when he reads what certain newspaper columnists write in the newspaper. She added that this constant reaction of anger and suppressed rage on his part brought on bleeding ulcers, and his physician recommended an emotional reconditioning.

I invited this man to see me and I explained to him the way his mind functions indicating how emotionally immature it was to get angry when others write articles with which he disapproves or disagrees.

He began to realize that he should give the newspaperman freedom to express himself even though the latter disagreed with him politically, religiously, or in any other way. In the same manner, the newspaperman would give him freedom to write a letter to the newspaper disagreeing with his published statements. He learned that he could disagree without being disagreeable. He awakened to the simple truth that it is never what a person says or does that affects him, it is his reaction to what is said or done that matters. This explanation was the cure for this man, and he realized that with a little practice he could master his morning tantrums. His wife told me, subsequently, that he laughed at himself and also at what the columnists say. They no longer have power to disturb, annoy, and irritate him. His ulcers have disappeared due to his emotional poise and serenity.

• I hate women, but I like men

A private secretary was very bitter toward some of the girls in her office because they were gossiping about her, and as she said, spreading vicious lies about her. She admitted that she did not like women. She said, "I hate women, but I like men." I discovered also that she spoke to the girls who were under her in the office in a very haughty, imperious, and irritable tone of voice. She pointed out that they took a delight in making things difficult for her. There was a certain pomposity in her way of speaking, and I could see where her tone of voice would affect some people unpleasantly.

If all the people in the office or factory annoy you, isn't it a possibility that the vibration, annoyance, and turmoil may be due to some subconscious pattern or mental projection from you? We know that a dog will react ferociously if you hate or fear dogs. Animals pick up your subconscious vibrations and react accordingly. Many undisciplined human beings are just as sensitive as dogs, cats, and other animals.

I suggested a process of prayer to this private secretary who hated women, explaining to her that when she began to identify herself with spiritual values and commenced to affirm the truths of life, her voice, mannerisms, and hatred of women would completely disappear. She was surprised to know that the emotion of hatred shows up in a person's speech, actions, in his writings, and in all phases of his life. She ceased reacting in the typical, resentful, and angry way. She established a pattern of prayer, which she practiced regularly, systematically, and conscien-tiously in the office.

The prayer was as follows: "I think, speak, and act lovingly, quietly, and peacefully. I now radiate love, peace, tolerance, and kindliness to all the girls who criticized me and gossiped about me. I anchor my thoughts on peace, harmony, and good will to all. Whenever I am about to react negatively, I say firmly to myself, 'I am going to think, speak, and act from the standpoint of the principle of harmony, health, and peace within myself.' Creative intelligence leads, rules, and guides me in all my ways."

The practice of this prayer transformed her life, and she found that all criticism and annoyance ceased. The girls became co-workers and friends along life's journey. She discovered that there is no one to change but myself.

• His inner speech held back his promotion

One day a salesman came to see me and described his difficulties in working with the sales manager of his organization. He had been with the company ten years and had received no promotion or recognition of any kind. He showed me his sales figures, which were greater proportionately than the other men in the territory. He said that the sales manager did not like him, that he was unjustly treated, and that at conferences the manager was rude to him, and at times ridiculed his suggestions.

I explained that undoubtedly the cause was to a great degree within himself, and that his concept and belief about his superior bore witness to the reaction of this man. The measure we mete, shall be measured to us again. His mental measure or concept of the sales manager was that he was mean and cantankerous. He was filled with bitterness and hostility toward the executive. On his way to work he conducted a vigorous conversation with himself filled with criticism, mental arguments, recriminations, and denunciations of his sales manager.

What he gave out mentally, he was inevitably bound to get back. This salesman realized that his inner speech was highly destructive because the intensity and force of his silent thoughts and emotions, and personally conducted mental condemnation and vilification of the sales manager entered into his own subconscious mind. This brought about the negative response from his boss as well as creating many other personal, physical, and emotional disorders.

He began to pray frequently as follows: "I am the only thinker in my universe. I am responsible for what I think about my boss. My sales manager is not responsible for the way I think about him. I refuse to give power to any person, place, or thing to annoy me or disturb me. I wish health, success, peace of mind, and happiness for my boss. I sincerely wish him well, and I know he is divinely guided in all his ways."

He repeated this prayer out loud slowly, quietly, and feelingly, knowing that his mind is like a garden, and that whatever he plants in the garden will come forth like seeds after their kind.

I also taught him to practice mental imagery prior to sleep in this way: He imagined that his sales manager was congratulating him on his fine work, on his zeal and enthusiasm, and on his wonderful response from customers. He felt the reality of all this, felt his handshake, heard the tone of his voice, and saw him smile. He made a real mental movie, dramatizing it to the best of his ability. Night after night he conducted this mental movie, knowing that his subconscious mind was the receptive plate on which his conscious imagery would be impressed.

Gradually by a process of what may be termed mental and spiritual osmosis, the impression was made on his subconscious mind, and the expression automatically came forth. The sales manager subsequently called him up to San Francisco, congratulated him, and gave him a new assignment as Division Sales Manager over one hundred men with a big increase in salary. He changed his concept and estimate of his boss, and the latter responded accordingly.

• Becoming emotionally mature

What the other person says or does cannot really annoy or irritate you except you permit him to disturb you. The only way he can annoy you is through your own thought. For example, if you get angry, you have to go through four stages in your mind: You begin to think about what he said. You decide to get angry and generate an emotion of rage. Then, you decide to act. Perhaps, you talk back and react in kind. You see that the thought, emotion, reaction, and action all take place in your mind.

When you become emotionally mature, you do not respond negatively to the criticism and resentment of others. To do so would mean that you had descended to that state of low mental vibration and become one with the negative atmosphere of the other. Identify yourself with your aim in life, and do not permit any person, place, or thing to deflect you from your inner sense of peace, tranquility, and radiant health.

• The meaning of love in harmonious human relations

Sigmund Freud, the Austrian founder of psychoanalysis, said that unless the personality has love, it sickens and dies. Love includes understanding, good will, and respect for the divinity in the other person. The more love and good will you emanate and exude, the more comes back to you.

If you puncture the other fellow's ego and wound his estimate of himself, you cannot gain his good will. Recognize that every man wants to be loved and appreciated, and made to feel important in the world. Realize that the other man is conscious of his true worth, and that, like yourself, he feels the dignity of being an expression of the One Life-Principle animating all men. As you do this consciously and knowingly, you build the other person up, and he returns your love and good will.

• He hated audiences

An actor told me that the audience booed and hissed him on his first appearance on the stage. He added that the play was badly written and that undoubtedly he did not play a good role. He admitted openly to me that for months afterward he hated audiences. He called them dopes, dummies, stupid, ignorant, gullible, etc. He quit the stage in disgust and went to work in a drugstore for a year.

One day a friend invited him to hear a lecture in Town Hall, New York City, on "How to Get Along With Ourselves." This lecture changed his life. He went back to the stage and began to pray sincerely for the audience and himself. He poured out love and good will every night before appearing on the stage. He made it a habit to claim that the peace of God filled the hearts of all-present, and that all present were lifted up and inspired. During each performance he sent out love vibrations to the audience. Today, he is a great actor, and he loves and respects people. His good will and esteem are transmitted to others and are felt by them.

• Handling difficult people

There are difficult people in the world who are twisted and distorted mentally. They are malconditioned. Many are mental delinquents, argumentative, uncooperative, cantankerous, cynical, and sour on life. They are sick psychologically. Many people have deformed and distorted minds, probably warped during childhood. Many have congenital deformities. You would not condemn a person who had tuberculosis, nor should you condemn a person who is mentally ill. No one, for example, hates or resents a hunchback; there are many mental hunchbacks. You should have compassion and understanding. To understand all is to forgive all.

• Misery loves company

The hateful, frustrated, distorted, and twisted personality is out of tune with the Infinite. He resents those who are peaceful, happy, and joyous. Usually he criticizes, condemns, and vilifies those who have been very good and kind to him. His attitude is this: Why should they be so happy when he is so miserable? He wants to drag them down to his own level. Misery loves company. When you understand this you remain unmoved, calm, and dispassionate.

• The practice of empathy in human relations

A girl visited me recently stating that she hated another girl in her office. She gave as her reason that the other girl was prettier, happier, and wealthier than she, and, in addition, was engaged to the boss of the company where they worked. One day after the marriage had taken place, the crippled daughter (by a former marriage) of the woman whom she hated came into the office. The child put her arms around her mother and said, "Mommy, mommy, I love my new daddy! Look what he gave me!" She showed her mother a wonderful new toy.

She said to me, "My heart went out to that little girl, and I knew how happy she must feel. I got a vision of how happy this woman was. All of a sudden I felt love for her, and I went into the office and wished her all the happiness in the world, and I meant it."

In psychological circles today, this is called empathy, which simply means the imaginative projection of your mental attitude into that of another. She projected her mental mood or the feeling of her heart into that of the other woman, and began to think and look out through the other woman's brain. She was actually thinking and feeling as the other woman, and also as the child, because she likewise had projected herself into the mind of the child. She was looking out from that vantage point on the child's mother.

If tempted to injure or think ill of another, project yourself mentally into the mind of Moses and think from the standpoint of the Ten Commandments.

• Appeasement never wins

Do not permit people to take advantage of you and gain their point by temper tantrums, crying jags, or so-called heart attacks. These people are dictators who try to enslave you and make you do their bidding. Be firm but kind, and refuse to yield. Appeasement never wins. Refuse to contribute to their delinquency, selfishness, and possessiveness. Remember, do that which is right. You are here to fulfill your ideal and remain true to the eternal verities and spiritual values of life, which are eternal.

Give no one in all the world the power to deflect you from your goal, your aim in life, which is to express your hidden talents to the world, to serve humanity, and to reveal more and more of God's wisdom, truth, and beauty to all people in the world. Remain true to your ideal. Know definitely and absolutely that whatever contributes to your peace, happiness, and fulfillment must of necessity bless all men who walk the earth. The harmony of the part is the harmony of the whole, for the whole is in the part, and the part is in the whole. All you owe the other, as Paul says, is love, and love is the fulfilling of the law of health, happiness, and peace of mind.

Ideas worth recalling

1. Your subconscious mind is a recording machine, which reproduces your habitual thinking. Think good of the other, and you are actually thinking good about yourself.

2. A hateful or resentful thought is a mental poison. Do not think ill of another for to do so is to think ill of yourself. You are the only thinker in your universe, and your thoughts are creative.

3. Your mind is a creative medium; therefore, what you think and feel about the other, you are bringing to pass in your own experience. This is the psychological meaning of the Golden Rule. As you would that man should think about you, think you about them in the same manner.

4. To cheat, rob, or defraud another brings lack, loss, and limitation to yourself. Your subconscious mind records your inner motivations, thoughts, and feelings. These being of a negative nature; loss, limitation, and trouble come to you in countless ways. Actually, what you do to the other, you are doing to yourself.

5. The good you do, the kindness proffered, the love and good will you send forth, will all come back to you multiplied in many ways.

6. You are the only thinker in your world. You are responsible for the way you think about the other. Remember, the other person is not responsible for the way you think about him. Your thoughts are reproduced. What are you thinking now about the other fellow?

7. Become emotionally mature and permit other people to differ from you. They have a perfect right to disagree with you, and you have the same freedom to disagree with them. You can disagree without being disagreeable.

8. Animals pick up your fear vibrations and snap at you. If you love animals, they will never attack you. Many undisciplined human beings are just as sensitive as dogs, cats, and other animals.

9. Your inner speech, representing your silent thoughts and feelings, is experienced in the reactions of others toward you.

10. Wish for the other what you wish for yourself. This is the key to harmonious human relations.

11. Change your concept and estimate of your employer. Feel and know he is practicing the Golden Rule and the Law of Love, and he will respond accordingly.

12. The other person cannot annoy you or irritate you except you permit him. Your thought is creative; you can bless him. If someone calls you a skunk, you have the freedom to say to the other, "God's peace fills your soul."

13. Love is the answer to getting along with others. Love is understanding, good will, and respecting the divinity of the other.

14. You would not hate a hunchback or cripple. You would have compassion. Have compassion and understanding for mental hunchbacks who have been conditioned negatively. To understand all is to forgive all.

15. Rejoice in the success, promotion, and good fortune of the other. In doing so, you attract good fortune to yourself.

16. Never yield to emotional scenes and tantrums of others. Appeasement never wins. Do not be a doormat. Adhere to that which is right. Stick to your ideal, knowing that the mental outlook, which gives you peace, happiness, and joy, is right, good, and true. What blesses you, blesses all.

17. All you owe any person in the world is love, and love is wishing for everyone what you wish for yourself—health, happiness, and all the blessings of life.

Chapter 17: How to Use Your Subconscious Mind for Forgiveness

Life plays no favorites. God is Life, and this Life-Principle is flowing through you this moment. God loves to express Himself as harmony, peace, beauty, joy, and abundance through you. This is called the will of God or the tendency of Life.

If you set up resistance in your mind to the flow of Life through you, this emotional congestion will get snarled up in your subconscious mind and cause all kinds of negative conditions. God has nothing to do with unhappy or chaotic conditions in the world. Man's negative and destructive thinking brings about all these conditions. Therefore, it is silly to blame God for your trouble or sickness.

Many persons habitually set up mental resistance to the flow of Life by accusing and reproaching God for the sin, sickness, and suffering of mankind. Others cast the blame on God for their pains, aches, and loss of loved ones, personal tragedies, and accidents. They are angry at God, and they believe He is responsible for their misery.

As long as people entertain such negative concepts about God, they will experience the automatic negative reactions from their subconscious minds. Actually, such people do not know that they are punishing themselves. They must see the truth, find release, and give up all condemnation, resentment, and anger against anyone or any power outside themselves. Otherwise, they cannot go forward into a healthy, happy, or creative activity. The minute these people entertain a God of love in their minds and hearts, and when they believe that God is their Loving Father who watches over them, cares for them, guides them, sustains and strengthens them, this concept and belief about God or the Life-Principle will be accepted by their subconscious mind, and they will find themselves blessed in countless ways.

• Life always forgives you

Life forgives you when you cut your finger. The subconscious intelligence within you sets about immediately to repair it. New cells build bridges over the cut. Should you take some tainted food by error, Life forgives you and causes you to regurgitate it in order to preserve you. If you burn your hand, the Life-Principle reduces the edema and congestion, and gives you new skin, tissue, and cells. Life holds no grudges against you, and it is always forgiving you. Life brings you back to health, vitality, harmony, and peace, if you cooperate by thinking in harmony with nature. Negative, hurtful memories, bitterness, and ill will clutter up and impede the free flow of the Life-Principle in you.

• How he banished that feeling of guilt

I knew a man who worked every night until about one o'clock in the morning. He paid no attention to his two boys or his wife. He was always too busy working hard. He thought people should pat him on the back because he was working so arduously and persistently past midnight every night. He had a blood pressure of over two hundred and was full of guilt. Unconsciously, he proceeded to punish himself by hard work and he completely ignored his children. A normal man does not do that. He is interested in his boys and in their development. He does not shut his wife out of his world.

I explained to him why he was working so arduously, "There is something eating you inside, otherwise, you would not act this way. You are punishing yourself, and you have to learn to forgive yourself." He did have a deep sense of guilt. It was toward a brother.

I explained to him that God was not punishing him, but that he was punishing himself. For example, if you misuse the laws of life, you will suffer accordingly. If you put your hand on a naked charged wire, you will get burned. The forces of nature are not evil; it is your use of them that determines whether they have a good or evil effect. Electricity is not evil; it depends on how you use it, whether to burn down a structure or light up a home. The only sin is ignorance of the law, and the only punishment is the automatic reaction of man's misuse of the law.

If you misuse the principle of chemistry, you may blow up the office or the factory. If you strike your hand on a board, you may cause your hand to bleed. The board is not for that purpose. Its purpose may be to lean upon or to support your feet.

This man realized that God does not condemn or punish anyone, and that all his suffering was due to the reaction of his subconscious mind to his own negative and destructive thinking. He had cheated his brother at one time, and the brother had now passed on. Still, he was full of remorse and guilt.

I asked him, "Would you cheat your brother now?"
He said, "No."
"Did you feel you were justified at the time?"
His reply was, "Yes."
"But, you would not do it now?"
He added, "No, I am helping others to know how to live."
I added the following comment, "You have a greater reason and understanding now. Forgiveness is to forgive yourself. Forgiveness is getting your thoughts in line with the divine law of harmony. Self-condemnation is called hell (bondage and restriction); forgiveness is called heaven (harmony and peace)."

The burden of guilt and self-condemnation was lifted from his mind, and he had a complete healing. The doctor tested his blood pressure, and it had become normal. The explanation was the cure.

• A murderer learned to forgive himself

A man who murdered his brother in Europe visited me many years ago. He was suffering from great mental anguish and torture believing that God must punish him. He explained that his brother had been having an affair with his wife, and that he had shot him on the spur of the moment. This had happened about fifteen years previous to his interview with me. In the meantime, this man had married an American girl and had been blessed with three lovely children. He was in a posi-tion where he helped many people, and he was a transformed man.

My explanation to him was that physically and psychologically he was not the same man who shot his brother, since scientists inform us that every cell of our bodies changes every eleven months. Moreover, mentally and spiritually he was a new man. He was now full of love and good will for humanity. The "old" man who committed the crime fifteen years before was mentally and spiritually dead. Actually, he was condemning an innocent man!

This explanation had a profound effect upon him, and he said it was as if a great weight had been lifted from his mind. He realized the significance of the following truth in the Bible: Come now, let us reason together, saith the Lord: though your sins be as scarlet, they shall be as white as snow; though they be red like crimson, they shall be as wool. ISAIAH 1:18.

• Criticism cannot hurt you without your consent

A schoolteacher told me that one of her associates criticized a speech she had given, saying to her that she spoke too fast, she swallowed some of her words, she couldn't be heard, her diction was poor, and her speech ineffective. This teacher was furious and full of resentment toward her critic.

She admitted to me that the criticisms were just. Her first reaction was really childish, and she agreed that the letter was really a blessing and a marvelous corrective. She proceeded immediately to supplement her deficiencies in her speech by enrolling in a course in public speaking at City College. She wrote and thanked the writer of the note for her interest, expressing appreciation for her conclusions and findings, which enabled the teacher to correct the matter at once.

• How to be compassionate

Suppose none of the things mentioned in the letter had been true of the teacher. The latter would have realized that her class material had upset the prejudices, superstitions, or narrow sectarian beliefs of the writer of the note, and that a psychologically ill person was simply pouring forth her resentment because a psychological boil had been hurt.

To understand this fact is to be compassionate. The next logical step would be to pray for the other person's peace, harmony, and understanding. You cannot be hurt when you know that you are master of your thoughts, reactions, and emotions. Emotions follow thoughts, and you have the power to reject all thoughts, which may disturb or upset you.

• Left at the altar

Some years ago I visited a church to perform a marriage ceremony. The young man did not appear, and at the end of two hours, the bride-to-be shed a few tears, and then said to me, "I prayed for divine guidance. This might be the answer for He never faileth."

That was her reaction—faith in God and all things good. She had no bitterness in her heart because as she said, "It must not have been right action because my prayer was for right action for both of us." Someone else having a similar experience would have gone into a tantrum, have had an emotional fit, required sedation, and perhaps needed hospitalization.

Tune in with the infinite intelligence within your subconscious depths, trusting the answer in the same way that you trusted your mother when she held you in her arms. This is how you can acquire poise and mental and emotional health.

• It is wrong to marry. Sex is evil and I am evil

Some time ago, I talked to a young lady aged twenty-two. She was taught that it was a sin to dance, to play cards, to swim, and to go out with men. She was threatened by her mother who told her she would burn eternally in hell-fire if she disobeyed her will and her religious teachings. This girl wore a black dress and black stockings. She wore no rouge, lipstick, or any form of make-up because her mother said that these things were sinful. Her mother told her that all men were evil, and that sex was of the devil and simply diabolic debauchery.

This girl had to learn how to forgive herself, as she was full of guilt. To forgive means to give for. She had to give up all these false beliefs for the truths of life and a new estimate of herself. When she went out with young men in the office where she worked, she had a deep sense of guilt and thought that God would punish her. Several eligible young men proposed to her, but she said to me, "It is wrong to marry. Sex is evil and I am evil." This was her conscience or early conditioning speaking.

She came to me once weekly for about ten weeks, and I taught her the workings of the conscious and subconscious mind as set forth in this book. This young girl gradually came to see that she had been completely brainwashed, mesmerized, and conditioned by an ignorant, superstitious, bigoted, and frus-trated mother. She broke away completely from her family and started to live a wonderful life.

At my suggestion she dressed up and had her hair attended to. She took lessons in dancing from a man, and she also took driving lessons. She learned to swim, play cards, and had a number of dates. She began to love He. She prayed for a divine companion by claiming that Infinite Spirit would attract to her a man who harmonized with her thoroughly. Eventually this came to pass. As she left my office one evening, there was a man waiting to see me and I casually introduced them. They are now married and harmonize with each other perfectly.

• Forgiveness is necessary for healing

Forgiveness of others is essential to mental peace and radiant health. You must forgive everyone who has ever hurt you if you want perfect health and happiness. Forgive yourself by getting your thoughts in harmony with divine law and order. You cannot really forgive yourself completely until you have forgiven others first. To refuse to forgive yourself is nothing more or less than spiritual pride or ignorance.

In the psychosomatic field of medicine today, it is being constantly stressed that resentment, condemnation of others, remorse, and hostility are behind a host of maladies ranging from arthritis to cardiac disease. They point out that these sick people, who were hurt, mistreated, deceived, or injured, were full of resentment and hatred for those who hurt them. This caused inflamed and festering wounds in their subconscious minds. There is only one remedy. They have to cut out and discard their hurts, and the one and only sure way is by forgiveness.

• Forgiveness is love in action

The essential ingredient in the art of forgiveness is the willingness to forgive. If you sincerely desire to forgive the other, you are fifty-one percent over the hurdle. I feel sure you know that to forgive the other does not necessarily mean that you like him or want to associate with him. You cannot be compelled to like someone, neither can a government legislate good will, love, peace, or tolerance. It is quite impossible to like people because someone in Washington issues an edict to that effect. We can, however, love people without liking them.

The Bible says, Love ye one another. This, anyone can do who really wants to do it. Love means that you wish for the other health, happiness, peace, joy, and all the blessings of life. There is only one prerequisite, and that is sincerity. You are not being magnanimous when you forgive, you are really being selfish, because what you wish for the other, you are actually wishing for yourself. The reason is that you are thinking it and you are feeling it. As you think and feel, so are you. Could anything be simpler than that?

• Technique of forgiveness

The following is a simple method, which works wonders in your life as you practice it: Quiet your mind, relax, and let go. Think of God and His love for you, and then affirm, "I fully and freely forgive (mention the name of the offender); I release him mentally and spiritually. I completely forgive everything connected with the matter in question. I am free, and he/she is free. It is a marvelous feeling. It is my day of general amnesty. I release anybody and everybody who has ever hurt me, and I wish for each and everyone health, happiness, peace, and all the blessings of life. I do this freely, joyously, and lovingly, and whenever I think of the person or persons who hurt me, I say, 'I have released you, and all the blessings of life are yours.' I am free and you are free. It is wonderful!"

The great secret of true forgiveness is that once you have forgiven the person, it is unnecessary to repeat the prayer. Whenever the person comes to your mind, or the particular hurt happens to enter your mind, wish the delinquent well, and say, "Peace be to you." Do this as often as the thought enters your mind. You will find that after a few days the thought of the person or experience will return less and less often, until it fades into nothingness.

• The acid test for forgiveness

There is an acid test for gold. There is also an acid test for forgiveness. If I should tell you something wonderful about someone who has wronged you, cheated you, or defrauded you, and you sizzled at hearing the good news about this person, the roots of hatred would still be in your subconscious mind, playing havoc with you.

Let us suppose you had a painful abscess on your jaw a year ago, and you told me about it. I would casually ask you if you had any pain now. You would automatically say, "Of course not, I have a memory of it but no pain." That is the whole story. You may have a memory of the incident but no sting or hurt any more. This is the acid test, and you must meet it psychologically and spiritually, otherwise, you are simply deceiving yourself and not practicing the true art of forgiveness.

115

• To understand all is to forgive all

When man understands the creative law of his own mind, he ceases to blame other people and conditions for making or marring his life. He knows that his own thoughts and feelings create his destiny. Furthermore, he is aware that externals are not the causes and conditioners of his life and his experiences. To think that others can mar your happiness that you are the football of a cruel fate that you must oppose and fight others for a living—all these and others like them are untenable when you understand that thoughts are things. The Bible says the same thing: For as a man thinketh in his heart, so is he. PROVERBS 23:7.

Pointers to review

1. God, or Life, is no respecter of persons. Life plays no favorites. Life, or God, seems to favor you when you align yourself with the principle of harmony, health, joy, and peace.

2. God, or Life, never sends disease, sickness, accident, or suffering. We bring these things on ourselves by our own negative destructive thinking based upon the law as we sow, so shall we reap.

3. Your concept of God is the most important thing in your life. If you really believe in a God of love, your subconscious mind will respond in countless blessings to you. Believe in a God of love.

4. Life, or God, holds no grudge against you. Life never condemns you. Life heals a severe cut on your hand. Life forgives you if you burn your finger. It reduces the edema and restores the part to wholeness and perfection.

5. Your guilt complex is a false concept of God and Life. God, or Life, does not punish or judge you. You do this to yourself by your false beliefs, negative thinking, and self-condemnation.

6. God, or Life, does not condemn or punish you. The forces of nature are not evil. The effect of their use depends on how you use the power within you. You can use electricity to kill someone or to light the house. You can use water to drown a child, or quench his thirst. Good and evil come right back to the thought and purpose in man's own mind.

7. God, or Life, never punishes. Man punishes himself by his false concepts of God, Life, and the Universe. His thoughts are creative, and he creates his own misery.

8. If another criticizes you, and these faults are within you, rejoice, give thanks, and appreciate the comments. This gives you the opportunity to correct the particular fault.

9. You cannot be hurt by criticism when you know that you are master of your thoughts, reactions, and emotions. This gives you the opportunity to pray and bless the other, thereby blessing yourself.

10. When you pray for guidance and right action, take what comes. Realize it is good and very good. Then there is no cause for self-pity, criticism, or hatred.

11. There is nothing good or bad, but thinking makes it so. There is no evil in sex, the desire for food, wealth, or true expression. It depends on how you use these urges, desires, or aspirations. Your desire for food can be met without killing someone for a loaf of bread.

12. Resentment, hatred, ill will, and hostility are behind a host of maladies. Forgive yourself and everybody else by pouring out love, life, joy, and good will to all those who have hurt you. Continue until such time as you meet them in your mind and you are at peace with them.

13. To forgive is to give something for. Give love, peace, joy, wisdom, and all the blessings of life to the other, until there is no sting left in your mind. This is really the acid test of forgiveness.

14. Let us suppose you had an abscess in your jaw about a year ago. It was very painful. Ask yourself if it is painful now. The answer is in the negative. Likewise, if someone has hurt you, lied about and vilified you, and said all manner of evil about you, is your thought of that person negative? Do you sizzle when he or she comes into your mind? If so, the roots of hatred are still there, playing havoc with you and your good. The only way

is to wither them with love by wishing for the person all the blessings of life, until you can meet the person in your mind, and you can sincerely react with a benediction of peace and good will. This is the meaning of forgive until seventy times seven.

Chapter 18: How Your Subconscious Removes Mental Blocks

The solution lies within the problem. The answer is in every question. If you are presented with a difficult situation and you cannot see your way clear, the best procedure is to assume that infinite intelligence within your subconscious mind knows all and sees all, has the answer, and is revealing it to you now. Your new mental attitude that the creative intelligence is bringing about a happy solution will enable you to find the answer. Rest assured that such an attitude of mind would bring order, peace, and meaning to all your undertakings.

• How to break or build a habit

You are a creature of habit. Habit is the function of your subconscious mind. You learned to swim, ride a bicycle, dance, and drive a car by consciously doing these things over and over again until they established tracks in your subconscious mind. Then, the automatic habit action of your subconscious mind took over. This is sometimes called second nature, which is a reaction of your subconscious mind to your thinking and acting.

You are free to choose a good habit or a bad habit. If you repeat a negative thought or act over a period of time, you will be under the compulsion of a habit. The law of your subconscious is compulsion.

• How he broke a bad habit

Mr. Jones said to me, "An uncontrollable urge to drink seizes me, and I remain drunk for two weeks at a time. I can't give up this terrible habit."

Time and time again these experiences had occurred to this unfortunate man. He had grown into the habit of drinking to excess. Although he had started drinking of his own initiative, he also began to realize that he could change the habit and establish a new one. He said that while through his will power he was able to suppress his desires temporarily, his continued efforts to suppress the many urges only made matters worse. His repeated failures convinced him that he was hopeless and powerless to control his urge or obsession. This idea of being powerless operated as a powerful suggestion to his subconscious mind and aggravated his weakness, making his life a succession of failures.

I taught him to harmonize the functions of the conscious and subconscious mind. When these two cooperate, the idea or desire implanted in the subconscious mind is realized. His reasoning mind agreed that if the old habit path or track had carried him into trouble, he could consciously form a new path to freedom, sobriety, and peace of mind. He knew that his destructive habit was automatic, but since it was acquired through his conscious choice, he realized that if he had been conditioned negatively, he also could be conditioned positively. As a result, he ceased thinking of the fact that he was powerless to overcome the habit. Moreover, he understood clearly that there was no obstacle to his healing other than his own thought. Therefore, there was no occasion for great mental effort or mental coercion.

• The power of his mental picture

This man acquired a practice of relaxing his body and getting into a relaxed, drowsy, meditative state. Then he filled his mind with the picture of the desired end, knowing his subconscious mind could bring it about the easiest way. He imagined his daughter congratulating him on his freedom, and saying to him, "Daddy, it's wonderful to have you home!" He had lost his family through drink. He was not allowed to visit them, and his wife would not speak to him.

Regularly, systematically, he used to sit down and meditate in the way outlined. When his attention wandered, he made it a habit to immediately recall the mental picture of his daughter with her smile and the scene of his home enlivened by her cheerful voice. All this brought about a reconditioning of his mind. It was a gradual process. He kept it up. He persevered knowing that sooner or later he would establish a new habit pattern in his subconscious mind.

I told him that he could liken his conscious mind to a camera, that his subconscious mind was the sensitive plate on which he registered and impressed the picture. This made a profound impression on him, and his whole aim was to firmly impress the picture on his mind and develop it there. Films are developed in the dark; likewise, mental pictures are developed in the darkroom of the subconscious mind.

• Focused attention

Realizing that his conscious mind was simply a camera, he used no effort. There was no mental struggle. He quietly adjusted his thoughts and focused his attention on the scene before him until he gradually became identified with the picture. He became absorbed in the mental atmosphere, repeating the mental movie frequently. There was no room for doubt that a healing would follow. When there was any temptation to drink, he would switch his imagination from any reveries of drinking bouts to the feeling of being at home with his family. He was successful because he confidently expected to experience the picture he was developing in his mind. Today he is president of a multimillion-dollar concern and is radiantly happy.

• He said a jinx was following him

Mr. Block said that he had been making an annual income of $20,000, but for the past three months all doors seemed to jam tightly. He brought clients up to the point where they were about to sign on the dotted line, and then at the eleventh hour the door closed. He added that perhaps a jinx was following him.

In discussing the matter with Mr. Block, I discovered that three months previously he had become very irritated, annoyed, and resentful toward a dentist who, after he had promised to sign a contract, had withdrawn at the last moment. He began to live in the unconscious fear that other clients would do the same, thereby setting up a history of frustration, hostility, and obstacles. He gradually built up in his mind a belief in obstruction and last minute cancellations until a vicious circle had been established. What I fear most has come upon me. Mr. Block realized that the trouble was in his mind, and that it was essential to change his mental attitude.

His run of so-called misfortune was broken in the following way: "I realize I am one with the infinite intelligence of my subconscious mind which knows no obstacle, difficulty, or delay. I live in the joyous expectancy of the best. My deeper mind responds to my thoughts. I know that the work of the infinite power of my subconscious cannot be hindered. Infinite intelligence always finishes successfully whatever it begins. Creative wisdom works through me bringing all my plans and purposes to completion. Whatever I start, I bring to a successful conclusion. My aim in life is to give wonderful service, and all those whom I contact are blessed by what I have to offer. All my work comes to full fruition in divine order."

He repeated this prayer every morning before going to call on his customers, and he also prayed each night prior to sleep. In a short time he had established a new habit pattern in his subconscious mind, and he was back in his old accustomed stride as a successful salesman.

• How much do you want what you want?

A young man asked Socrates how he could get wisdom. Socrates replied, "Come with me." He took the lad to a river, pushed the boy's head under the water, held it there until the boy was gasping for air, then relaxed and released his head. When the boy regained his composure, he asked him, "What did you desire most when you were under water?"

"I wanted air," said the boy.

Socrates said to him, "When you want wisdom as much as you wanted air when you were immersed in the water, you will receive it."

Likewise, when you really have an intense desire to overcome any block in your life, and you come to a clear-cut decision that there is a way out, and that is the course you wish to follow, then victory and triumph are assured.

If you really want peace of mind and inner calm, you will get it. Regardless of how unjustly you have been treated, or how unfair the boss has been, or what a mean scoundrel someone has proved to be, all this makes no difference to you when you awaken to your mental and spiritual powers. You know what you want, and you will definitely refuse to let the thieves (thoughts) of hatred, anger, hostility, and ill will rob you of peace, harmony, health, and happiness. You cease to become upset by people, conditions, news, and events by identifying your thoughts immediately with your aim in life. Your aim is peace, health, inspiration, harmony, and abundance. Feel a river of peace flowing through you now. Your thought is the immaterial and invisible power, and you choose to let it bless, inspire, and give you peace.

• Why he could not be healed

This is a case history of a married man with four children who was supporting and secretly living with another woman during his business trips. He was ill, nervous, irritable, and cantankerous, and he could not sleep without drugs. The doctor's medicine failed to bring down his high blood pressure of over two hundred. He had pains in numerous organs of his body, which doctors could not diagnose or relieve. To make matters worse, he was drinking heavily.

The cause of all this was a deep unconscious sense of guilt. He had violated the marriage vows, and this troubled him. The religious creed he was brought up on was deeply lodged in his subconscious mind, and he drank excessively to heal the wound of guilt. Some invalids take morphine and codeine for severe pains; he was taking alcohol for the pain or wound in his mind. It was the old story of adding fuel to the fire.

• The explanation and the cure

He listened to the explanation of how his mind worked. He faced his problem, looked at it, and gave up his dual role. He knew that his drinking was an unconscious attempt to escape. The hidden cause lodged in his subconscious mind had to be eradicated; then the healing would follow.

He began to impress his subconscious mind three or four times a day by using the following prayer: "My mind is full of peace, poise, balance, and equilibrium. The infinite lies stretched in smiling repose within me. I am not afraid of anything in the past, the present, or the future. The infinite intelligence of my subconscious mind leads, guides, and directs me in all ways. I now meet every situation with faith, poise, calmness, and confidence. I am now completely free from the habit. My mind is full of inner peace, freedom, and joy. I forgive myself; then I am forgiven. Peace, sobriety, and confidence reign supreme in my mind."

He repeated this prayer frequently as outlined; being fully aware of what he was doing and why he was doing it. Knowing what he was doing gave him the necessary faith and confidence. I explained to him that as he spoke these statements out loud, slowly, lovingly, and meaningfully, they would gradually sink down into his subconscious mind. Like seeds, they would grow after their kind. These truths, on which he concentrated, went in through his eyes, his ears heard the sound, and the healing vibrations of these words reached his subconscious mind and obliterated all the negative mental patterns which caused all the trouble. Light dispels darkness. The constructive thought destroys the negative thought. He became a transformed man within a month.

• Refusing to admit it

If you are an alcoholic or drug addict, admit it. Do not dodge the issue. Many people remain alcoholics because they refuse to admit it.

Your disease is instability, an inner fear. You are refusing to face life, and so you try to escape your responsibilities through the bottle. As an alcoholic you have no free will, although you think you have, and you may even boast about your will power. If you are a habitual drunkard and say bravely, "I will not touch it any more," you have no power to make this assertion come true, because you do not know where to locate the power.

You are living in a psychological prison of your own making, and you are bound by your beliefs, opinions, training, and environmental influences. Like most people, you are a creature of habit. You are conditioned to react the way you do.

• Building in the idea of freedom

You can build the idea of freedom and peace of mind into your mentality so that it reaches your subconscious depths. The latter, being all-powerful, will free you from all desire for alcohol. Then, you will have the new understanding of how your mind works, and you can truly back up your statement and prove the truth to yourself.

• Fifty-one percent healed

If you have a keen desire to free yourself from any destructive habit, you are fifty-one percent healed already. When you have a greater desire to give up the bad habit than to continue it, you will not experience too much difficulty in gaining complete freedom.

Whatever thought you anchor the mind upon, the latter magnifies. If you engage the mind on the concept of freedom (freedom from the habit) and peace of mind, and if you keep it focused on this new direction of attention, you generate feelings and emotions, which gradually emotionalizes the concept of freedom and peace. Whatever idea you emotionalize is accepted by your subconscious and brought to pass. Your Subconscious Removes Mental Blocks

• The law of substitution

Realize that something good can come out of your suffering. You have not suffered in vain. However, it is foolish to continue to suffer.

If you continue as an alcoholic, it will bring about mental and physical deterioration and decay. Realize that the power in your subconscious is backing you up. Even though you may be seized with melancholia, you should begin to imagine the joy of freedom that is in store for you. This is the law of substitution. Your imagination took you to the bottle; let it take you now to freedom and peace of mind. You will suffer a little bit, but it is for a constructive purpose. You will bear it like a mother in the pangs of childbirth, and you will, likewise, bring forth a child of the mind. Your subconscious will give birth to sobriety.

• Cause of alcoholism

The real cause of alcoholism is negative and destructive thinking; for as a man thinketh, so is he. The alcoholic has a deep sense of inferiority, inadequacy, defeat, and frustration, usually accompanied by a deep inner hostility. He has countless alibis as to his reason for drinking, but the sole reason is in his thought life.

• Three magic steps

The first step: Get still; quiet the wheels of the mind. Enter into a sleepy, drowsy state. In this relaxed, peaceful, receptive state, you are preparing for the second step.

The second step: Take a brief phrase, which can readily be graven on the memory, and repeat it over and over as a lullaby. Use the phrase, "Sobriety and peace of mind are mine now, and I give thanks." To prevent the mind from wandering, repeat it aloud or sketch its pronunciation with the lips and tongue as you say it mentally. This helps its entry into the subconscious mind. Do this for five minutes or more. You will find a deep emotional response.

The third step: Just before going to sleep, practice what Johann von Goethe, German author, used to do. Imagine a friend, a loved one in front of you. Your eyes are closed, you are relaxed and at peace. The loved one or friend is subjectively present, and is saying to you, "Congratulations!" You see the smile; you hear the voice. You mentally touch the hand; it is all real and vivid. The word congratulations imply complete freedom. Hear it over and over again until you get the subconscious reaction, which satisfies.

• Keep on keeping on

When fear knocks at the door of your mind, or when worry, anxiety, and doubt cross your mind, behold your vision, your goal. Think of the infinite power within your subconscious mind, which you can generate by your thinking and imagining, and this will give you confidence, power, and courage. Keep on, persevere, until the day breaks, and the shadows flee away.

Pointers to review

1. The solution lies within the problem. The answer is in every question. Infinite intelligence responds to you as you call upon it with faith and confidence.

2. Habit is the function of your subconscious mind. There is no greater evidence of the marvelous power of your subconscious than the force and sway habit holds in your life. You are a creature of habit.

3. You form habit patterns in your subconscious mind by repeating a thought and act over and over again until it establishes tracks in the subconscious mind and becomes automatic, such as swimming, dancing, typing, walking, driving your car, etc.

4. You have freedom to choose. You can choose a good habit or a bad habit. Prayer is a good habit.

5. Whatever mental picture, backed by faith, you behold in your conscious mind, and your subconscious mind will bring to pass.

6. The only obstacle to your success and achievement is your own thought or mental image.

7. When your attention wanders, bring it back to the contemplation of your good or goal. Make a habit of this. This is called disciplining the mind.

8. Your conscious mind is the camera, and your subconscious mind is the sensitive plate on which you register or impress the picture.

9. The only jinx that follows anyone is a fear thought repeated over and over in the mind. Break the jinx by knowing that whatever you start you will bring to a conclusion in divine order. Picture the happy ending and sustain it with confidence.

10. To form a new habit, you must be convinced that it is desirable. When your desire to give up the bad habit is greater than your desire to continue, you are fifty-one percent healed already.

11. The statements of others cannot hurt you except through your own thoughts and mental participation. Identify yourself with your aim, which is peace, harmony, and joy. You are the only thinker in your universe.

12. Excessive drinking is an unconscious desire to escape. The cause of alcoholism is negative and destructive thinking. The cure is to think of freedom, sobriety, and perfection, and to feel the thrill of accomplishment.

13. Many people remain alcoholics because they refuse to admit it.

14. The law of your subconscious mind, which held you in bondage and inhibited your freedom of action, will give you freedom and happiness. It depends on how you use it.

15. Your imagination took you to the bottle; let it take you to freedom by imagining you are free.

16. The real cause of alcoholism is negative and destructive thinking. As a man thinketh in his heart [subconscious mind], so is he.

17. When fear knocks at the door of your mind, let faith in God and all things good open the door.

Chapter 19: How to Use Your Subconscious Mind to Remove Fear

One of our students told me that he was invited to speak at a banquet. He said he was panic-stricken at the thought of speaking before a thousand people. He overcame his fear this way: For several nights he sat down in an armchair for about five minutes and said to himself slowly, quietly, and positively, "I am going to master this fear. I am overcoming it now. I speak with poise and confidence. I am relaxed and at ease." He operated a definite law of mind and overcame his fear.

The subconscious mind is amenable to suggestion and is controlled by suggestion. When you still your mind and relax, the thoughts of your conscious mind sink down into the subconscious through a process similar to osmosis, whereby fluids separated by a porous membrane intermingle. As these positive seeds, or thoughts, sink into the subconscious area, they grow after their kind, and you become poised, serene, and calm.

• Man's greatest enemy

It is said that fear is man's greatest enemy. Fear is behind failure, sickness, and poor human relations. Millions of people are afraid of the past, the future, old age, insanity, and death. Fear is a thought in your mind, and you are afraid of your own thoughts.

A little boy can be paralyzed with fear when he is told there is a boogieman under his bed that is going to take him away. When his father turns on the light and shows him there is no boogieman, he is freed from fear. The fear in the mind of the boy was as real as if there really was a boogieman there. He was healed of a false thought in his mind. The thing he feared did not exist. Likewise, most of your fears have no reality. They are merely a conglomeration of sinister shadows and shadows that have no reality.

• Do the thing you fear

Ralph Waldo Emerson, philosopher and poet, said, "Do the thing you are afraid to do, and the death of fear is certain."

There was a time when the writer of this chapter was filled with unutterable fear when standing before an audience. The way I overcame it was to stand before the audience, do the thing I was afraid to do, and the death of fear was certain.

When you affirm positively that you are going to master your fears, and you come to a definite decision in your conscious mind, you release the power of the subconscious, which flows in response to the nature of your thought.

• Banishing stage fright

A young lady was invited to an audition. She had been looking forward to the interview. However, on three previous occasions, she had failed miserably due to stage fright.

She possessed a very good voice, but she was certain that when the time came for her to sing, she would be seized with stage fright. The subconscious mind takes your fears as a request, proceeds to manifest them, and brings them into your experience. On three previous auditions she sang wrong notes, and she finally broke down and cried. The cause, as previously outlined, was an involuntary autosuggestion, i.e., a silent fear thought emotionalized and subjectified.

She overcame it by the following technique: Three times a day she isolated herself in a room. She sat down comfortably in an armchair, relaxed her body, and closed her eyes. She stilled her mind and body to the best of her ability. Physical inertia favors passivity and renders the mind more receptive to suggestion. She counteracted the fear suggestion by its converse, saying to herself, "I sing beautifully. I am poised, serene, confident, and calm."

She repeated the words slowly, quietly, and with feeling from five to ten times at each sitting. She had three such "sittings" every day and one immediately prior to sleep at night. At the end of a week she was completely poised and confident, and gave a definitely outstanding audition. Carry out the above procedure, and the death of fear is certain.

• Fear of failure

Occasionally young men from the local university come to see me, as well as schoolteachers, who often seem to suffer from suggestive amnesia at examinations. The complaint is always the same: "I know the answers after the examination is over, but I can't remember the answers during the examination."

The idea, which realizes itself, is the one to which we invariably give concentrated attention. I find that each one is obsessed with the idea of failure. Fear is behind the temporary amnesia, and it is the cause of the whole experience.

One young medical student was the most brilliant person in his class, yet he found himself failing to answer simple questions at the time of written or oral examinations. I explained to him that the reason was he had been worrying and was fearful for several days previous to the examination. These negative thoughts became charged with fear.

Thoughts enveloped in the powerful emotion of fear are realized in the subconscious mind. In other words, this young man was requesting his subconscious mind to see to it that he failed, and that is exactly what it did. On the day of the examination he found himself stricken with what is called, in psychological circles, suggestive amnesia.

• How he overcame the fear

He learned that his subconscious mind was the storehouse of memory, and that it had a perfect record of all he had heard and read during his medical training. Moreover, he learned that the subconscious mind was responsive and reciprocal. The way to be en rapport with it was to be relaxed, peaceful, and confident.

Every night and morning he began to imagine his mother congratulating him on his wonderful record. He would hold an imaginary letter from her in his hand. As he began to contemplate the happy result, he called forth a corresponding or reciprocal response or reaction in himself. The all-wise and omnipotent power of the subconscious took over, dictated, and directed his conscious mind accordingly. He imagined the end, thereby willing the means to the realization of the end. Following this procedure, he had no trouble passing subsequent examinations. In other words, the subjective wisdom took over, compelling him to give an excellent account of himself.

• Fear of water, mountains, closed places, etc.

There are many people who are afraid to go into an elevator, climb mountains, or even swim in the water. It may well be that the individual had unpleasant experiences in the water in his youth, such as having been thrown forcibly into the water without being able to swim. He might have been forcibly detained in an elevator, which failed to function properly, causing resultant fear of closed places.

I had an experience when I was about ten years of age. I accidentally fell into a pool and went down three times. I can still remember the dark water engulfing my head, and my gasping for air until another boy pulled me out at the last moment. This experience sank into my subconscious mind, and for years I feared the water.

An elderly psychologist said to me, "Go down to the swimming pool, look at the water, and say out loud in strong tones, 'I am going to master you. I can dominate you.' Then go into the water, take lessons, and overcome it." This I did, and I mastered the water. Do not permit water to master you. Remember, you are the master of the water.

When I assumed a new attitude of mind, the omnipotent power of the subconscious responded, giving me strength, faith, and confidence, and enabling me to overcome my fear.

• Master technique for overcoming any particular fear

The following is a process and technique for overcoming fear, which I teach from the platform. It works like a charm. Try it!

Suppose you are afraid of the water, a mountain, an interview, an audition, or you fear closed places. If you are afraid of swimming, begin now to sit still for five or ten minutes three or four times a day, and imagine you are swimming. Actually, you are swimming in your mind. It is a subjective experience. Mentally you have projected yourself into the water. You feel the chill of the water and the movement of your arms and legs. It is all real, vivid, and a joyous activity of the mind. It is not idle daydreaming, for you know that what you are experiencing in your imagination will be developed in your subconscious mind. Then you will be compelled to express the image and likeness of the picture you impressed on your deeper mind. This is the law of the subconscious.

You could apply the same technique if you are afraid of mountains or high places. Imagine you are climbing the mountain, feel the reality of it all, enjoy the scenery, knowing that as you continue to do this mentally, you will do it physically with ease and comfort.

• He blessed the elevator

I knew an executive of a large corporation who was terrified to ride in an elevator. He would walk up five flights of stairs to his office every morning. He said that he began to bless the elevator every night and several times a day. He finally overcame his fear. This was how he blessed the elevator: "The elevator in our building is a wonderful idea. It came out of the universal mind. It is a boon and a blessing to all our employees. It gives wonderful service. It operates in divine order. I ride in it in peace and joy. I remain silent now while the currents of life, love, and understanding flow through the patterns of my thought. In my imagination I am now in the elevator, and I step out into my office. The elevator is full of our employees. I talk to them, and they are friendly, joyous, and free. It is a wonderful experience of freedom, faith, and confidence. I give thanks."

He continued this prayer for about ten days, and on the eleventh day, he walked into the elevator with other members of the organization and felt completely free.

• Normal and abnormal fear

Man is born only with two fears, the fear of falling and the fear of noise. These are an alarm system given you by nature as a means of self-preservation. Normal fear is good. You hear an automobile coming down the road, and you step aside to survive. The momentary fear of being run over is overcome by your action. All other fears were given to you by parents, relatives, teachers, and all those who influenced your early years.

• Abnormal fear

Abnormal fear takes place when man lets his imagination run riot. I knew a woman who was invited to go on a trip around the world by plane. She began to cut out of the newspapers all reports of airplane catastrophes. She pictured herself going down in the ocean, being drowned, etc. This is abnormal fear. Had she persisted in this, she would undoubtedly have attracted what she feared most.

Another example of abnormal fear is that of a businessman in New York, who was very prosperous and successful. He had his own private mental motion picture of which he was the director. He would run this mental movie of failure, bankruptcy, empty shelves, and no bank balance until he sank into a deep depression. He refused to stop this morbid imagery and kept reminding his wife that "this can't last," "there will be a recession," "I feel sure we will go bankrupt," etc.

His wife told me that he finally did go into bankruptcy, and all the things he imagined and feared came to pass. The things he feared did not exist, but he brought them to pass by constantly fearing, believing, and expecting financial disaster. Job said, the thing I feared has come upon me.

There are people who are afraid that something terrible will happen to their children, and that some dread catastrophe will befall them. When they read about an epidemic or rare disease, they live in fear that they will catch it, and some imagine they have the disease already. All this is abnormal fear.

• The answer to abnormal fear

Move mentally to the opposite. To stay at the extreme of fear is stagnation plus mental and physical deterioration. When fear arises, there immediately comes with it a desire for something opposite to the thing feared. Place your attention on the thing immediately desired. Get absorbed and engrossed in your desire, knowing that the subjective always overturns the objective. This attitude will give you confidence and lift your spirits. The infinite power of your subconscious mind is moving on your behalf, and it cannot fail. Therefore, peace and assurance are yours.

• Examine your fears

The president of a large organization told me that when he was a salesman he used to walk around the block five or six times before he called on a customer. The sales manager came along one day and said to him "Don't be afraid of the boogie man behind the door. There is no boogieman. It is a false belief."

The manager told him that whenever he looked at his own fears he stared them in the face and stood up to them, looking them straight in the eye. Then they faded and shrank into insignificance.

• He landed in the jungle

A chaplain told me of his experiences in the Second World War. He had to parachute from a damaged plane and land in the jungle. He said he was frightened, but he knew there were two kinds of fear, normal and abnormal, which we have previously pointed out.

He decided to do something about the fear immediately and began to talk to himself saying, "John, you can't surrender to your fear. Your fear is a desire for safety and security, and a way out."

He began to claim; "Infinite intelligence which guides the planets in their courses is now leading and guiding me out of this jungle."

He kept saying this out loud to himself for ten minutes or more. "Then," he added, "Something began to stir inside me. A mood of confidence began to seize me, and I began to walk. After a few days, I miraculously came out of the jungle, and was picked up by a rescue plane."

His changed mental attitude saved him. His confidence and trust in the subjective wisdom and power within him was the solution to his problem.

He said, "Had I begun to bemoan my fate and indulge my fears, I would have succumbed to the monster fear, and probably would have died of fear and starvation."

• He dismissed himself

The general manager of an organization told me that for three years he feared he would lose his position. He was always imagining failure. The thing he feared did not exist, save as a morbid anxious thought in his own mind. His vivid imagination dramatized the loss of his job until he became nervous and neurotic. Finally he was asked to resign.

Actually, he dismissed himself. His constant negative imagery and fear suggestions to his subconscious mind caused the latter to respond and react accordingly. It caused him to make mistakes and foolish decisions, which resulted in his failure as a general manager. His dismissal would never have happened if he had immediately moved to the opposite in his mind.

• They plotted against him

During a recent world lecture tour, I had a two-hour conversation with a prominent government official. He had a deep sense of inner peace and serenity. He said that all the abuse he receives politically from newspapers and the opposition party never disturb him. His practice is to sit still for fifteen minutes in the morning and realize that in the center of him is a deep still ocean of peace. Meditating in this way, he generates tremendous power, which overcomes all manner of difficulties and fears.

Some time previously, a colleague called him at midnight and told him a group of people was plotting against him. This is what he said to his colleague, "I am going to sleep now in perfect peace. You can discuss it with me at 10:00 A.M. tomorrow."

He said to me, "I know that no negative thought can ever manifest except I emotionalize the thought and accept it mentally. I refuse to entertain their suggestion of fear. Therefore, no harm can come to me."

Notice how calm he was, how cool, how peaceful! He did not start getting excited, tearing his hair, or wringing his hands. At his center he found the still water, an inner peace, and there was a great calm.

• Deliver yourself from all your fears

Use this perfect formula for casting out fear. I sought the Lord, and He heard me, and delivered me from all my fears. PSALM 34:4. The Lord is an ancient word meaning law—the power of your subconscious mind.

Learn the wonders of your subconscious, and how it works and functions. Master the techniques given to you in this chapter. Put them into practice now, today! Your subconscious will respond, and you will be free of all fears. I sought the Lord, and He heard me, and delivered me from all my fears.

Pointers to review

1. Do the thing you are afraid to do, and the death of fear is certain. Say to yourself and mean it, "I am going to master this fear," and you will.

2. Fear is a negative thought in your mind. Supplant it with a constructive thought. Fear has killed millions. Confidence is greater than fear. Nothing is more powerful than faith in God and the good.

3. Fear is man's greatest enemy. It is behind failure, sickness, and bad human relations. Love casts out fear. Love is an emotional attachment to the good things of life. Fall in love with honesty, integrity, justice, good will, and success. Live in the joyous expectancy of the best, and invariably the best will come to you.

4. Counteract the fear suggestions with the opposite, such as "I sing beautifully; I am poised, serene, and calm." It will pay fabulous dividends.

5. Fear is behind amnesia at oral and written examination time. You can overcome this by affirming frequently, "I have a perfect memory for everything I need to know," or you can imagine a friend congratulating you on your brilliant success on the examination. Persevere and you will win.

6. If you are afraid to cross water, swim. In your imagination swim freely, joyously. Project yourself into the water mentally. Feel the chill and thrill of swimming across the pool. Make it vivid. As you do this subjectively, you will be compelled to go into the water and conquer it. This is the law of your mind.

7. If you are afraid of closed places, such as elevators, lecture halls, etc., mentally ride in an elevator blessing all its parts and functions. You will be amazed how quickly the fear will be dissipated.

8. You were born with only two fears, the fear of falling and the fear of noise. All your other fears were acquired. Get rid of them.

9. Normal fear is good. Abnormal fear is very bad and destructive. To constantly indulge in fear thoughts results in abnormal fear, obsessions, and complexes. To fear something persistently causes a sense of panic and terror.

10. You can overcome abnormal fear when you know the power of your subconscious mind can change conditions and bring to pass the cherished desires of your heart. Give your immediate attention and devotion to your desire which is the opposite of your fear. This is the love that casts out fear.

11. If you are afraid of failure, give attention to success. If you are afraid of sickness, dwell on your perfect health. If you are afraid of an accident, dwell on the guidance and protection of God. If you are afraid of death, dwell on Eternal Life. God is Life, and that is your life now.

12. The great law of substitution is the answer to fear. Whatever you fear has its solution in the form of your desire. If you are sick, you desire health. If you are in the prison of fear, you desire freedom. Expect the good. Mentally concentrate on the good, and know that your subconscious mind answers you always. It never fails.

13. The things you fear do not really exist except as thoughts in your mind. Thoughts are creative. This is why Job said; the thing I feared has come upon me. Think good and good follows.

14. Look at your fears; hold them up to the light of reason. Learn to laugh at your fears. That is the best medicine.

15. Nothing can disturb you but your own thought. The suggestions, statements, or threats of other persons have no power. The power is within you, and when your thoughts are focused on that which is good, then God's power is with your thoughts of good. There is only one Creative Power, and It moves as harmony. There are no divisions of quarrels in it. Its source is Love. This is why God's power is with your thoughts of good.

Chapter 20: How to Stay Young in Spirit Forever

Your subconscious mind never grows old. It is timeless, ageless, and endless. It is a part of the universal mind of God, which was never born, and it will never die.

Fatigue or old age cannot be predicated on any spiritual quality or power. Patience, kindness, veracity, humility, good will, peace, harmony, and brotherly love are attributes and qualities, which never grow old. If you continue to generate these qualities here on this plane of life, you will always remain young in spirit.

I remember reading an article in one of our magazines some years ago, which stated that a group of eminent medical men at the De Courcy Clinic, in Cincinnati, Ohio, reported that years alone are not responsible for bringing about degenerative disorders. These same physicians stated that it is the fear of time, not time itself, that has a harmful aging effect on our minds and bodies, and that the neurotic fear of the effects of time may well be the cause of premature aging.

During the many years of my public life, I have had occasion to study the biographies of the famous men and women who have continued their productive activities into the years well beyond the normal span of life. Some of them achieve their greatness in old age. At the same time, it has been my privilege to meet and to know countless individuals of no prominence who, in their lesser sphere, belonged to those hardy mortals who have proved that old age of itself does not destroy the creative powers of the mind and body.

• He had grown old in his thought life

A few years ago I called on an old friend in London, England. He was over 80 years of age, very ill, and obviously was yielding to his advancing years. Our conversation revealed his physical weakness, his sense of frustration, and a general deterioration almost approaching lifelessness. His cry was that he was useless and that no one wanted him. With an expression of hopelessness he betrayed his false philosophy, "We are born, grow up, become old, good for nothing, and that's the end."

This mental attitude of futility and worthlessness was the chief reason for his sickness. He was looking forward only to senescence, and after that—nothing. Indeed, he had grown old in his thought life, and his subconscious mind brought about all the evidence of his habitual thinking.

• Age is the dawn of wisdom

Unfortunately, many people have the same attitude as this unhappy man. They are afraid of what they term "old age," the end, and extinction, which really means that they are afraid of life. Yet, life is endless. Age is not the flight of years, but the dawn of wisdom.

Wisdom is an awareness of the tremendous spiritual powers in your subconscious mind and the knowledge of how to apply these powers to lead a full and happy life. Get it out of your head once and for all that 65, 75, or 85 years of age is synonymous with the end for you or anybody else. It can be the beginning of a glorious, fruitful, active, and most productive life pattern, better than you have ever experienced. Believe this, expect it, and your subconscious will bring it to pass.

• Welcome the change

Old age is not a tragic occurrence. What we call the aging process is really change. It is to be welcomed joyfully and gladly as each phase of human life is a step forward on the path, which has no end. Man has powers, which transcend his bodily powers. He has senses, which transcend his five physical senses.

Scientists today are finding positive indisputable evidence that something conscious in man can leave his present body and travel thousands of miles to see, hear, touch, and speak to people even though his physical body never leaves the couch on which it reclines.

Man's life is spiritual and eternal. He need never grow old for Life, or God, cannot grow old. The Bible says that God is Life. Life is self-renewing, eternal, indestructible, and is the reality of all men.

• Evidence for survival

The evidence gathered by the psychical research societies both in Great Britain and America is overwhelming. You may go into any large metropolitan library and get volumes on The Proceedings of the Psychical Research Society based on findings of distinguished scientists on survival following so-called death. You will find a startling report on scientific experiments establishing the reality of life after death in The Case for Psychic Survival by Hereward Carrington, Director of the American Psychical Institute.

• Life is

A woman asked Thomas Edison, the electrical wizard, "Mr. Edison, what is electricity?"
He replied, "Madame, electricity is. Use it."

Electricity is a name we give an invisible power which we do not fully comprehend, but we learn all we can about the principle of electricity and its uses. We use it in countless ways.

The scientist cannot see an electron with his eyes, yet he accepts it as a scientific fact, because it is the only valid conclusion, which coincides with his other experimental evidence. We cannot see life. However, we know we are alive. Life is, and we are here to express it in all its beauty and glory.

• Mind and spirit do not grow old

The man who thinks or believes that the earthly cycle of birth, adolescence, youth, maturity, and old age is all there is to life, is indeed to be pitied. Such a man has no anchor, no hope, no vision, and to him life has no meaning.

This type of belief brings frustration, stagnation, cynicism, and a sense of hopelessness resulting in neurosis and mental aberrations of all kinds. If you cannot play a fast game of tennis, or swim as fast as your son, or if your body has slowed down, or you walk with a slow step, remember life is always clothing itself anew. What men call death is but a journey to a new city in another dimension of life.

I say to men and women in my lectures that they should accept what we call old age gracefully. Age has its own glory, beauty, and wisdom, which belong to it. Peace, love, joy, beauty, happiness, wisdom, good will, and understanding are qualities, which never grow old or die.

Ralph Waldo Emerson, poet and philosopher, said, "We do not count a man's years until he has nothing else to count."

Your character, the quality of your mind, your faith, and your convictions are not subject to decay.

• You are as young as you think you are

I give public lectures in Caxton Hall, London, England, every few years, and following one of these lectures, a surgeon said to me, "I am 84 years of age. I operate every morning, visit patients in the afternoons, and I write for medical and other scientific journals in the evening."

His attitude was that he was as useful as he believed himself to be, and that he was as young as his thoughts. He said to me, "It's true what you said, 'Man is as strong as he thinks he is, and as valuable as he thinks he is.'"

This surgeon has not surrendered to advancing years. He knows that he is immortal. His final comment to me was, "If I should pass on tomorrow, I would be operating on people in the next dimension, not with a surgeon's scalpel, but with mental and spiritual surgery."

• Your gray hairs are an asset

Don't ever quit a job and say, "I am retired; I am old; I am finished." That would be stagnation, death, and you would be finished. Some men are old at 30, while others are young at 80. The mind is the master weaver, the architect, the designer, and the sculptor. George Bernard Shaw was active at 90, and the artistic quality of his mind had not relaxed from active duty.

I meet men and women who tell me that some employers almost slam the door in their faces when they say they are over 40. This attitude on the part of the employers is to be considered cold, callous, evil, and completely void of compassion and understanding. The total emphasis seems to be on youth, i.e., you must be under 35 years of age to receive consideration. The reasoning behind this is certainly very shallow. If the employer would stop and think, he would realize that the man or woman was not selling his age or gray hair, rather, he was willing to give of his talents, his experience, and his wisdom gathered through years of experience in the market place of life.

• Age is an asset

Your age should be a distinct asset to any organization, because of your practice and application through the years of the principles of the Golden Rule and the law of love and good will. Your gray hair, if you have any, should stand for greater wisdom, skill, and understanding. Your emotional and spiritual maturity should be a tremendous blessing to any organization.

A man should not be asked to resign when he is 65 years of age. That is the time of life when he could be most useful in handling personnel problems, making plans for the future, making decisions, and guiding others in the realm of creative ideas based on his experience and insight into the nature of the business.

• Be your age
A motion-picture writer in Hollywood told me that he had to write scripts which would cater to the twelve-year-old mind.

This is a tragic state of affairs if the great masses of people are expected to become emotionally and spiritually mature. It means that the emphasis is placed on youth in spite of the fact that youth stands for inexperience, lack of discernment, and hasty judgment.

• I can keep up with the best of them
I am now thinking of a man 65 years of age who is trying frantically to keep young. He swims with young men every Sunday, goes on long hikes, plays tennis, and boasts of his prowess and physical powers, saying, "Look, I can keep up with the best of them!" He should remember the great truth: As a man thinketh in his heart, so is he. PROV. 23:7.
Diets, exercises, and games of all kinds will not keep this man young. It is necessary for him to observe that he grows old or remains young in accordance with his processes of thinking. Your subconscious mind is conditioned by your thoughts. If your thoughts are constantly on the beautiful, the noble, and the good, you will remain young regardless of the chronological years.

• Fear of old age
Job said, The thing which I greatly feared is come upon me. There are many people who fear old age and are uncertain about the future, because they anticipate mental and physical deterioration as the years advance. What they think and feel comes to pass.
You grow old when you lose interest in life, when you cease to dream, to hunger after new truths, and to search for new worlds to conquer. When your mind is open to new ideas, new interests, and when you raise the curtain and let in the sunshine and inspiration of new truths of life and the universe, you will be young and vital.

• You Lave much to give
If you are 65 or 95 years of age, realize you have much to give. You can help stabilize, advise, and direct the younger generation. You can give the benefit of your knowledge, your experience, and your wisdom. You can always look ahead for at all times you are gazing into infinite life. You will find that you can never cease to unveil the glories and wonders of life. Try to learn something new every moment of the day, and you will find your mind will always be young.

• One hundred and ten years old
Some years ago while lecturing in Bombay, India, I was introduced to a man who said he was 110 years old. He had the most beautiful face I have ever seen. He seemed

transfigured by the radiance of an inner light. There was a rare beauty in his eyes indicating he had grown old in years with gladness and with no indication that his mind had dimmed its lights.

• Retirement—a new venture

Be sure that your mind never retires. It must be like a parachute, which is no good unless it opens up. Be open and receptive to new ideas. I have seen men of 65 and 70 retire. They seemed to rot away, and in a few months passed on. They obviously felt that life was at an end.

Retirement can be a new venture, a new challenge, a new path, the beginning of the fulfillment of a long dream. It is inexpressibly depressing to hear a man say, "What shall I do now that I am retired?" He is saying in effect, "I am mentally and physically dead. My mind is bankrupt of ideas."

All this is a false picture. The real truth is that you can accomplish more at 90 than you did at 60, because each day you are growing in wisdom and understanding of life and the universe through your new studies and interest.

• He graduated to a better job

An executive, who lives near me, was forced to retire a few months ago because he had reached the age of 65. He said to me, "I look upon my retirement as promotion from kindergarten to the first grade." He philosophized in this manner: He said that when he left high school, he went up the ladder by going to college. He realized this was a step forward in his education and understanding of life in general. Likewise, he added, now he could do the things he had always wanted to do, and therefore, his retirement was still another step forward on the ladder of life and wisdom.

He came to the wise conclusion that he was no longer going to concentrate on making a living. Now he was going to give all his attention to living life. He is an amateur photographer, and he took additional courses on the subject. He took a trip around the world and took movies of famous places. He now lectures before various groups, lodges, and clubs, and is in popular demand.

There are countless ways of taking an interest in something worthwhile outside yourself. Become enthusiastic over new creative ideas, make spiritual progress, and continue to learn and to grow. In this manner you remain young in heart, because you are hungering and thirsting after new truths, and your body will reflect your thinking at all times.

• You must be a producer and not a prisoner of society

The newspapers are taking cognizance of the fact that the voting population of the elderly in California elections is increasing by leaps and bounds. This means that their voices will be heard in the legislature of the state and also in the halls of Congress. I believe there will be enacted a federal law prohibiting employers from discrimination against men and women because of age.

A man of 65 years may be younger mentally, physically, and physiologically than many men at 30. It is stupid and ridiculous to tell a man he cannot be hired because he is over 40. It is like saying to him that he is ready for the scrap heap or the junk pile.

What is a man of 40 or over to do? Must he bury his talents and hide his light under a bushel? Men, who are deprived and prevented from working because of age must be sustained by government treasuries at county, state, and federal levels. The many organizations who refuse to hire them and benefit from their wisdom and experience will be taxed to support them. This is a form of financial suicide.

Man is here to enjoy the fruit of his labor, and he is here to be a producer and not a prisoner of society, which compels him to idleness.

Man's body slows down gradually as he advances through the years, but his conscious mind can be made much more active, alert, alive, and quickened by the inspiration from his subconscious mind. His mind, in reality, never grows old. Job said, Oh that I were as in months past, as in the days when God preserved me; When his candle shined upon my head, and when by his light I walked through darkness; As I was in the days of my youth, when the secret of God was upon my tabernacle. JOB 29:2-4.

• Secret of youth

To recapture the days of your youth, feel the miraculous, healing, self-renewing power of your subconscious mind moving through your whole being. Know and feel that you are inspired, lifted up, rejuvenated, revitalized, and recharged spiritually. You can bubble over with enthusiasm and joy, as in the days of your youth, for the simple reason that you can always mentally and emotionally recapture the joyous state.

The candle, which shines upon your head, is divine intelligence, and reveals to you everything you need to know; it enables you to affirm the presence of your good, regardless of appearances. You walk by the guidance of your subconscious mind, because you know that the dawn appears and the shadows flee away.

• Get a vision

Instead of saying, "I am old," say, "I am wise in the way of the Divine Life." Don't let the corporation, newspapers, or statistics hold a picture before you of old age, declining years, decrepitude, senility, and uselessness. Reject it, for it is a lie. Refuse to be hypnotized by such propaganda. Affirm life—not death. Get a vision of yourself as happy, radiant, successful, serene, and powerful.

• Your mind does not grow old

Former President Herbert Hoover, now 88 years old, is very active and is performing monumental work. I interviewed him a few years ago in his suite at the Waldorf-Astoria, New York City. I found him healthy, happy, vigorous, and full of life and enthusiasm. He was keeping several secretaries busy handling his correspondence and was himself writing books of a political and historical nature. Like all great men, I found him affable, genial, amiable, loving, and most understanding.

His mental acumen and sagacity gave me the thrill of a lifetime. He is a deeply religious man, and is full of faith in God and in the triumph of the eternal truth of life. He was subjected to a barrage of criticism and condemnation in the years of the great depression, but he weathered the storm and did not grow old in hatred, resentment, ill will, and bitterness. On the contrary, he went into the silence of his soul, and communing with the Divine Presence within him, he found the peace, which is the power at the heart of God.

• His mind active at ninety-nine

My father learned the French language at 65 years of age, and became an authority on it at 70. He made a study of Gaelic when he was over 60, and became an acknowledged and famous teacher of the subject. He assisted my sister in a school of higher learning and continued to do so until he passed away at 99. His mind was as clear at 99 as it was when he was 20. Moreover, his handwriting and his reasoning powers had improved with age. Truly, you are as old as you think and feel.

• We need our senior citizens

Marcus Porcius Cato, the Roman patriot, learned Greek at 80. Madame Ernestine Schumann-Heink, the great German-American contralto, reached the pinnacle of her musical success after she became a grandmother. It is wonderful to behold the accomplishments of the oldsters. General Douglas MacArthur, Harry S. Truman, General Dwight David Eisenhower, and American financier Bernard Baruch are interesting, active, and contributing their talents and wisdom to the world.

The Greek philosopher Socrates, learned to play musical instruments when he was 80 years old. Michelangelo was painting his greatest canvases at 80. At 80, Cios Simonides won the prize for poetry, Johann von Goethe finished Faust, and Leopold von Ranke commenced his History of the World, which he finished at 92.

Alfred Tennyson wrote a magnificent poem, "Crossing the Bar," at 83. Isaac Newton was hard at work close to 85. At 88 John Wesley was directing, preaching, and guiding Methodism. We have several men of 95 years who come to my lec-tures, and they tell me they are in better health now than they were at 20.

Let us place our senior citizens in high places and give them every opportunity to bring forth the flowers of Paradise.

If you are retired, get interested in the laws of life and the wonders of your subconscious mind. Do something you have always wanted to do. Study new subjects, and investigate new ideas.

Pray as follows: As the hart panteth after the water brooks, so panteth my soul after thee, O God. PSALM 42:1.

• The fruits of old age

His flesh shall be fresher than a child's: he shall return to the days of his youth. JOB 33:25.

Old age really means the contemplation of the truths of God from the highest standpoint. Realize that you are on an endless journey, a series of important steps in the ceaseless, tireless, endless ocean of life. Then, with the Psalmist you will say, They shall still bring forth fruit in old age; they shall be fat and flourishing. PSALM 92:14.

But the fruit of the Spirit is love, joy, peace, patience, gentleness, goodness, faith, meekness, temperance: against such there is no law.

You are a son of Infinite Life, which knows no end, and you are a child of Eternity.

Ideas worth recalling

1. Patience, kindness, love, good will, joy, happiness, wisdom, and understanding are qualities, which never grow old. Cultivate them and express them, and remain young in mind and body.

2. Some research physicians say that the neurotic fear of the effects of time may well be the cause of premature aging.

3. Age is not the flight of years; it is the dawn of wisdom in the mind of man.

4. The most productive years of your life can be from 65 to 95.

5. Welcome the advancing years. It means you are moving higher on the path of life, which has no end.

6. God is Life, and that is your life now. Life is self-renewing, eternal, and indestructible, and is the reality of all men. You live forever, because your life is God's life.

7. Evidence of survival after death is overwhelming. Study Proceedings of Psychical Research Society of Great Britain and America in your library. Outstanding scientists base the work on the scientific research for over 75 years.

8. You cannot see your mind, but you know you have a mind. You cannot see spirit, but you know that the spirit of the game, the spirit of the artist, the spirit of the musician, and the spirit of the speaker is real. Likewise, the spirit of goodness, truth, and beauty moving in your mind and heart are real. You cannot see life, but you know you are alive.

9. Old age may be called the contemplation of the truths of God from the highest standpoint. The joys of old age are greater than those of youth. Your mind is engaged in spiritual and mental athletics. Nature slows down your body so that you may have the opportunity to meditate on things divine.

10. We do not count a man's years until he has nothing else to count. Your faith and convictions are not subject to decay.

11. You are as young as you think you are. You are as strong as you think you are. You are as useful as you think you are. You are as young as your thoughts.

12. Your gray hair is an asset. You are not selling your gray hairs. You are selling your talent, abilities, and wisdom, which you have garnered through the years.

13. Diets and exercises won't keep you young. As a man thinketh, so is he.

14. Fear of old age can bring about physical and mental deterioration. The thing I greatly feared has come upon me.

15. You grow old when you cease to dream, and when you lose interest in life. You grow old if you are irritable, crotchety, petulant, and cantankerous. Fill your mind with the truths of God and radiate the sunshine of His love—this is youth.

16. Look ahead, for at all times you are gazing into infinite life.

17. Your retirement is a new venture. Take up new studies and new interests. You can now do the things you always wanted to do when you were so busy making a living. Give your attention to living life.

18. Become a producer and not a prisoner of society. Don't hide your light under a bushel.

19. The secret of youth is love, joy, inner peace, and laughter. In Him there is fullness of joy. In Him there is no darkness at all.

20. You are needed. Some of the great philosophers, artists, scientists, writers, and others accomplished their greatest work after they were 80 years old.

21. The fruits of old age are love, joy, peace, patience, gentleness, goodness, faith, meekness, and temperance.

22. You are a son of Infinite Life, which knows no end. You are a child of Eternity. You are wonderful!

How to Attract Money

Dr. Joseph Murphy

© Copyright 2006 – BN Publishing

www.bnpublishing.com

info@bnpublishing.com

Printed in the U.S.A.

YOUR RIGHT TO BE RICH

It is your right to be rich. You are here to lead the abundant life, and to be happy, radiant, and free. You should, therefore, have all the money you need to lead a full, happy, prosperous life.

There is no virtue in poverty; the latter is a mental disease, and it should be abolished from the face of the earth. You are here to grow, expand, and unfold - spiritually, mentally, and materially. You have the inalienable right to fully develop and express yourself along all lines. You should surround yourself with beauty and luxury.

Why be satisfied with just enough to go around when you can enjoy the riches of the Infinite? In this book you will learn to make friends with money, and you will always have a surplus. Your desire to be rich is a desire for a fuller, happier, more wonderful life. It is a cosmic urge. It is good and very good.

Begin to see money in its true significance: as a symbol of exchange. It means to you freedom from want; it means beauty, luxury, abundance, and refinement.

As you read this chapter, you are probably saying, "I want more money." "I am worthy of a higher salary than I am receiving." "I believe most people are inadequately compensated." One of the reasons many people do not have more money is that they are silently or openly condemning it. They refer to money as "filthy lucre," or they believe that "Love of money is the root of all evil," etc. Another reason they do not prosper is that they have a sneaky, subconscious feeling there is some virtue in poverty; this subconscious pattern may be due to early childhood training, superstition, or it could be based on a false interpretation of the scriptures.

There is no virtue in poverty; it is a disease like any other mental disease. If you were physically ill, you would think there was something wrong with you; you would seek help, or do something about the condition at once. Likewise, if you do not have money constantly circulating in your life, there is something radically wrong with you.

Money is only a symbol; it has taken many forms as a medium of exchange down through the centuries, such as salt, beads, and trinkets of various kinds. In early times, man's wealth was determined by the number of sheep or oxen he had. It is much more convenient to write a check than to carry some sheep around with you to pay your bills.

God does not want you to live in a hovel or to go hungry. God wants you to be happy, prosperous, and successful. God is always successful in all His undertakings, whether He makes a star or a cosmos!

You may wish to take a trip around the world, study art in foreign countries, go to college, or send your children to a superior school. You certainly wish to bring up your children in lovely surroundings, so that they might learn to appreciate beauty, order, symmetry, and proportion. You were born to succeed, to win, to conquer all difficulties, and to have all your faculties fully developed. If there is financial lack in your life do something about it. Get away immediately from all superstitious beliefs about money. Do not ever regard money as evil or filthy. If you do, you cause it to take wings and fly away from you. Remember that you lose what you condemn.

Suppose, for example, you found gold, silver, lead, copper, or iron in the ground. Would you pronounce these things evil? God pronounced all things good. The evil comes from man's darkened understanding, from his unillumined mind, from his false interpretation of life, and his misuse of Divine Power. Uranium, lead, or some other metal could have been used as a medium of exchange. We use paper bills, checks, etc.; surely the piece of paper is not evil; neither is the check. Physicists and scientists know today that the only difference between one metal and another is the number and rate of motion of the electrons revolving around a central nucleus. They are now changing one metal into another through a bombardment of the atoms in the powerful cyclotron. Gold under certain conditions becomes mercury. It will be only a little while until gold, silver, and other metals will be made synthetically in the chemical laboratory. I cannot imagine seeing anything evil in electrons, neutrons, protons, and isotopes.

The piece of paper in your pocket is composed of electrons and protons arranged differently; their number and rate of motion is different; that is the only way the paper differs from the silver in your pocket.

Some people will say, "Oh, people kill for money. They steal for money!" It has been associated with countless crimes, but that does not make it evil.

A man may give another $50 to kill someone; he has misused money in using it for a destructive purpose. You can use electricity to kill someone or to light the house. You can use water to quench the baby's thirst, or use it to drown the child. You can use fire to warm the child, or burn it to death.

Another illustration would be if you brought some earth from your garden and put it in your coffee cup for breakfast: that would be your evil; yet the earth is not evil; neither is the coffee. The earth is misplaced; it belongs in your garden. Similarly, if a needle were stuck in your thumb, it would be your evil; the needle or pin belongs in the pincushion, not in your thumb.

We know the forces or the elements of nature are not evil; it depends on our use of them whether they bless or hurt us.

A man said to me one time, "I am broke. I do not like money; it is the root of all evil." Love of money to the exclusion of everything else will cause you to become lopsided and unbalanced. You are here to use your power or authority wisely. Some men crave power; others crave money. If you set your heart on money, and say, "That is all I want. I am going to give all my attention to amassing money; nothing else matters," you can get money and attain a fortune, but you have forgotten that you are here to lead a balanced life.

For example, if you belong to some cult, or religious group, and become fanatical about it, excluding yourself from your friends, society, and social activities, you will become unbalanced, inhibited, and frustrated. Nature insists on a balance. If all your time is devoted to external things and possessions, you will find yourself hungry for peace of mind, harmony, love, joy, or perfect health. You will find that you cannot buy anything that is real. You can amass a fortune, or have millions of dollars; this is not evil or bad.

Love of money to the exclusion of everything else results in frustration, disappointment, and disillusionment; in that sense it is the root of your evil.

By making money your sole aim, you simply made a wrong choice. You thought that was all you wanted, but you found after all your efforts that it was not only the money you needed. What you really desired was true place, peace of mind, and abundance. You could have the million or many millions, if you wanted them, and still have peace of mind, harmony, perfect health, and Divine expression.

Everyone wants enough money, and not just enough to go around. He wants abundance and to spare; he should have it. The urges, desires, and impulses we have for food, clothing, homes, better means of transportation, expression, procreation, and abundance are all God-given, Divine, and good, but we may misdirect these impulses, desires, and urges, resulting in evil or negative experiences in our lives.

Man does not have an evil nature; there is no evil nature in you; it is God, the Universal Wisdom, or Life seeking expression through you.

For example, a boy wants to go to college, but he does not have enough money. He sees other boys in the neighborhood going off to college and the university; his desire increases. He says to himself, "I want an education, too." Such a youth may steal or embezzle money for the purpose of going to college. The desire to go to college was basically and fundamentally good; he misdirected that desire or urge by violating the laws of society, the cosmic law of harmony, or the golden rule; then he finds himself in trouble.

However, if this boy knew the laws of mind, and his unqualified capacity through the use of the Spiritual Power to go to college, he would be free and not in jail. Who put him in jail? He placed himself there. The policeman who locked him up in prison was an instrument of the man-made laws which he violated. He first imprisoned himself in his mind by stealing and hurting others. Fear and a guilt consciousness followed; this is the prison of the mind, followed by the prison walls made of bricks and stones.

Money is a symbol of God's opulence, beauty, refinement, and abundance, and it should be used wisely, judiciously, and constructively to bless humanity in countless ways. It is merely a symbol of the economic health of the nation. When your blood is circulating freely, you are healthy. When money is circulating freely in your life, you are economically healthy. When people begin to hoard money, to put it away in tin boxes, and become charged with fear, there is economic illness.

The crash of 1929 was a psychological panic; it was fear seizing the minds of people everywhere. It was a sort of negative, hypnotic spell.

You are living in a subjective and objective world. You must not neglect the spiritual food, such as peace of mind, love, beauty, harmony, joy, and laughter.

Knowledge of the spiritual power is the means to the Royal Road to Riches of all kinds, whether your desire is spiritual, mental, or material. The student of the laws of mind, or the student of the spiritual principle, believes and knows absolutely that regardless of the economic situation, stock market fluctuation, depression, strikes, war, or other conditions and circumstances, he will always be amply supplied regardless of what form money may take. The reason for this is he abides in the consciousness of wealth. The student has convinced himself in his mind that wealth is forever flowing freely in his life and there is always a Divine surplus. Should there be a war tomorrow and all the student's present holdings become valueless, as the German marks did after the First World War, he would still attract wealth and be cared for, regardless of the form the new currency took.

Wealth is a state of consciousness; it is a mind conditioned to Divine supply forever flowing. The scientific thinker looks at money or wealth like the tide; i.e., it goes out, but it always comes back. The tides never fail; neither will man's supply when he trusts a tireless, changeless, immortal Presence which is Omnipresent and flowing ceaselessly. The man who knows the workings of the subconscious mind is never, therefore, worried about the economic situation, stock market panics, devaluation, or inflation of currency, since he abides in the consciousness of God's eternal supply. Such a man is always supplied and watched over by an over-shadowing Presence.

As you consciously commune with the Divine Presence, claiming and knowing that It leads and guides you in all your ways, that It is a Lamp unto your feet, and a Light on your path, you will be Divinely prospered and sustained beyond your wildest dreams.

Here is a simple way for you to impress your subconscious mind with the idea of constant supply or wealth: Quiet the wheels of your mind. Relax! Let go! Immobilize the attention. Get into a sleepy, drowsy, meditative state of mind; this reduces effort to the minimum; then, in a quiet, relaxed, passive way, reflect on the following simple truths: Ask yourself where do ideas come from? Where does wealth come from? Where did you come from? Where did your brain and your mind come from? You will be led back to the One Source.

You find yourself on a spiritual, working basis now. It will no longer insult your intelligence to realize that wealth is a state of mind. Take this little phrase; repeat it slowly four or five minute three or four times a day quietly to yourself, particularly before you go to sleep: "Money is forever circulating freely in my life, and there is always a Divine surplus." As you do this regularly and systematically, the idea of wealth will be conveyed to your deeper mind, and you will develop a wealth consciousness. Idle, mechanical repetition will not succeed in building the consciousness of wealth. Begin to feel the truth of what you affirm. You know what you are doing, and why you are doing it. You know your deeper self is responsive to what you consciously accept as true.

In the beginning, people who are in financial difficulties do not get results with such affirmations as, "I am wealthy," "I am prosperous," "I am successful"; such statements may cause their conditions to get worse. The reason is the subconscious mind will only accept the dominant of two ideas, or the dominant mood or feeling. When they say, "I am prosperous," their feeling of lack is greater, and something within them says, "No, you are not prosperous, you are broke." The feeling of lack is dominant, so that each affirmation calls forth the mood of lack, and more lack becomes theirs. The way to overcome this for beginners is to affirm what the conscious and subconscious mind will agree on; then there will be no contradiction. Our subconscious mind accepts our beliefs, feelings, convictions, and what we consciously accept as true.

A man could engage the cooperation of his subconscious mind by saying, "I am prospering every day." "I am growing in wealth and in wisdom every day." "Every day my wealth is multiplying." "I am advancing, growing, and moving forward financially." These and similar statements would not create any conflict in the mind.

For instance, if a salesman has only ten cents in his pocket, he could easily agree that he could have more tomorrow. If he sold a pair of shoes tomorrow, there is nothing within him which says his sales could not increase. He could use statements, such as, "My sales are increasing every day." "I am advancing and moving forward." He would find these would be sound psychologically and acceptable to his mind, and they would produce desirable fruit.

The spiritually advanced students who quietly, knowingly, and feelingly say, "I am prosperous," "I am successful," "I am wealthy," get wonderful results also. Why would this be true? When they think, feel, or say, "I am prosperous," they mean God is All Supply or Infinite Riches, and what is true of God is true of them. When they say, "I am wealthy," they know God is Infinite Supply, the Inexhaustible Treasure-House, and what is true of God is, therefore, true of them, for God is within them.

Many men get wonderful results by dwelling on three abstract ideas, such as health, wealth, and success. *Health* is a Divine Reality or quality of God. *Wealth* is of God; it is eternal and endless. *Success* is of God; God is always successful in all His undertakings.

The way they produce remarkable results is to stand before a mirror as they shave, and repeat for five or ten minutes: "Health, wealth, and success." They do not say, "I am healthy," or "I am successful;" they create no opposition in their minds. They are quiet and relaxed; thus the mind is receptive and passive; then they repeat these words. Amazing results follow. All they are doing is identifying with truths that are eternal, changeless, and timeless.

You can develop a wealth consciousness. Put the principles enunciated and elaborated on in this book to practice, and your desert will rejoice and blossom as the rose.

I worked with a young boy in Australia many years ago, who wanted to become a physician and surgeon, but he had no money; nor had he graduated from high school. For expenses, he used to clean doctors' offices, wash windows, and do odd repair jobs. He told me that every night as he went to sleep, he used to see a diploma on a wall with his name in big, bold letters. He used to clean and shine the diplomas in the medical building where he worked; it was not hard for him to engrave the diploma in his mind and develop it there. I do not know how long he continued this imaging, but it must have been for some months.

Results followed as he persisted. One of the doctors took a great liking to this young boy, and after training him in the art of sterilizing instruments, giving hypodermic injections, and other miscellaneous first aid work, he became a technical assistant in his office. The doctor sent him to high school and also to college at his own expense.

Today this man is a prominent doctor in Montreal, Canada. He had a dream! A clear image in his mind! *His wealth was in his mind.*

Wealth is your idea, desire, talent, urge for service, capacity to give to mankind, your ability for usefulness to society, and your love for humanity in general.

This young boy operated a great law unconsciously. Troward says, "Having seen the end, you have willed the means to the realization of the end." The *end* in this boy's case was to be a physician. To imagine, see, and feel the reality of being a doctor now, to live with that idea, sustain it, nourish it, and to love it until through his imagination it penetrated the layers of the subconscious, became a conviction, and paved the way to the fulfillment of his dreams.

He could have said, "I have no education." "I do not know the right people." "I am too old to go to school now." "I have no money; it would take years, and I am not intelligent." He would then be beaten before he started. His wealth was in his use of the Spiritual Power within him which responded to his thought.

The means or the way in which our prayer is answered is always hidden from us, except that occasionally we may intuitively perceive a part of the process. The *ways* are not known. The only thing man has to do is to imagine and accept the end in his mind, and leave its unfoldment to the subjective wisdom within.

Oftentimes the question is asked, "What should I do after meditating on the end and accepting my desire in consciousness?" The answer is simple: You will be compelled to do whatever is necessary for the unfoldment of your ideal. The law of the subconscious is compulsion. The law of life is action and reaction. What we do is the automatic response to our inner movements of the mind, inner feeling, and conviction.

A few months ago as I went to sleep, I imagined I was reading one of my most popular books, *Magic of Faith,* in French. I began to realize and imagine this book going into all French-speaking nations. For several weeks I did this every night, falling asleep with the imaginary French edition of *Magic of Faith* in my hands.

Just before Christmas in 1954, 1 received a letter from a leading publisher in Paris, France, enclosing a contract drawn up, asking me to sign it, giving him permission to publish and promote abroad to all French-speaking countries the French edition of *Magic of Faith.*

You might ask me what did I do about the publishing of this book after prayer? I would have to say, "Nothing!" The subjective wisdom took over, and brought it to pass in its own way, which was a far better way than any method I could consciously devise.

All of our external movements, motions, and actions follow the inner movements of the mind. Inner action precedes all outer action. Whatever steps you take physically, or what you seem to do objectively will all be a part of a pattern which you were compelled to fulfill.

Accepting the end wills the means to the realization of the end. Believe that you have it now, and you shall receive it.

We must cease denying our good. Realize that the only thing that keeps us from the riches that lie all around us is our mental attitude, or the way we look at God, life, and the world in general. Know, believe, and act on the positive assumption that there is no reason why you cannot have, be, and do whatever you wish to accomplish through the great laws of God.

Your knowledge of how your mind works is your savior and redeemer. Thought and feeling are your destiny. You possess everything by right of consciousness. The consciousness of health produces health; the consciousness of wealth produces wealth. The world seems to deny or oppose what you pray for; your senses sometimes mock and laugh at you.

If you say to your friend that you are opening up a new business for yourself, he may proceed to give you all the reasons why you are bound to fail. If you are susceptible to his hypnotic spell, he may instill fear of failure in your mind. As you become aware of the spiritual power which is one and indivisible, and which responds to your thought, you will reject the darkness and ignorance of the world and know that you possess all the equipment, power and knowledge to succeed.

To walk on the Royal Road to Riches, you must not place obstacles and impediments on the pathway of others; neither must you be jealous or envious of others. Actually, when you entertain these negative states of mind, you are hurting and injuring yourself, because you are thinking and feeling it. "The suggestion," as Quimby said, "you give to another, you are giving to yourself." This is the reason that the law of the golden rule is a cosmic, divine law.

I am sure you have heard men say, "That fellow has a racket." "He is a racketeer." "He is getting money dishonestly." "He is a faker." "I knew him when he had nothing." "He is crooked, a thief, and a swindler." If you analyze the man who talks like that, he is usually in want or suffering from some financial or physical illness. Perhaps his former college friends went up the ladder of success and excelled him; now he is bitter and envious of their progress. In many instances this is the cause of his downfall. Thinking negatively of these classmates, and condemning their wealth, causes the wealth and prosperity he is praying for to vanish and flee away. He is condemning the things he is praying for. He is praying two ways. On the one hand he is saying, "God is prospering me," and in the next breath, silently or audibly, he is saying, "I resent that fellow's wealth." Always make it a special point to bless the other person, and rejoice in his prosperity and success; when you do, you bless and prosper yourself.

If you go into the bank, and you see your competitor across the street deposit twenty times more than you do, or you see him deposit ten thousand dollars, rejoice and be exceedingly glad to see God's abundance being manifested through one of his sons. You are then blessing and exalting what you are praying for. What you bless, you multiply. What you condemn, you lose.

If you are working in a large organization, and you are silently thinking of and resenting the fact that you are underpaid, that you are not appreciated, and that you deserve more money and greater recognition, you are subconsciously severing your ties with that organization. You are setting a law in motion; then the superintendent or manager says to you, "We have to let you go." You dismissed yourself. The manager was simply the instrument through which your own negative mental state was confirmed. In other words, he was a messenger telling you what you conceived as true about yourself. It was an example of the law of action and reaction. The *action* was the internal movement of your mind; the *reaction* was the response of the outer world to conform to your inner thinking.

Perhaps as you read this, you are thinking of someone who has prospered financially by taking advantage of others, by defrauding them, by selling them unsound investments in property, etc. The answer to this is obvious, because if we rob, cheat, or defraud another, we do the same to ourselves. In reality, in this case we are actually hurting or robbing from ourselves. We are in a mood of lack in the first place, which is bound to attract loss to us. The loss may come in many ways; it may come in loss of health, prestige, peace of mind, social status, sickness in the home, or in business. It may not necessarily come in loss of money. We must not be shortsighted and think that the loss has to come in just dollars and cents.

Isn't it a wonderful feeling to place your head on the pillow at night, and feel you are at peace with the whole world, and that your heart is full of goodwill toward all? There are some people who have accumulated money the wrong way, by trampling on others, trickery, deceit, and chicanery. What is the price? Sometimes it is mental and physical disease, guilt complexes, insomnia, or hidden fears. As one man said to me, "Yes, I rode roughshod over others. I got what I wanted, but I got cancer doing it." He realized he had attained his wealth in the wrong way.

You can be wealthy and prosperous without hurting anyone. Many men are constantly robbing themselves; they steal from themselves: peace of mind, health, joy, inspiration, happiness, and the laughter of God. They may say that they have never stolen, but is it true? Every time we resent another, or are jealous, or envious of another's wealth or success, we are stealing from ourselves.

I remember in the early days of the war reading about a woman in Brooklyn, New York, who went around from store to store buying up all the coffee she could. She knew it was going to be rationed; she was full of fear that there would not be enough for her. She bought as much as she could, and stored it in the cellar. That evening she went to church services. When she came home, burglars had broken down the door, stolen not only the coffee, but silverware, money, jewelry, and other things.

This good woman said what they all say, "Why did this happen to me when I was at church? I never stole from anyone."

Is it true? Was she not in the consciousness of lack and fear when she began to hoard supplies of coffee? Her mood and fear of lack were sufficient to bring about loss in her home and possessions. She did not have to put her hand on the cash register or rob a bank;

her fear of lack produced lack. This is the reason that many people who are what society calls, "Good citizens," suffer loss. They are good in the worldly sense; i.e., they pay their taxes; they obey the laws, vote regularly, and are generous to charities, but they are resentful of others' possessions, their wealth, or social position. If they would like to take money when no one was looking, such an attitude is definitely and positively a state of lack, and may cause the person who indulges in such a mental state to attract charlatans or knaves who may swindle or cheat them in some business transaction.

Before the outer thief robs us, we have first robbed ourselves. There must be an inner thief, before the outer one appears.

A man can have a guilt complex, and accuse himself constantly. I knew such a man; he was very honest as a teller in a bank. He never stole any money, but he had an illicit romance; he was supporting another woman, and denying his family. He lived in fear that he would be discovered; a deep sense of guilt resulted. Fear follows guilt. Fear causes a contraction of the muscles and mucous membranes; acute sinusitis developed. Medication gave him only temporary relief.

I explained to this client the cause of his trouble, and told him the cure was to give up his outside affair. He said he couldn't; she was his soul mate, and that he had tried. He was always condemning and accusing himself.

One day he was accused by one of the officials of the bank of having embezzled some money; it looked serious for him, as the evidence was circumstantial. He became panic-stricken, and realized the only reason he was wrongfully accused was that he had been accusing and condemning himself. He saw how mind operates. Inasmuch as he was always accusing himself on the inner plane, he would be accused on the outer.

He immediately broke off the relationship with the other woman due to the shock of being accused of embezzling, and began to pray for Divine harmony and understanding between himself and the bank official. He began to claim, "There is nothing hidden that is not revealed. The peace of God reigns supreme in the minds and hearts of all concerned."

Truth prevailed. The whole matter was dissolved in the light of truth. Another young man was discovered as the culprit. The bank teller knew that only through prayer was he saved from a jail sentence.

The great law is, "As you would that men should think about you, think you about them in the same manner. As you would that men should feel about you, feel you also about them in like manner."

Say from your heart, "I wish for every man who walks the earth, what I wish for myself. The sincere wish of my heart is, therefore, peace, love, joy, abundance, and God's blessings to all men everywhere." Rejoice and be glad in the progression, advancement, and prosperity of all men. Whatever you claim as true for yourself, claim it for all men everywhere. If you pray for happiness and peace of mind, let your claim be peace and happiness for all. Do not ever try to deprive another of any joy. If you do, you deprive yourself. When the ship comes in for your friend, it comes in for you also.

If someone is promoted in your organization, be glad and happy. Congratulate him, rejoice in his advancement and recognition. If you are angry or resentful, you are demoting yourself. Do not try to withhold from another his God-given birthright to happiness, success, achievement, abundance, and all good things.

Hatred and resentment rot and corrode the heart, causing us to become full of scars, impurities, toxins, and poisons. Fill your minds with peace, harmony, faith, joy, honesty, integrity, loving kindness, and gentleness.

If you are seeking wisdom regarding investments, or if you are worried about your stocks or bonds, quietly claim, "Infinite Intelligence governs and watches over all my financial transactions, and whatsoever I do shall prosper." Do this frequently and you will find that your investments will be wise; moreover, you will be protected from loss, as you will be prompted to sell your securities or holdings before any loss accrues to you.

Let the following prayer be used daily by you regarding your home, business, and possessions: "The overshadowing Presence which guides the planets on their course and causes the sun to shine, watches over all my possessions, home, business, and all things that are mine. God is my fortress and vault. All my possessions are secure in God. It is wonderful." By reminding yourself daily of this great truth, and by observing the laws of

Love, you will always be guided, watched over, and prospered in all your ways. You will never suffer from loss, for you have chosen the Most High as your Counsellor and Guide. The envelope of God's Love surrounds, enfolds, and encompasses you at all times. You rest in the Everlasting Arms of God.

All of us should seek an inner guidance for our problems. If you have a financial problem, repeat this before you retire at night: "Now I shall sleep in peace. I have turned this matter over to the God-Wisdom within. It knows only the answer. As the sun rises in the morning, so will my answer be resurrected. I know the sunrise never fails." Then go off to sleep.

Do not fret, fuss and fume over a problem. Night brings counsel. Sleep on it. Your intellect cannot solve all your problems. Pray for the Light that is to come. Remember that the dawn always comes; then the shadows flee away. Let your sleep every night be a contented bliss.

You are not a victim of circumstances, except you believe you are. You can rise and overcome any circumstance or condition. You will have different experiences as you stand on the rock of spiritual Truth, steadfast, and faithful to your deeper purposes and desires.

In large stores, the management employs store detectives to prevent people from stealing; they catch a number every day trying to get something for nothing. All such people are living in the consciousness of lack and limitation, and they are stealing from themselves, attracting at the same time all manner of loss. These people lack faith in God, and the understanding of how their minds work. If they would pray for true place, Divine expression, and supply, they would find work; then by honesty, integrity, and perseverance they would become a credit to themselves and society at large.

The *poor states* of consciousness are always with us in this sense, that no matter how much wealth you now have, there is something you want with all your heart. It may be a problem of health; perhaps a son or daughter needs guidance, or harmony is lacking in the home. At that moment you are poor.

We could not know what abundance was, except we were conscious of lack. Whether it be the king of England or the boy in the slums, we are all born into limitation and into the race belief. It is through these limitations we grow. We could never discover the Inner Power, except through problems and difficulties; these are our *poor states* which prod us in seeking the solution. We could not know what joy was, except we could shed a tear of sorrow. We must be aware of poverty, to seek liberation and freedom, and ascend into God's opulence.

The *poor states*, such as fear, ignorance, worry, lack, and pain, are not bad when they cause you to seek the opposite. When you get into trouble, and get kicked from pillar to post; when you ask negative, heart-rending questions, such as "Why are all these things happening to me? Why does there seem to be a jinx following me?" light will come into your mind. Through your suffering, pain, or misery you will discover the truth which sets you free.

Through dissatisfaction we are led to satisfaction. All those studying the laws of life have been dissatisfied with something. They have had some problem or difficulty which they could not solve; or they were not satisfied with the man-made answers to life's riddles. They have found their answer in the God-Presence within themselves - the pearl of great price - the precious jewel. The Bible says, "I sought the Lord, and I found him, and He delivered me from all my fears."

When you realize your ambition or desire, you will be satisfied for only a brief period of time; then the urge to expand will come again. This is Life seeking to express Itself at higher levels through you. When one desire is satisfied, another comes, etc. to infinity. You are here to grow. Life is progression; it is not static. You are here to go from glory to glory; there is no end, for there is no end to God's glory.

We are all poor in the sense we are forever seeking more light, wisdom, happiness, and greater joy out of life. God is Infinite, and never in Eternity could you exhaust the glory, beauty, and wisdom which is within; this is how wonderful you are.

In the absolute state all things are finished, but in the relative world we must awaken to that glory which was ours before the world was. No matter how wise you are, you are seeking more wisdom; so you are still poor. No matter how intelligent you are in the field of mathematics, physics, or astronomy, you are only scratching the surface. You are still poor. The journey is ever onward, upward, and Godward. It is really an awakening process, whereby you realize creation is finished. When you know God does not have to learn, grow, expand, or unfold, you begin to gradually awaken from the dream of limitation and become alive in God. As the scales of fear, ignorance, race belief, and mass hypnosis fall from your eyes, you begin to see as God sees. The blind spots are removed; then you begin to see the world as God made it; for we begin to see it through God's eyes. Now you say, "Behold, the Kingdom of Heaven is at hand!"

Feed the "poor" within you; clothe the naked ideas, and give them form by believing in the reality of the idea, trusting the great Fabricator within to clothe it in form and objectify it. Now your word (idea) shall become flesh (take form). When you are hungry (poor states), you seek food. When worried, you seek peace. When you are sick, you seek health; when you are weak, you seek strength. Your desire for prosperity is the voice of God in you telling you that abundance is yours; therefore, through your poor state, you find the urge to grow, to expand, to unfold, to achieve, and to accomplish your desires.

A pain in your shoulder is a blessing in disguise; it tells you to do something about it at once. If there were no pain and no indication of trouble, your arm might fall off on the street. Your pain is God's alarm system telling you to seek His Peace and His Healing Power, and move from darkness to Light. When cold, you build a fire. When you are hungry, you eat. When you are in lack, enter into the mood of opulence and plenty. Imagine the end; rejoice in it. Having imagined the end, and felt it as true, you have willed the means to the realization of the end.

When you are fearful and worried, feed your mind with the great truths of God that have stood the test of time and will last forever. You can receive comfort by meditating on the great Psalms. For example: "The Lord is my shepherd; I shall not want." "God is my refuge, my salvation, whom shall I fear?" "God is an ever-present help in time of trouble." "My God; in Him will I trust." "He shall cover me with His feathers, and under His wings shall I rest." "One with God is a majority." "If God be for me, who can be against me?" Let the healing vibrations of these truths flood your mind and heart; then you will crowd out of your mind all your fears, doubts, and worries through this meditative process.

Imbibe another great spiritual truth: "A merry heart maketh a cheerful countenance." "A merry heart hath a continual feast." "A merry heart doeth good like a medicine; a broken spirit drieth the bones." Begin *now* to stir up the gift of God by completely rejecting the evidence of senses, the tyranny and despotism of the race mind, and give complete recognition to the spiritual Power within you as the only Cause, the only Power, and the only Presence. Know that it is a responsive and beneficent Power. Turn to It devotedly with assurance, trust, and love; it will respond to you as love, peace, guidance, and prosperity.

It will be your Comforter, Guide, Counsellor, and your heavenly Father. You will then say, "God is Love. I have found Him, and He truly has delivered me from all my fears." Furthermore, you will find yourself in green pastures, where abundance and all of God's riches flow freely through you.

Say to yourself freely and joyously during the day, "I walk in the consciousness of the Presence of God all day long." "His fullness flows through me at all times, filling up all the empty vessels in my life."

When you are filled full of the feeling of being what you long to be, your prayer is answered. Are all the vessels full in your life? Look under health, wealth, love, and expression. Are you fully satisfied on all levels? Is there something lacking in one of these four? All that you seek, no matter what it is, comes under one of these classifications.

•

If you say, "All I want is truth or wisdom," you are expressing the desire of all men everywhere. That is what everyone wants, even though he or she may word it differently. Truth or wisdom is the over-all desire of every man; this comes under the classification of expression. You wish to express more and more of God here and now.

Through your lack, limitation, and problems, you grow in God's Light, and you discover yourself. There is no other way whereby you could discover yourself.

If you could not use your powers two ways, you would never discover yourself; neither would you ever deduce a law governing you. If you were compelled to be good, or compelled to love, that would not be love. You would then be an automaton. You have freedom to love, because you can give it, or retain it. If compelled to love, there is no love. Aren't you flattered when some woman tells you she loves you and wants you? She has chosen you from all the men in the world. She does not have to love you. If she were forced to love you, you would not be flattered or happy about it.

You have freedom to be a murderer or a holy man. That is the reason that we praise such men as Lincoln and others. They decided to choose the good; we praise them for their choice. If we believe that circumstances, conditions, events, age, race, religious training, or early environment can preclude the possibility of our attaining a happy, prosperous life, we are thieves and robbers. All that is necessary to express happiness and prosperity is to *feel* happy and prosperous. The feeling of wealth produces wealth. States of consciousness manifest themselves. Feeling is the law, and the law is feeling.

Your desire for prosperity is really the promise of God saying that His riches are yours; accept this promise without any mental reservation.

Quimby likened prayer to a lawyer pleading the case before the judge. This teacher of the laws of mind said he could prove the defendant was not guilty as charged, but that the person was a victim of lies and false beliefs. You are the judge; you render your own verdict; then you are set free. The negative thoughts of lack, poverty, and failure are all false; they are all lies; there is nothing to back them up.

You know there is only one spiritual Power, one primal cause, and you, therefore, cease giving power to conditions, circumstances, and opinions of men. Give all Power to the Spiritual Power within you, knowing that It will respond to your thought of abundance and prosperity. Recognizing the supremacy of the Spirit within, and the Power of your own thought or mental image, is the way to opulence, freedom, and constant supply. Accept the abundant life in your own mind. Your mental acceptance and expectancy of wealth has its own mathematics and mechanics of expression. As you enter into the mood of opulence, all things necessary for the abundant life will come to pass. You are now the judge arriving at a decision in the courthouse of your mind. You have, like Quimby, produced indisputable evidence showing how the laws of your mind work, and you are now free from fear. You have executed and chopped the heads off all the fear and superstitious thoughts in your mind. Fear is the signal for action; it is not really bad; it tells you to move to the opposite, which is faith in God and all positive values.

Let this be your daily prayer; write it in your heart: "God is the source of my supply. That supply is my supply now. His riches flow to me freely, copiously, and abundantly. I am forever conscious of my true worth. I give of my talents freely, and I am wonderfully, divinely compensated. Thank you, Father! "

THE ROAD TO RICHES

Riches are of the mind. Let us suppose for a moment that a physician's diploma was stolen together with his office equipment. I am sure you would agree that his wealth was in his mind. He could still carry on, diagnose disease, prescribe, operate, and lecture on materia medica. Only his symbols were stolen; he could always get additional supplies. His riches were in his mental capacity, knowledge to help others, and his ability to contribute to humanity in general.

You will always be wealthy when you have an intense desire to contribute to the good of mankind. Your urge for service - i.e., to give of your talents to the world - will always find a response in the heart of the universe.

I knew a man in New York during the financial crisis of 1929 who lost everything he had including his home and all his life's savings. I met him after a lecture which I had given at one of the hotels in the city. This was what he said: "I lost everything. I made a million dollars in four years. I will make it again. All I have lost is a symbol. I can again attract the symbol of wealth in the same way that honey attracts flies." I followed the career of this man for several years to discover the key to his success. The key may seem strange to you; yet it is a very old one. The name he gave the key was, "Change water into wine!" He knew it was the answer to perfect health, happiness, peace of mind, and prosperity.

Wine means the realization of your desires, urges, plans, dreams, propositions, etc.; in other words, it is the things you wish to accomplish, achieve, and bring forth.

Water refers to your mind or consciousness. Water takes the shape of any vessel into which it is poured; likewise, whatever you feel and believe as true will become manifest in your world; thus you are always changing water into wine.

You determine, mould, fashion, and shape your own destiny through right thought, feeling, and beliefs. You can solve any problem, overcome any situation; you are born to succeed, to win, and to triumph.

The above man who was in a financial crisis used to say to himself frequently during the days when he was without funds, "I can change water into wine!" These words meant to him, "I can exchange the poverty ideas in my mind for the realization of my present desires or needs which are wealth and financial supply."

His mental attitude (water) was, "Once I made a fortune honestly. I will make it again (wine)." His regular affirmation consisted of, "I attracted the symbol (money) once, I am attracting it again. I know this, and feel it is true (wine)."

This man went to work as a salesman for a chemical organization. Ideas for the better promotion of their products came to him; he passed them on to his organization. It was not long until he became vice president. Within four years the company made him president. His constant mental attitude was, "I can change water into wine!"

Say to yourself as the above-mentioned chemical salesman did: "I can make the invisible ideas, urges, dreams, and desires of mine visible, because I have discovered a simple, universal law of mind."

The law he demonstrated is the law of action and reaction. It means your external world, body, circumstances, environment, and financial status are always a perfect reflection of your inner thinking, beliefs, feelings, and convictions. This being true, you can now change your inner pattern of thought by dwelling on the idea of success, wealth, and peace of mind. As you busy your mind with these latter concepts, these ideas will gradually seep into your mentality like seeds planted in the ground. As all seeds (thoughts and ideas) grow after their kind, so will your habitual thinking and feeling manifest in prosperity, success, and peace of mind. Wise thought (action) is followed by right action (reaction).

You can acquire riches when you become aware of the fact that prayer is a marriage feast. The *feast* is a psychological one; you meditate on (mentally eat of) your good or your desire until you become *one* with it.

I will now cite a case history from my files relating how a young girl succeeded in transforming "water into wine." She operated a very beautiful hair salon. Her mother became ill, and she had to devote considerable time at home, neglecting her business. During her absence two of her assistants embezzled funds. She was forced into bankruptcy, lost her home, and found herself deeply in debt. She was unable to pay hospital bills for her mother, and she was now unemployed.

I explained to this woman the magic formula of changing water into wine. Again we made it clear to her that *wine* means answered prayer or the objectification of her ideal.

She was quarreling with the outside world. She said, "Look at the facts: I have lost everything; it is a cruel world. I cannot pay my bills. I do not pray, for I have lost hope." She was so absorbed and engrossed in the material world, that she was completely oblivious to the internal cause of her situation. As we talked, she began to understand that she had to resolve the quarrel in her mind.

No matter what your desire or ideal is as you read this book, you will also find some thought or idea in your mind opposed to it. For example, your desire may be for health; perhaps there are several thoughts such as these in your mind simultaneously: "I can't be healed. I have tried, but it is no use; it's getting worse." "I don't know enough about spiritual mind healing."

As you study yourself, don't you have a tug of war in your mind? Like this girl, you find environment and external affairs challenging your desire of expression, wealth, and peace of mind.

True prayer is a mental marriage feast, and it teaches us all how to resolve the mental conflict. In prayer, you "write" what you *believe* in your own mind. Emerson said, "A man is what he thinks all day long." By your habitual thinking you make your own mental laws of belief. By repeating a certain train of thought you establish definite opinions and beliefs in the deeper mind called the subconscious; then such mental acceptances, beliefs, and opinions direct and control all the outer actions. To understand this and begin to apply it is the first step in changing "water into wine," or changing lack and limitation into abundance and opulence. The man who is unaware of his own inner spiritual powers is, therefore, subject to race beliefs, lack, and limitation.

When you wish to accomplish something, such as finding work, supply, and a way out of your problem - suggestions of lack come to you, such as, "There is no hope. All is lost. I can't accomplish it; it is hopeless." This is the voice from the outside world saying to you,

"They have no wine," or "Look at the facts." This is your feeling of lack, limitation, or bondage speaking.

How do you meet the challenge of circumstances and conditions? By now you are getting

acquainted with the laws of mind, which are as follows: "As I think and feel inside, so is my outside world; i.e., my body, finances, environment, social position, and all phases of my external relationship to the world and man." Your internal, mental movements and imagery govern, control, and direct the external plane in your life.

Thought and feeling are your destiny. Thought charged with feeling and interest is always subjectified, and becomes manifest in your world. *Prayer* is a marriage of thought and feeling, or your idea and emotion; this is what the marriage feast relates.

Any idea or desire of the mind felt as true comes to pass, whether it is good, bad, or indifferent. Knowing the law now that what you imagine and feel in your mind, you will express, manifest, or experience in the outside, enables you to begin to discipline your mind.

When the suggestion of lack, fear, doubt, or despair (they have no wine) comes to your mind, immediately reject it mentally by focusing your attention at once on the answered prayer, or fulfillment of your desire.

A suggestion of lack has no power; the power is resident in your own thought and feeling. What does God mean to you? *God* is the Name given to the One Spiritual Power. *God* is the One Invisible Source from Which all things flow.

When your thoughts are constructive and harmonious, the Spiritual Power, being responsive to your thought, flows as harmony, health, and abundance. Practice the wonderful discipline of completely rejecting every thought of lack by immediately recognizing the availability of the Spiritual Power, and Its response to your constructive thoughts and imagery.

Whatever the mind dwells upon, it multiplies, magnifies, and causes it to grow until finally the mind becomes qualified with the new state of consciousness. You are then conditioned positively, whereas before you were conditioned negatively.

The spiritual man in prayer moves from the mood of lack to the mood of confidence, peace, and trust in the Spiritual Power within himself. Since his trust and faith are in the Spiritual Power, his mood and feelings register a feeling of triumph or victory; this will bring about the solution or the answer to your prayer. The length of time may be a moment, hour, week, or month, depending on the faith and state of consciousness of the individual.

In prayer we must cleanse our mind of false beliefs, fear, doubt, and anxiety by becoming completely detached from the evidence of senses and the external world. In the peacefulness and quietude of your mind, wherein you have stilled the wheels of your mind, meditate on the joy of the answered prayer until that inner certitude comes, *whereby you know that you know*. When you have succeeded in being *one* with your desire, you have succeeded in the mental marriage – or the union of your feeling with your idea.

I am sure you wish to be married (one with) to health, harmony, success, and achievement in your mind at this moment. Every time you pray you are trying to realize your desires or ideals. You want to be mentally identified with the concepts of peace, success, well-beng, and perfect health.

You must fill your mind to the brim, meaning you must become filled full of the feeling of being what you long to be. When you succeed in filling your mind with the ideal you wish to accomplish or express, you are full to the brim; then you cease praying about it; for you feel its reality in your mind. You *know!* It is a finished state of consciousness. You are at peace about it.

Whatever is impregnated in our subconscious mind is always objectified on the screen of space; consequently, when we enter a state of conviction that our prayer is answered, we have given the command.

You are always governing your mental feast. During the day thousands of thoughts, suggestions, opinions, sights, and sounds reach your eyes and ears. You can reject them as unfit for mental consumption or entertain them, as you choose. Your conscious, reasoning, intellectual mind is the governor of the feast. When you consciously choose to entertain, meditate, feast upon, and imagine your heart's desire as true, it becomes a living embodiment and a part of your expression to it. In other words, what is impressed subjectively is expressed objectively. Your senses or conscious mind see the objectification of your good. When the conscious mind becomes aware of "water made into wine," it becomes aware of the answered prayer. *Water* might be called, also, the invisible, formless, spiritual power, unconditioned consciousness. *Wine* is conditioned consciousness, or the mind giving birth to its beliefs and convictions.

The *servants* which draw the water for you represent the mood of peace, confidence, and faith. According to your faith or feeling, your good is attracted or drawn to you.

Love is the fulfilling of the law. Love is really an emotional attachment, a sense of oneness with your good. You must be true to that which you love. You must be loyal to your purpose or to your ideal. We are not being true to the one we love when we are flirting or mentally entertaining other marriages with fear, doubt, worry, anxiety, or false beliefs. Love is a state of oneness, a state of fulfillment. (Refer to the book by the author,

Love is Freedom.)

When this simple drama was explained to the beauty operator mentioned above, she became rich mentally. She understood this drama, and she put it into practice in her life. This is how she prayed: She knew that the *water* (her own mind) would flow, and fill up all the *empty vessels* in response to her new way of thinking and feeling.

At night this client became very quiet and still, relaxed her body, and began to use constructive imagery. The steps she used are as follows:

First step: She began to imagine the local bank manager was congratulating her on her wonderful deposits in the bank. She kept imagining that for about five minutes.

The second step: In her imagination she heard her mother saying to her, "I am so happy about your wonderful, new position." She continued to hear her say this in a happy, joyous way for about three to five minutes.

The third step: She vividly imagined the writer was in front of her performing her marriage ceremony. This woman heard me saying as the officiating minister, "I now pronounce you man and wife." Completing this routine, she went off to sleep feeling filled full, i.e., sensing and feeling within herself the joy of the answered prayer.

Nothing happened for three weeks; in fact, things got much worse, but she persevered, refusing to take, "No," for her answer. She knew that in order to grow spiritually, she, too, had to perform her first miracle by changing her fear to faith, her mood of lack to a mood of opulence and prosperity, by changing consciousness (water) into the conditions, circumstances, and experiences she wished to express.

Consciousness, Awareness, Beingness, Principle, Spirit, or whatever Name you give It, is the cause of all; It is the only Presence and Power. The Spiritual Power or Spirit within us is the cause and substance of all things. All things - birds, trees, stars, sun, moon, earth, gold, silver, and platinum - are its manifestations. It is the cause and substance of all things.

Understanding this, she knew that *water* (consciousness) could become supply in the form of money, true place, or true expression for herself, health for her mother, as well as companionship and fullness of life. She saw this simple - yet profound - truth in the twinkling of an eye, and she said to me, "I *accept* my good."

She knew that nothing is hidden from us; all of God is within us, waiting for our discovery and inquiry.

In less than a month this young girl got married. The writer performed the ceremony. I pronounced the words she heard me say over and over again in her meditative, relaxed state, "I now pronounce you man and wife!"

Her husband gave her a check for $24,000 as a wedding present, as well as a trip around the world. Her new expression as a beauty operator was to beautify her home and garden, and make the desert of her mind rejoice and blossom as the rose.

She changed "water into wine." *Water* or her consciousness became charged or conditioned by her constant, true, happy imagery. These images, when sustained regularly, systematically, and with faith in the developing powers of the deeper mind, will come out of the darkness (subconscious mind) into light (objectified on the screen of space).

There is one important rule: Do not expose this newly developed film to the shattering light of fear, doubt, despondency, and worry. Whenever worry or fear knocks at your door, immediately turn to the picture you developed in your mind, and say to yourself, "A beautiful picture is being developed now in the dark house of my mind." Mentally pour on that picture your feeling of joy, faith, and understanding. You know you have operated a psychological, spiritual law, for what is impressed shall be expressed. It is wonderful!

The following is a sure, certain way for developing and manifesting all the material riches and supply you need all the days of your life. If you apply this formula sincerely and honestly, you should be amply rewarded on the external plane. I will illustrate this by telling you of a man who came to see me in London in desperate, financial straits. He was a member of the Church of England, and had studied the working of the subconscious mind to some extent.

I told him to say frequently during the day, "God is the source of my supply, and all my needs are met at every moment of time and point of space." Think also of all the animal life in this world, and of all the galaxies of space which are now being taken care of by an Infinite Intelligence. Notice how nature is lavish, extravagant, and bountiful.

He began to realize that since he was born, he had been taken care of, fed by his mother, clothed by his father, and watched over by tender, loving parents. This man got a job and was paid in a wonderful way. He reasoned that it was illogical to assume that the Principle of Life which gave him life and always took care of him, would suddenly cease to respond to him.

He realized that he had cut off his own supply by resenting his employer, self-condemnation, criticism of himself, and by his own sense of unworthiness. He had psychologically severed the cord which joined him to the Infinite Source of all things - the Indwelling Spirit or Life Principle, called by some, "Consciousness or Awareness."

Man is not fed like the birds; he must consciously commune with the Indwelling Power and Presence, and receive guidance, strength, vitality, and all things necessary for the fulfillment of his needs.

This is the formula which he used to change water into the wine of abundance and financial success. He realized God or the Spiritual Power within him was the cause of all; furthermore, he realized that if he could sell himself the idea that wealth was his by Divine right, he would manifest abundance of supply.

The affirmation he used was, "God is the source of my supply. All my financial and other needs are met at every moment of time and point of space; there is always a Divine surplus." This simple statement repeated frequently, knowingly, and intelligently, conditioned his mind to a prosperity consciousness.

All he had to do was to sell himself this positive idea, in the same way a good salesman has to sell himself on the merits of his product. Such a person is convinced of the integrity of his company, the high quality of the product, the good service which it will give the customer, and the fact that the price is right, etc.

I told him whenever negative thoughts came to his mind, which would happen, not to fight or quarrel with them in any way, but simply go back to the spiritual, mental formula, and repeat it quietly and lovingly to himself. Negative thoughts came to him in avalanches at times, in the form of a flood of negativity. Each time he met them with the positive, firm, loyal conviction: "God supplies all my needs; there is a Divine surplus in my life."

He said that as he drove his car, and went through his day's routine, a host of sundry, miscellaneous, negative concepts crowded his mind from time to time, such as "There is no hope." "You are broke." Each time such negative thoughts came, he refused their mental admission by turning to the Eternal Source of wealth, health, and all things which he knew to be his own spiritual awareness. Definitely and positively he claimed, "God is the source of my supply, and that supply is mine now!" Or, "There is a Divine solution. God's wealth is my wealth," and other affirmative, positive statements which charged his mind with hope, faith, expectancy, and ultimately a conviction in an ever-flowing fountain of riches, supplying all his needs copiously, joyously, and endlessly.

The negative flood of thoughts came to him as often as fifty times in an hour; each time he refused to open the door of his mind to these gangsters, assassins, and thieves which he knew would only rob him of peace, wealth, success, and all good things. Instead he opened the door of his mind to the idea of God's Eternal Life Principle of supply flowing through him as wealth, health, energy, power, and all things necessary to lead a full and happy life here.

As he continued to do this, the second day not so many thieves knocked at his door; the third day, the flow of negative visitors was less; the fourth day, they came intermittently, hoping for admission, but receiving the same mental response: "No entrance! I accept only thoughts and concepts which activate, heal, bless, and inspire my mind!"

He reconditioned his consciousness or mind to a wealth consciousness. The negative thoughts, such as fear, lack, worry, anxiety, came, but they received no response from his mind. He was now immune, God-intoxicated, and seized by a divine faith in an ever-expanding consciousness of abundance and financial supply. This man did not lose everything; neither did he go into bankruptcy. He was given extended credit; his business improved; new doors opened up, and he prospered.

Remember always in the prayer process, you must be loyal to your ideal, purpose, and objective. Many people fail to realize wealth and financial success, because they pray two ways. They affirm God is their supply, and that they are Divinely prospered, but a few minutes later they deny their good by saying, "I can't pay this bill." "I can't afford this, that, or the other thing." Or they say to themselves: "A jinx is following me." "I can't ever make ends meet." "I never have enough to go around." All such statements are highly destructive and neutralize your positive prayers. This is what is called "praying two ways."

You must be faithful to your plan or your goal. You must be true to your knowledge of the Spiritual Power. Cease making negative marriages, i.e., uniting with negative thoughts, fears, and worries.

Prayer is like a captain directing the course of his ship. You must have a destination. You must know where you are going. The captain of the ship, knowing the laws of navigation, regulates his course accordingly. If the ship is turned from its course by storms or unruly waves, he calmly redirects it along its true course.

You are the captain on the bridge, and you are giving the orders in the way of thoughts, feelings, opinions, beliefs, moods, and mental tones. Keep your eye on the beam. *You go where your vision is!* Cease, therefore, looking at all the obstacles, delays, and impediments that would cause you to go off your course. Be definite and positive. Decide where you are going. Know that your mental attitude is the ship which will take you from the mood of lack and limitation, to the mood and feeling of opulence, and to the belief in the inevitable law of God working for you.

Quimby, who was a doctor, a wonderful student, and teacher of the mental and spiritual laws of mind, said, "Man acts as he is acted upon." What moves you now? What is it that determines your response to life? The answer is as follows: Your ideas, beliefs, and opinions activate your mind and condition you to the point that you become, as Quimby stated, "An expression of your beliefs." This illustrates the truth of Quimby's statement: "Man is belief expressed." Another popular statement of Quimby's was, "Our minds mingle like atmospheres, and each person has his identity in that atmosphere." When you were a child, you were subject to the moods, feelings, beliefs, and the general mental atmosphere of the home. The fears, anxieties, superstitions, as well as the religious faith and convictions of the parents were impressed on your mind.

Let us say the child had been brought up in a poverty-stricken home, in which there was never enough to go around, financially speaking; he heard constantly the complaint of lack and limitation. You could say, like Salter in his conditioned reflex therapy, that the child was conditioned to poverty. The young man may have a poverty complex based on his early experiences, training, and beliefs, but he can rise above any situation and become free; this is done through the power of prayer.

I knew a young boy, aged 17, who was born in a place called, "Hell's Kitchen," in New York. He listened to some lectures I was giving in Steinway Hall, New York, at the time. This boy realized that he had been the victim of negative, destructive thinking, and that if he did not redirect his mind along constructive channels, the world-mind with its fears, failures, hates, and jealousies would move in and control him. "Man acts as he is acted upon."

It stands to reason, as Quimby knew, that if man will not take charge of his own house (mind), the propaganda, false beliefs, fears, and worries of the phenomenalistic world will act as a hypnotic spell over him.

We are immersed in the race mind which believes in sickness, death, misfortune, accident, failures, disease, and diverse disasters. Identify yourself mentally and emotionally with the Eternal Verities which have stood the test of time.

This young man decided to think and plan for himself. He decided to take the Royal Road to Riches by accepting God's abundance here and now, and to fill his mind with spiritual concepts and perceptions. He knew, as he did this, he would automatically crowd out of his mind all negative patterns. He adopted a simple process called, "scientific imagination." He had a wonderful voice, but it was not cultivated or developed. I told him the image he gave attention to in his mind would be developed in his deeper mind and come to pass. He understood this to be a law of mind - a law of action and reaction - i.e., the response of the deeper mind to the mental picture held in the conscious mind.

This young man would sit down quietly in his room at home, relax his whole body, and vividly imagine himself singing before a microphone. He would actually reach out for the "feel" of the instrument. He would hear me congratulate him on his wonderful contract and tell him how magnificent his voice was. By giving his attention and devotion to this mental image regularly and systematically, a deep impression was made on his subconscious mind.

A short time elapsed, and an Italian voice instructor in New York gave him free lessons several times a week, because he saw his possibilities. He got a contract which sent him abroad to sing in the salons of Europe, Asia, South Africa, and other places. His financial worries were over, for he also received a wonderful salary. His hidden talents and ability to release them were his real riches. These talents and powers within all of us are God-given; let us release them.

Did you ever say to yourself, "How can I be more useful to my fellow creatures?" "How can I contribute more to humanity?"

A minister-friend of mine told me that in his early days he and his church suffered financially. His technique or process was this simple prayer which worked wonders for him, "God reveals to me better ways to present the truths of God to my fellow creatures." Money poured in; the mortgage was paid in a few years, and he has never worried about money since.

As you read this chapter, you have now learned that the inner feelings, moods, and beliefs of man always control and govern his external world. The inner movements of the mind control the outer movements. To change the outside, you I must change the inside. "As in Heaven, so on earth;" or as in my mind or consciousness, so is it in my body, circumstances, and environment.

There are no hidden secrets that cannot be revealed. For example, if you are sick, you are revealing a mental and emotional pattern which is the cause. If you are upset, or if you receive tragic news, notice how you reveal it in your face, eyes, gestures, tonal qualities, also in your gait, and posture. As a matter of fact, your whole body reveals your inner distress. You could, of course, through mental discipline and prayer remain absolutely poised, serene, and calm, refusing to betray your hidden feelings or mental states. You could order the muscles of your body to relax, be quiet, and be still; they would have to obey you. Your eyes, face, and lips would not betray any sign of grief, anger, or despondency. On the other hand, with a little discipline, through prayer and meditation, you could reverse the entire picture. Even though you had received disturbing news, regardless of its grave nature, you could show and exhibit joy, peace, relaxation, and a vibrant, buoyant nature. No one would ever know that you were the recipient of so-called bad news.

Regardless of what kind of news you received today, you could go to the mirror, look at your face, lips, eyes, and your gestures, as you tell yourself and imagine you have heard the news of having received a vast fortune. Dramatize it, feel it, thrill to it, and notice how your whole body responds to the inner thrill.

You can reverse any situation through prayer. Busy your mind with the concepts of peace, success, wealth, and happiness. Identify yourself with these ideas mentally, emotionally, and pictorially.

Get a picture of yourself as you want to be; retain that image; sustain it with joy, faith, and expectancy; finally you will succeed in experiencing its manifestation.

I say to people who consult me regarding financial lack to "marry wealth." Some see the point; others do not. As all Bible students know, your *wife* is what you are mentally joined to, united with, or at one with.

In other words, what you conceive and believe, you give conception. If you believe the world is cold, cruel, and harsh, that it is a "dog eat dog" way of life, that is your concept; you are married to it, and you will have children or issue by that marriage. The children from such a mental marriage or belief will be your experiences, conditions, and circumstances, together with all other events in your life. All your experiences and reactions to life will be the image and likeness of the ideas which fathered them.

Look at the many wives the average man is living with, such as fear, doubt, anxiety, criticism, jealousy, and anger; these play havoc with his mind. Marry wealth by claiming, feeling, and believing: "God supplies all my needs according to his riches in glory." Or take the following statement, and repeat it over and over again knowingly until your consciousness is conditioned by it, or it becomes part of your meditation: "I am Divinely expressed, and I have a wonderful income." Do not say this in a parrot-like fashion, but know that your train of thought is being engraved in your deeper mind, and it becomes a conditioned state of consciousness. Let the phrase become meaningful to you. Pour life, love, and feeling on it, making it alive.

One of my class-students recently opened a restaurant. He phoned me, saying that he got married to a restaurant; he meant that he had made up his mind to be very successful, diligent, and persevering, and to see that his business prospered. This man's wife (mental) was his belief in the accomplishment of his desire or wish.

Identify yourself with your aim in life, and cease mental marriages with criticism, self-condemnation, anger, fear, and worry. Give attention to your chosen ideal, being full of faith and confidence in the inevitable law of prosperity and success. You will accomplish nothing by loving your ideal one minute, and denying it the next minute; this is like mixing acid and alkali, and you will get an inert substance. In going along the Royal Road to Riches, you must be faithful to your chosen ideal (your wife).

Let Divine Wisdom be your guide. Let the subjective Wisdom within you lead, guide, and govern you in all your ways. Turn over your request to this Indwelling Presence, knowing in your heart and soul that it will dissipate the anxiety, heal the wound, and restore your soul to equanimity and tranquility. Open your mind and heart, and say, "God is my pilot. He leads me. He prospers me. He is my counsellor." Let your prayer be night and morning, "I am a channel through which God's riches flow ceaselessly, copiously, and freely." Write that prayer in your heart, inscribe it in your mind. Keep on the beam of God's glory!

The man who does not know the inner workings of his own mind is full of burdens, anxieties, and worries; he has not learned how to cast his burden on the Indwelling Presence and go free.

The Zen monk was asked by his disciple, "What is Truth?" He replied in a symbolic way by taking the bag off his back, and placing it on the ground.

The disciple then asked him, "Master, how does it work?"

The Zen monk, still silent, placed the bag on his back, and walked on down the road singing to himself. The bag is your burden, or your problem. You cast it on the subjective Wisdom which knows all, and has the "know how" of accomplishment. It knows only the answer.

Placing the bag again on his back means though I still have the problem, I now have mental rest and relief from the burden, because I have invoked the Divine Wisdom on my behalf; therefore, I sing the song of triumph, knowing that the answer to my prayer is on the way, and I sing for the joy that is set before me. It is wonderful.

Every man, when he first enters a knowledge of the laws of the mind, sets out with high spirits and ambitions. He is the new broom which sweeps clean, and he is full of good intentions; oftentimes he forgets the Source of power. He does not remain faithful to the Principle within him, which is scientific and effectual, that would lift him out of his negative experiences and set him on the high road to freedom and peace of mind. He begins to indulge mentally and emotionally with ideas and thoughts extraneous to his announced aim and goal. In other words, he is not faithful to his ideal or wife.

Know that the subjective or deeper self within you will accept your request, and being the great fabricator, it will bring it to pass in its own way. All you do is release your request with faith and confidence, in the same way you would cast a seed on the ground, or mail a letter to a friend, knowing the answer would come.

Did you ever go between two great rocks and listen to the echo of your voice? This is the way the Life Principle within you answers. You will hear the echo of your own voice. Your voice is your inner, mental movement of the mind – your inner, psychological journey where you feasted mentally on an idea until you were full; then you rested.

Knowing this law and how to use it, be sure you never become drunk with power, arrogance, pride, or conceit. Use the law to bless, heal, inspire, and lift up others, as well as yourself.

Man misuses the law by selfishly taking advantage of his fellow man; if you do, you hurt and attract loss to yourself. Power, security, and riches are not to be obtained externally. They come from the treasure-house of eternity within. We should realize that the good wine is always present, for God is the Eternal Now. Regardless of present circumstances, you can prove your good is ever-present by detaching yourself mentally from the problem, going on the High Watch, and going about your Father's business.

To go on the High Watch is to envision your good, to dwell on the new concept of yourself, to become married to it, and sustain the happy mood by remaining faithful - full of faith every step of the way - knowing that the wine of joy, the answered prayer, is on the way. "Now is the day of salvation." "The kingdom of heaven is at hand."

You can - this moment - travel psychologically in your mind, and enter mentally through

Divine imagination into any desired state. The wealth, health, or invention you wish to introduce are all invisible at first. Everything comes out of the Invisible. You must subjectively possess riches, before you can objectively possess wealth. The feeling of wealth produces wealth; for wealth is a state of consciousness. *A state of consciousness* is what you think, feel, believe, and mentally give consent to.

A teacher in California receiving over five or six thousand dollars a year looked in a window at a beautiful ermine coat that was priced at $8,000. She said, "It would take me years to save that amount of money. I could never afford it. Oh, how I want it!" She listened to our lectures on Sunday mornings. By ceasing to marry these negative concepts, she learned that she could have a coat, car, or anything she wished without hurting anybody on the face of the earth.

I told her to imagine she had the coat on, to feel its beautiful fur, and to get the feel of it on her. She began to use the power of her imagination prior to sleep at night. She put the imaginary coat on her, fondled it, caressed it, like a child does with her doll. She continued to do this, and finally felt the thrill of it all.

She went to sleep every night wearing this imaginary coat and being so happy in possessing it. Three months went by, and nothing happened. She was about to waiver, but she reminded herself that it is the sustained mood which demonstrates. The solution will come to the person who does not waver, but always goes about with the perfume of His Presence with him. The answer comes to the man who walks in the light that "It is done!" You are always using the *perfume of His Presence* when you sustain the happy, joyous mood of expectancy, knowing your good is on the way. You saw it in the unseen, and you know you will see it in the seen.

The sequel to the teacher's drama of the mind is interesting. One Sunday morning after our lecture, a man accidentally stepped on her toe, apologized profusely, asked her where she lived, and offered to drive her home. She accepted gladly. Shortly after, he proposed marriage, gave her a beautiful diamond ring, and said to her, "I saw the most wonderful coat; you would simply look radiant wearing it!" It was the coat she admired three months previously. (The salesman said over one hundred wealthy women looked at the coat, admired it immensely, but for some reason always selected another garment.)

Through your capacity to choose, imagine the reality of what you have selected, and through faith and perseverance, *you can* realize your goal in life. All the riches of heaven are here now within you, waiting to be released. Peace, joy, love, guidance, inspiration, goodwill, and abundance all exist now. All that is necessary in order to express God's riches is for you to leave the present now (your limitation), enter into the mental vision or picture, and in a happy, joyous mood become one with your ideal. Having seen and felt your good in moments of high exaltation, you know that in a little while you shall see your ideal objectively as you walk through time and space. As within, so without. As above, so below. As in heaven so on earth. In other words, you will see your beliefs expressed. Man *is* belief expressed!

Thought Vibration
or
the Law of Attraction in the Thought World

William Walker Atkinson

CONTENTS

Law of Attraction

The Universe is governed by Law - one great Law. Its manifestations are multiform, but viewed from the Ultimate there is but one Law. We are familiar with some of its manifestations, but are almost totally ignorant of certain others. Still we are learning a little more every day - the veil is being gradually lifted. We speak learnedly of the Law of Gravitation, but ignore that equally wonderful manifestation, THE LAW OF ATTRACTION IN THE THOUGHT WORLD. We are familiar with that wonderful manifestation of Law which draws and holds together the atoms of which matter is composed - we recognize the power of the law that attracts bodies to the earth, that holds the circling worlds in their places, but we close our eyes to the mighty law that draws to us the things we desire or fear, that makes or mars our lives.

When we come to see that Thought is a force - a manifestation of energy -having a magnet-like power of attraction, we will begin to understand the why and wherefore of many things that have heretofore seemed dark to us. There is no study that will so well repay the student for his time and trouble as the study of the workings of this mighty law of the world of Thought - the Law of Attraction. When we think we send out vibrations of a fine ethereal substance, which are as real as the vibrations manifesting light, heat, electricity, magnetism. That these vibrations are not evident to our five senses is no proof that they do not exist. A powerful magnet will send out vibrations and exert a force sufficient to attract to itself a piece of steel weighing a hundred pounds, but we can neither see, taste, smell, hear nor feel the mighty force. These thought vibrations, likewise, cannot be seen, tasted, smelled, heard nor felt in the ordinary way; although it is true there are on record cases of persons peculiarly sensitive to psychic impressions who have perceived powerful thought-waves, and very many of us can testify that we have distinctly felt the thought vibrations of others, both whilst in the presence of the sender and at a distance. Telepathy and its kindred phenomena are not idle dreams. Light and heat are manifested by vibrations of a far lower intensity than those of Thought, but the difference is solely in the rate of vibration. The annals of science throw an interesting light upon this question. Prof. Elisha Gray, an eminent scientist, says in his little book, "The Miracles of Nature": "There is much food for speculation in the thought that there exist sound-waves that no human ear can hear, and color-waves of light that no eye can see. The long, dark, soundless space between 40,000 and 400,000,000,000,000 vibrations per second, and the infinity of range beyond 700,000,000,000,000 vibrations per second, where light ceases, in the universe of motion, makes it possible to indulge in speculation."

M. M. Williams, in his work entitled "Short Chapters in Science," says: "There is no gradation between the most rapid undulations or tremblings that produce our sensation of sound, and the slowest of those which give rise to our sensations of gentlest warmth. There is a huge gap between them, wide enough to include another world of motion, all lying between our world of sound and our world of heat and light; and there is no good reason whatever for supposing that matter is incapable of such intermediate activity, or that such activity may not give rise to intermediate sensations, provided there are organs for taking up and sensifying their movements." I cite the above authorities merely to give you food for thought, not to attempt to demonstrate to you the fact that thought vibrations exist. The last-named fact has been fully established to the satisfaction of numerous investigators of the subject, and a little reflection will show you that it coincides with your own experiences. We often hear repeated the well-known Mental Science statement, "Thoughts are Things," and we say these words over without consciously realizing just what is the meaning of the statement. If we fully comprehended the truth of the statement and the natural consequences of the truth back of it, we should understand many things which have appeared dark to us, and would be able to use the wonderful power, Thought Force, just as we use any other manifestation of Energy. As I have said, when we think we set into motion vibrations of a very high degree, but just as real as the vibrations of light, heat, sound, electricity. And when we understand the laws governing the production and transmission of these vibrations we will be able to use them in our daily life, just as we do the better known forms of energy. That we cannot see, hear, weigh or measure these vibrations is no proof that they do not exist. There exist waves of sound which no human ear can hear, although some of these are undoubtedly registered by the ear of some of the insects, and others are caught by delicate scientific instruments invented by man; yet there is a great gap between the sounds registered by the most delicate instrument and the limit which man's mind, reasoning by analogy, knows to be the boundary line between sound waves and some other forms of vibration. And there are light waves which the eye of man does not register, some of which may be detected by more delicate instruments, and many more so fine that the instrument has not yet been invented which will detect them, although improvements are being made every year and the unexplored field gradually lessened. As new instruments are invented, new vibrations are registered by them -and yet the vibrations were just as real before the invention of the instrument as afterward. Supposing that we had no instruments to register magnetism - one might be justified in denying the existence of that mighty force, because it could not be tasted, felt, smelt, heard, seen, weighted or measured. And yet the mighty magnet would still send out waves of force sufficient to draw to it pieces of steel weighing hundreds of pounds. Each form of vibration requires its own form of instrument for registration. At present the human brain seems to be the only instrument capable of registering thought waves, although occultists say that in this century scientists will invent apparatus sufficiently delicate to catch and register such impressions. And from present indications it looks as if the invention named might be expected at any time. The demand exists and undoubtedly will be soon supplied. But to those who have experimented along the lines of practical telepathy no further proof is required than the results of their own experiments. We are sending out thoughts of greater or less intensity all the time, and we are reaping the results of such thoughts. Not only do our thought waves influence ourselves and others, but they have a drawing power -they attract to us the thoughts of others, things, circumstances, people, "luck," in accord with the character of the thought uppermost in our minds. Thoughts of Love will attract to us the Love of others; circumstances and surroundings in accord with the thought; people who are of like thought. Thoughts of Anger, Hate, Envy, Malice and Jealousy will draw to us the foul brood of kindred thoughts emanating from the minds of others; circumstances in which we will be called upon to manifest these vile thoughts and will receive them in turn from others; people who will manifest inharmony; and so on. A strong thought or a thought long continued, will make us the center of attraction for the corresponding thought waves of others. Like attracts like in the Thought World - as ye sow so shall ye reap. Birds of a feather flock together in the Thought World - curses like chickens come home to roost, and bringing their friends with them. The man or woman who is filled with Love sees Love on all sides and attracts the Love of others. The man with hate in his heart gets all the Hate he can stand. The man who thinks Fight generally runs up against all the Fight he wants before he gets through. And so it goes, each gets what he calls for over the wireless telegraphy of the Mind. The man who rises in the morning feeling "grumpy" usually manages to have the whole family in the same mood before the breakfast is over. The "nagging" woman generally finds enough to gratify her "nagging" propensity during the day. This matter of Thought Attraction is a serious one. When you stop to think of it you will see that a man really makes his own surroundings, although he blames others for it. I have known people who understood this law to hold a positive, calm thought and be absolutely unaffected by the inharmony surrounding them. They were like the vessel from which the oil had been poured on the troubled waters - they rested safely and calmly whilst the tempest raged around them. One is not at the mercy of the fitful storms of Thought after he has learned the workings of the Law. We have passed through the age of physical force on to the age of intellectual supremacy, and are now entering a new and almost unknown field, that of psychic power. This field has its established laws and we should acquaint ourselves with them or we will be crowded to the wall as are the ignorant on the planes of effort. I will endeavor to make plain to you the great underlying principles of this new field of energy which is opening up before us, that you may be able to make use of this great power and apply it for legitimate and worthy purposes, just as men are using steam, electricity and other forms of energy today.

Thought Waves and their Process of Reproduction

LIKE a stone thrown into the water, thought produces ripples and waves which spread out over the great ocean of thought. There is this difference, however: the waves on the water move only on a level plane in all directions, whereas thought waves move in all directions from a common center, just as do the rays from the sun. Just as we here on earth are surrounded by a great sea of air, so are we surrounded by a great sea of Mind. Our thought waves move through this vast mental ether, extending, however, in all directions, as I have explained, becoming somewhat lessened in intensity according to the distance traversed, because of the friction occasioned by the waves coming in contact with the great body of Mind surrounding us on all sides. These thought waves have other qualities differing from the waves on the water. They have the property of reproducing themselves; in this respect they resemble sound waves rather than waves upon the water. Just as a note of the violin will cause the thin glass to vibrate and "sing," so will a strong thought tend to awaken similar vibrations in minds attuned to receive it. Many of the "stray thoughts" which come to us are but reflections or answering vibrations to some strong thought sent out by another. But unless our minds are attuned to receive it, the thought will not likely affect us. If we are thinking high and great thoughts, our minds acquire a certain keynote corresponding to the character of the thoughts we have been thinking. And, this keynote once established, we will be apt to catch the vibrations of other minds keyed to the same thought. On the other hand, let us get into the habit of thinking thoughts of an opposite character, and we will soon be echoing the low order of thought emanating from the minds of the thousands thinking along the same lines. We are largely what we have thought ourselves into being, the balance being represented by the character of the suggestions and thought of others, which have reached us either directly by verbal suggestions or telepathically by means of such thought waves. Our general mental attitude, however, determines the character of the thought waves received from others as well as the thoughts emanating from ourselves. We receive only such thoughts as are in harmony with the general mental attitude held by ourselves; the thoughts not in harmony affecting us very little, as they awaken no response in us. The man who believes thoroughly in himself and maintains a positive strong mental attitude of Confidence and Determination is not likely to be affected by the adverse and negative thoughts of Discouragement and Failure emanating from the minds of other persons in whom these last qualities predominate. At the same time these negative thoughts, if they reach one whose mental attitude is pitched on a low key, deepen his negative state and add fuel to the fire which is consuming his strength, or, if you prefer this figure, serve to further smother the fire of his energy and activity. We attract to us the thoughts of others of the same order of thought. The man who thinks success will be apt to get into tune with the minds of others thinking likewise, and they will help him, and he them. The man who allows his mind to dwell constantly upon thoughts of failure brings himself into close touch with the minds of other "failure" people, and each will tend to pull the other down still more. The man who thinks that all is evil is apt to see much evil, and will be brought into contact with others who will seem to prove his theory. And the man who looks for good in everything and everybody will be likely to attract to himself the things and people corresponding to his thought. We generally see that for which we look. You will be able to carry this idea more clearly if you will think of the Marconi wireless instruments, which receive the vibrations only from the sending instrument which has been attuned to the same key, while other telegrams are passing through the air in near vicinity without affecting the instrument. The same law applies to the operations of thought. We receive only that which corresponds to our mental attunement. If we have been discouraged, we may rest assured that we have dropped into a negative key, and have been affected not only by our own thoughts but have also received the added depressing thoughts of similar character which are constantly being sent out from the minds of other unfortunates who have not yet learned the law of attraction in the thought world. And if we occasionally rise to heights of enthusiasm and energy, how quickly we feel the inflow of the courageous, daring, energetic, positive thoughts being sent out by the live men and women of the world. We recognize this without much trouble when we come in personal contact with people and feel their vibrations, depressing or invigorating, as the case may be. But the same law operates when we are not in their presence, although less strongly.

The mind has many degrees of pitch, ranging from the highest positive note to the lowest negative note, with many notes in between, varying in pitch according to their respective distance from the positive or negative extreme. When your mind is operating along positive lines you feel strong, buoyant, bright, cheerful, happy, confident and courageous, and are enabled to do your work well, to carry out your intentions, and progress on your roads to Success. You send out strong positive thought, which affects others and causes them to co-operate with you or to follow your lead, according to their own mental keynote. When you are playing on the extreme negative end of the mental keyboard you feel depressed, week, passive, dull, fearful, cowardly. And you find yourself unable to make progress or to succeed. And your effect upon others is practically nil. You are led by, rather than leading others, and are used as a human doormat or football by more positive persons. In some persons the positive element seems to predominate, and in others the negative quality seems to be more in evidence. There are, of course, widely varying degrees of positiveness and negativeness, and B may be negative to A, while positive to C. When two people first meet there is generally a silent mental conflict in which their respective minds test their quality of positiveness, and fix their relative position toward each other. This process may be unconscious in many cases, but it occurs nevertheless. The adjustment is often automatic, but occasionally the struggle is so sharp - the opponents being so well matched - that the matter forces itself into the consciousness of the two people. Sometimes both parties are so much alike in their degrees of positiveness that they fail to come to terms, mentally; they never really are able to get along with each other, and they are either mutually repelled and separate or else stay together amid constant broils and wrangling. We are positive or negative to everyone with whom we have relations. We may be positive to our children, our employees and dependents, but we are at the same time negative to others to whom we occupy inferior positions, or whom we have allowed to assert themselves over us. Of course, something may occur and we will suddenly become more positive than the man or woman to whom we have heretofore been negative. We frequently see cases of this kind. And as the knowledge of these mental laws becomes more general we will see many more instances of persons asserting themselves and making use of their newfound power. But remember you possess the power to raise the keynote of your mind to a positive pitch by an effort of the will. And, of course, it is equally true that you may allow yourself to drop into a low, negative note by carelessness or a weak will. There are more people on the negative plane of thought than on the positive plane, and consequently there are more negative thought vibrations in operation in our mental atmosphere. But, happily for us, this is counterbalanced by the fact that a positive thought is infinitely more powerful than a negative one, and if by force of will we raise ourselves to a higher mental key we can shut out the depressing thoughts and may take up the vibrations corresponding with our changed mental attitude. This is one of the secrets of the affirmations and autosuggestions used by the several schools of Mental Science and other New Thought cults. There is no particular merit in affirmations of themselves, but they serve a twofold purpose: (1) They tend to establish new mental attitudes within us and act wonderfully in the direction of character- building - the science of making ourselves over. (2) They tend to raise the mental keynote so that we may get the benefit of the positive thought waves of others on the same plane of thought. Whether or not we believe in them, we are constantly making affirmations. The man who asserts that he can and will do a thing - and asserts it earnestly - develops in himself the qualities conducive to the well doing of that thing, and at the same time places his mind in the proper key to receive all the thought waves likely to help him in the doing. If, on the other hand, one says and feels that he is going to fail, he will choke and smother the thoughts coming from his own subconscious mentality which are intended to help him, and at the same time will place himself in tune with the Failure-thought of the world - and there is plenty of the latter kind of thought around, I can tell you. Do not allow yourselves to be affected by the adverse and negative thoughts of those around you. Rise to the upper chambers of your mental dwelling, and key yourself up to a strong pitch, away above the vibrations on the lower planes of thought. Then you will not only be immune to their negative vibrations but will be in touch with the great body of strong positive thought coming from those of your own plane of development. My aim will be to direct and train you in the proper use of thought and will, that you may have yourself well in hand and may be able to strike the positive key at any moment you may feel it necessary. It is not necessary to strike the extreme note on all occasions. The better plan is to keep yourself in a comfortable key, without much strain, and to have the means at command whereby you can raise the pitch at once when occasion demands. By this knowledge you will not be at the mercy of the old automatic action of the mind, but may have it well under your own control. Development of the will is very much like the development of a muscle -a matter of practice and gradual improvement. At first it is apt to be tiresome, but at each trial one grows stronger until the new strength becomes real and permanent. Many of us have made ourselves positive under sudden calls or emergencies. We are in the habit of "bracing up" when occasion demands. But by intelligent practice you will be so much strengthened that your habitual state will be equal to your "bracing up" stage now, and then when you find it necessary to apply the spur you will be able to reach a stage not dreamed of at present. Do not understand me as advocating a high tension continuously. This is not at all desirable, not only because it is apt to be too much of a strain upon you but also because you will find it desirable to relieve the tension at times and become receptive that you may absorb impressions. It is well to be able to relax and assume a certain degree of receptiveness, knowing that you are always able to spring back to the more positive state at will. The habitually strongly positive man loses much enjoyment and recreation. Positive, you give out expressions; receptive, you take in impressions. Positive, you are a teacher; receptive, a pupil. It is not only a good thing to be a good teacher, but it is also very important to be a good listener at times.

A Talk about the Mind

MAN has but one mind, but he has many mental faculties, each faculty being capable of functioning along two different lines of mental effort. There are no distinct dividing lines separating the two several functions of a faculty, but they shade into each other as do the colors of the spectrum. An Active effort of any faculty of the mind is the result of a direct impulse imparted at the time of the effort. A Passive effort of any faculty of the mind is the result of either a preceding Active effort of the same mind; an Active effort of another along the lines of suggestion; Thought Vibrations from the mind of another; Thought impulses from an ancestor, transmitted by the laws of heredity (including impulses transmitted from generation to generation from the time of the original vibratory impulse imparted by the Primal Cause - which impulses gradually unfold, and unsheath, when the proper state of evolutionary development is reached).

The Active effort is new-born - fresh from the mint, whilst the Passive effort is of less recent creation, and, in fact, is often the result of vibratory impulses imparted in ages long past. The Active effort makes its own way, brushing aside the impeding vines and kicking from its path the obstructing stones. The Passive effort travels along the beaten path. A thought-impulse, or motion-impulse, originally caused by an Active effort of faculty, may become by continued repetition, or habit, strictly automatic, the impulse given it by the repeated Active effort developing a strong momentum, which carries it on, along Passive lines, until stopped by another Active effort or its direction changed by the same cause. On the other hand, thought-impulses, or motion-impulses, continued along Passive lines may be terminated or corrected by an Active effort. The Active function creates, changes or destroys. The Passive function carries on the work given it by the Active function and obeys orders and suggestions. The Active function produces the thought-habit, or motion-habit, and imparts to it the vibrations, which carry it on along the Passive lines thereafter. The Active function also has the power to send forth vibrations which neutralize the momentum of the thought-habit, or motion-habit; it also is able to launch a new thought-habit, or motion-habit, with stronger vibrations, which overcomes and absorbs the first thought, or motion, and substitutes the new one. All thought-impulses, or motion-impulses, once started on their errands, continue to vibrate along passive lines until corrected or terminated by subsequent impulses imparted by the Active function, or other controlling power. The continuance of the original impulse adds momentum and force to it, and renders its correction or termination more difficult. This explains that which is called "the force of habit." I think that this will be readily understood by those who have struggled to overcome a habit which had been easily acquired. The Law applies to good habits as well as bad. The moral is obvious. Several of the faculties of the mind often combine to produce a single manifestation. A task to be performed may call for the combined exercise of several faculties, some of which may manifest by Active effort and others by Passive effort.

The meeting of new conditions - new problems - calls for the exercise of Active effort; whilst a familiar problem, or task, can be easily handled by the Passive effort without the assistance of his more enterprising brother. There is in Nature an instinctive tendency of living organisms to perform certain actions, the tendency of an organized body to seek that which satisfies the wants of its organism. This tendency is sometimes called Appetency. It is really a Passive mental impulse, originating with the impetus imparted by the Primal Cause, and transmitted along the lines of evolutionary development, gaining strength and power as it progresses. The impulse of the Primal Cause is assisted by the powerful upward attraction exerted by THE ABSOLUTE. In plant life this tendency is plainly discernible, ranging form the lesser exhibitions in the lower types to the greater in the higher types. It is that which is generally spoken of as the "life-force" in plants. It is, however, a manifestation of rudimentary mentation, functioning along the lines of Passive effort. In some of the higher forms of plant life there appears a faint color of independent "life action" - a faint indication of choice of volition. Writers on plant life relate many remarkable instances of this phenomenon. It is, undoubtedly, an exhibition of rudimentary Active mentation. In the lower animal kingdom a very high degree of Passive mental effort is found. And, varying in degree in the several families and species, a considerable amount of Active mentation is apparent. The lower animal undoubtedly possesses Reason only in a lesser degree than man, and, in fact, the display of volitional mentation exhibited by an intelligent animal is often nearly as high as that shown by the lower types of man or by a young child.

As a child, before birth, shows in its body the stages of the physical evolution of man, so does a child, before and after birth - until maturity -manifest the stages of the mental evolution of man. Man, the highest type of life yet produced, at least upon this planet, shows the highest form of Passive mentation, and also a much higher development of Active mentation than is seen in the lower animals, and yet the degrees of that power vary widely among the different races of men. Even among men of our race the different degrees of Active mentation are plainly noticeable; these degrees not depending by any means upon the amount of "culture," social position or educational advantages possessed by the individual: Mental Culture and Mental Development are two very different things. You have but to look around you to see the different stages of the development of Active mentation in man. The reasoning of many men is scarcely more than Passive mentation, exhibiting but little of the qualities of volitional thought. They prefer to let other men think for them. Active mentation tires them and they find the instinctive, automatic, Passive mental process much easier. Their minds work along the lines of least resistance. They are but little more than human sheep, Among the lower animals and the lower types of men Active mentation is largely confined to the grosser faculties - the more material plane; the higher mental faculties working along the instinctive, automatic lines of the Passive function. As the lower forms of life progressed in the evolutionary scale, they developed new faculties which were latent within them. These faculties always manifested in the form of rudimentary Passive functioning, and afterwards worked up through higher Passive forms, until the Active functions were brought into play. The evolutionary process still continues, the invariable tendency being toward the goal of highly developed Active mentation. This evolutionary progress is caused by the vibratory impulse imparted by the Primal Cause, aided by the uplifting attraction of THE ABSOLUTE. This law of evolution is still in progress, and man is beginning to develop new powers of mind, which, of course, are first manifesting themselves along the lines of Passive effort. Some men have developed these new faculties to a considerable degree, and it is possible that before long Man will be able to exercise them along the line of their Active functions. In fact, this power has already been attained by a few. This is the secret of the Oriental occultists, and of some of their Occidental brethren. The amenability of the mind to the will can be increased by properly directed practice. That which we are in the habit of referring to as the "strengthening of the Will" is in reality the training of the mind to recognize and absorb the Power Within. The Will is strong enough, it does not need strengthening, but the mind needs to be trained to receive and act upon the suggestions of the Will. The Will is the outward manifestation of the I AM. The Will current is flowing in full strength along the spiritual wires; but you must learn how to raise the trolley-pole to touch it before the mental car will move. This is a somewhat different idea from that which you have been in the habit of receiving from writers on the subject of Will Power, but it is correct, as you will demonstrate to your own satisfaction if you will follow up the subject by experiments along the proper lines. The attraction of THE ABSOLUTE is drawing man upward, and the vibratory force of the Primal Impulse has not yet exhausted itself. The time of evolutionary development has come when man can help himself. The man who understands the Law can accomplish wonders by means of the development of the powers of the mind; whilst the man who turns his back upon the truth will suffer from his lack of knowledge of the Law. He who understands the laws of his mental being, develops his latent powers and uses them intelligently. He does not despise his Passive mental functions, but makes good use of them also, charges them with the duties for which they are best fitted, and is able to obtain wonderful results from their work, having mastered them and trained them to do the bidding of the Higher Self. When they fail to do their work properly he regulates them, and his knowledge prevents him from meddling with them unintelligently, and thereby doing himself harm. He develops the faculties and powers latent within him and learns how to manifest them along the line of Active mentation as well as Passive. He knows that the real man within him is the master to whom both Active and Passive functions are but tools. He has banished Fear, and enjoys Freedom. He has found himself. HE HAS LEARNED THE SECRET OF THE I AM.

Mind Building

MAN can build up his mind and make it what he wills. In fact, we are mind-building every hour of our lives, either consciously or unconsciously. The majority of us are doing the work unconsciously, but those who have seen a little below the surface of things have taken the matter in hand and have become conscious creators of their own mentality. They are no longer subject to the suggestions and influences of others but have become masters of themselves. They assert the "I," and compel obedience from the subordinate mental faculties. The "I" is the sovereign of the mind, and what we call WILL is the instrument of the "I." Of course, there is something back of this, and the Universal Will is higher than the Will of the Individual, but the latter is in much closer touch with the Universal Will than is generally supposed, and when one conquers the lower self, and asserts the "I," he becomes in close touch with the Universal Will and partakes largely of its wonderful power. The moment one asserts the "I," and "finds himself," he establishes a close connection between the Individual Will and the Universal Will. But before he is able to avail himself of the mighty power at his command, he must first effect the Mastery of the lower self. Think of the absurdity of Man claiming to manifest powers, when he is the slave of the lower parts of his mental being, which should be subordinate. Think of a man being the slave of his moods, passions, animal appetites and lower faculties, and at the same time trying to claim the benefits of the Will. Now, I am not preaching asceticism, which seems to me to be a confession of weakness. I am speaking of Self-Mastery - the assertion of the "I" over the subordinate parts of oneself. In the higher view of the subject, this "I" is the only real Self, and the rest is the non-self; but our space does not permit the discussion of this point, and we will use the word "self" as meaning the entire man. Before a man can assert the "I" in its full strength he must obtain the complete mastery of the subordinate parts of the self. All things are good when we learn to master them, but no thing is good when it masters us. Just so long as we allow the lower portions of the self to give us orders, we are slaves. It is only when the "I" mounts his throne and lifts the scepter, that order is established and things assume their proper relation to each other. We are finding no fault with those who are swayed by their lower selves -they are in a lower grade of evolution, and will work up in time. But we are calling the attention of those who are ready, to the fact that the Sovereign must assert his will, and that the subjects must obey. Orders must be given and carried out. Rebellion must be put down, and the rightful authority insisted upon. And the time to do it is Now. You have been allowing your rebellious subjects to keep the King from his throne. You have been allowing the mental kingdom to be misgoverned by irresponsible faculties. You have been the slaves of Appetite, Unworthy Thoughts, Passion and Negativeness. The Will has been set aside and Low Desire has usurped the throne. It is time to re-establish order in the mental kingdom. You are able to assert the mastery over any emotion, appetite, passion or class of thoughts by the assertion of the Will. You can order Fear to go to the rear; Jealousy to leave your presence; Hate to depart from your sight; Anger to hide itself; Worry to cease troubling you; Uncontrolled Appetite and Passion to bow in submission and to become humble slaves instead of masters - all by the assertion of the "I." You may surround yourself with the glorious company of Courage, Love and Self-Control, by the same means. You may put down the rebellion and secure peace and order in your mental kingdom if you will but utter the mandate and insist upon its execution. Before you march forth to empire, you must establish the proper internal condition -must show your ability to govern you own kingdom. The first battle is the conquest of the lesser self by the Real Self.

AFFIRMATION

I AM Asserting the Mastery of My Real Self

Repeat these words earnestly and positively during the day at least once an hour, and particularly when you are confronted with conditions which tempt you to act on the lines of the lesser self instead of following the course dictated by the Real Self. In the moment of doubt and hesitation say these words earnestly, and your way will be made clear to you. Repeat them several times after you retire and settle yourself to sleep. But be sure to back up the words with the thought inspiring them, and do not merely repeat them parrot-like. Form the mental image of the Real Self asserting its mastery over the lower planes of your mind - see the King on his Throne. You will become conscious of an influx of new thought, and things which have seemed hard for you will suddenly become much easier. You will feel that you have yourself well in hand, and that YOU are the master and not the slave. The thought you are holding will manifest itself in action, and you will steadily grow to become that which you have in mind.

EXERCISE

Fix the mind firmly on the higher Self and draw inspiration from it when you feel led to yield to the promptings of the lower part of your nature. When you are tempted to burst into Anger - assert the "I," and your voice will drop. Anger is unworthy of the developed Self. When you feel vexed and cross, remember what you are, and rise above your feeling. When you feel Fearful, remember that the Real Self fears nothing, and assert Courage. When you feel Jealousy inciting, think of your higher nature, and laugh. And so on, asserting the Real Self and not allowing the things on the lower plane of mentality to disturb you. They are unworthy of you, and must be taught to keep their places. Do not allow these things to master you - they should be your subjects, not your masters. You must get away from this plane, and the only way to do so is to cut loose from these phases of thought which have been "running things" to suit themselves. You may have trouble at the start, but keep at it and you will have that satisfaction which comes only from conquering the lower parts of our nature. You have been a slave long enough - now is the time to free yourselves. If you will follow these exercises faithfully you will be a different being by the end of the year, and will look back with a pitying smile to your former condition. But it takes work. This is not child's play but a task for earnest men and women, Will YOU make the effort?

The Secret of the Will

WHILE psychologists may differ in their theories regarding the nature of the Will, none deny its existence, nor question its power. All persons recognize the power of strong Will - all see how it may be used to overcome the greatest obstacles. But few realize that the Will may be developed and strengthened by intelligent practice. They feel that they could accomplish wonders if they had a strong Will, but instead of attempting to develop it, they content themselves with vain regrets. They sigh, but do nothing. Those who have investigated the subject closely know that Will Power, with all its latent possibilities and mighty powers, may be developed, disciplined, controlled and directed, just as may be any other of Nature's forces. It does not matter what theory you may entertain about the nature of the Will, you will obtain the results if you practice intelligently. Personally, I have a somewhat odd theory about the Will. I believe that every man has, potentially, a strong Will, and that all he has to do is to train his mind to make use of it. I think that in the higher regions of the mind of every man is a great store of Will Power awaiting his use. The Will current is running along the psychic wires, and all that it is necessary to do is to raise the mental trolley-pole and bring down the power for your use. And the supply is unlimited, for your little storage battery is connected with the great powerhouse of the Universal Will Power, and the power is inexhaustible. Your Will does not need training - but your Mind does. The mind is the instrument and the supply of Will Power is proportionate to the fineness of the instrument through which it manifests. But you needn't accept this theory if you don't like it. This lesson will fit your theory as well as mine. He who has developed his mind so that it will allow the Will Power to manifest through it, has opened up wonderful possibilities for himself. Not only has he found a great power at his command, but he is able to bring into play, and use, faculties, talents and abilities of whose existence he has not dreamed. This secret of the Will is the magic key which opens all doors. The late Donald G. Mitchell once wrote: "Resolve is what makes a man manifest; not puny resolve, but crude determination; not errant purpose -but that strong and indefatigable will which treads down difficulties and danger, as a boy treads down the heaving frost-lands of winter; which kindles his eye and brain with a proud pulse-beat toward the unattainable. Will makes men giants." Many of us feel that if we would but exert our Will, we might accomplish wonders. But somehow we do not seem to want to take the trouble - at any rate; we do not get to the actual willing point. We put it off from time to time, and talk vaguely of "some day," but that some day never comes. We instinctively feel the power of the Will, but we haven't enough energy to exercise it, and so drift along with the tide, unless perhaps some friendly difficulty arises, some helpful obstacle appears in our path, or some kindly pain stirs us into action, in either of which cases we are compelled to assert our Will and thus begin to accomplish something. The trouble with us is that we do not want to do the thing enough to make us exert our Will Power. We don't want to hard enough.

We are mentally lazy and of weak Desire. If you do not like the word Desire substitute for it the word "Aspiration." (Some people call the lower impulses Desires, and the higher,

Aspirations - it's all a matter of words, take you choice.) That is the trouble. Let a man be in danger of losing his life - let a woman be in danger of losing a great love - and you will witness a startling exhibition of Will Power from an unexpected source. Let a woman's child be threatened with danger, and she will manifest a degree of Courage and Will that sweeps all before it. And yet the same woman will quail before a domineering husband, and will lack the Will to perform a simple task. A boy will do all sorts of work if he but considers it play, and yet he can scarcely force himself to cut a little firewood. Strong Will follows strong Desire. If you really want to do a thing very much, you can usually develop the Will Power to accomplish it. The trouble is that you have not really wanted to do these things, and yet you blame your Will. You say that you do want to do it, but if you stop to think you will see that you really want to do something else more than the thing in question. You are not willing to pay the price of attainment. Stop a moment and analyze this statement and apply it in your own case, You are mentally lazy - that's the trouble. Don't talk to me about not having enough Will. You have a great storehouse of Will awaiting your use, but you are too lazy to use it. Now, if you are really in earnest about this matter, get to work and first find out what you really want to do - then start to work and do it. Never mind about the Will Power - you'll find a full supply of that whenever you need it. The thing to do is to get to the point where you will resolve to do. That the real test - the resolving.

Think of these things a little, and make up your mind whether or not you really want to be a Willer sufficiently hard to get to work. Many excellent essays and books have been written on this subject, all of which agree regarding the greatness of Will Power, the most enthusiastic terms being used; but few have anything to say about how this power may be acquired by those who have it not, or who possess it in but a limited degree. Some have given exercises designed to "strengthen" the Will, which exercises really strengthen the Mind so that it is able to draw upon its store of power. But they have generally overlooked the fact that in autosuggestion is to be found the secret of the development of the mind so that it may become the efficient instrument of the Will.

AUTOSUGGESTION

I AM Using My Will Power

Say these words several times earnestly and positively, immediately after finishing this article. Then repeat them frequently during the day, at least once an hour, and particularly when you meet something that calls for the exercise of Will Power. Also repeat them several times after you retire and settle yourself for sleep. Now, there is nothing in the words unless you back them up with the thought. In fact, the thought is "the whole thing," and the words only pegs upon which to hang the thought. So think of what you are saying, and mean what you say. You must use Faith at the start, and use the words with a confident expectation of the result. Hold the steady thought that you are drawing on your storehouse of Will Power, and before long you will find that thought is taking form in action, and that your Will Power is manifesting itself. You will feel an influx of strength with each repetition of the words. You will find yourself overcoming difficulties and bad habits, and will be surprised at how things are being smoothed out for you.

EXERCISE

Perform at least one disagreeable task each day during the month.. If there is any especially disagreeable task which you would like to shirk, that is the one for you to perform. This is not given to you in order to make you self-sacrificing or meek, or anything of that sort - it is given you to exercise your Will. Anyone can do a pleasant thing cheerfully, but it takes Will to do the unpleasant thing cheerfully; and that is how you must do the work. It will prove a most valuable discipline to you. Try it for a month and you will see where "it comes in." If you shirk this exercise you had better stop right here and acknowledge that you do not want Will Power, and are content to stay where you are and remain a weakling.

How to become immune to injurious Thought Attraction

THE first thing to do is to begin to "cut out" Fear and Worry. Fear-thought is the cause of much unhappiness and many failures. You have been told this thing over and over again, but it will bear repeating. Fear is a habit of mind which has been fastened upon us by negative race-thought, but from which we may free ourselves by individual effort and perseverance. Strong expectancy is a powerful magnet. He of the strong, confident desire attracts to him the things best calculated to aid him - persons, things circumstances, surroundings; if he desires them hopefully, trustfully, confidently, calmly. And, equally true, he who Fears a thing generally manages to start into operation forces which will cause the thing he feared to come upon him. Don't you see, the man who Fears really expects the feared thing, and the eyes of the Law is the same as if he really had wished for or desired it? The Law is operative in both cases - the principle is the same. The best way to overcome the habit of Fear is to assume the mental attitude of Courage, just as the best way to get rid of darkness is to let in the light. It is a waste of time to fight a negative thought-habit by recognizing its force and trying to deny it out of existence by mighty efforts. The best, surest, easiest and quickest method is to assume the existence of the positive thought desired in its place; and by constantly dwelling upon the positive thought, manifest it into objective reality. Therefore, instead of repeating, "I'm not afraid," say boldly, "I am full of Courage," "I am Courageous." You must assert, "There's nothing to fear," which, although in the nature of a denial, simply denies the reality of the object causing fear rather than admitting the fear itself and then denying it. To overcome fear, one should hold firmly to the mental attitude of Courage. He should think Courage, say Courage, act Courage. He should keep the mental picture of Courage before him all the time, until it becomes his normal mental attitude. Hold the ideal firmly before you and you will gradually grow to its attainment - the ideal will become manifest. Let the word "Courage" sink deeply into your mind, and then hold it firmly there until the mind fastens it in place. Think of yourself as being Courageous - see yourself as acting with Courage in trying situations. Realize that there is nothing to Fear - that Worry and Fear never helped anyone, and never will. Realize that Fear paralyzes effort, and that Courage promotes activity. The confident, fearless, expectant, "I Can and I Will" man is a mighty magnet. He attracts to himself just what is needed for his success. Things seem to come his way, and people say he is "lucky." Nonsense! "Luck" has nothing to do with it. It's all in the Mental Attitude. And the Mental Attitude of the "I Can't" or the "I'm Afraid" man also determines his measure of success. There's no mystery whatsoever about it. You have but to look about you to realize the truth of what I have said. Did you ever know a successful man who did not have the "I Can and I will" thought strong within him? Why, he will walk all around the "I Can't" man, who has perhaps even more ability. The first mental attitude brought to the surface latent qualities, as well as attracted help from outside; whilst the second mental attitude not only attracted "I Can't" people and things, but also kept the man's own powers from manifesting themselves. I have demonstrated the correctness of these views, and so have many others, and the number of people who know these things is

200

growing every day. Don't waste your Thought-Force, but use it to advantage. Stop attracting to yourself failure, unhappiness, inharmony, sorrow - begin now and send out a current of bright, positive, happy thought. Let your prevailing thought be "I Can and I Will;" think "I Can and I Will;" dream "I Can and I Will;" say "I Can and I Will;" and act "I Can and I Will". Live on the "I Can and I and Will" plane, and before you are aware of it, you will feel the new vibrations manifesting themselves in action; will see them bring results; will be conscious of the new point of view; will realize that your own is coming to you. You will feel better, act better, see better, BE better in every way, after you join the "I Can and I Will" brigade. Fear is the parent of Worry, Hate, Jealousy, Malice, Anger, Discontent, Failure and all the rest. The man who rids himself of Fear will find that the rest of the brood has disappeared. The only way to be Free is to get rid of Fear. Tear it out by the roots. I regard the conquest of Fear as the first important step to be taken by those who wish to master the application of Thought Force. So long as Fear masters you, you are in no condition to make progress in the realm of Thought, and I must insist that you start to work at once to get rid of this obstruction. You CAN do it - if you only go about it in earnest. And when you have ridded yourself of the vile thing, life will seem entirely different to you - you will feel happier, freer, stronger, more positive, and will be more successful in every undertaking of Life.

Start it today, make up your mind that this intruder must GO - do not compromise matters with him, but insist upon an absolute surrender on his part. You will find the task difficult at first, but each time you oppose him he will grow weaker, and you will be stronger. Shut off his nourishment -starve him to death - he cannot live in a thought atmosphere of Fearlessness. So, start to fill your mind with good, strong, Fearless thoughts - keep yourself busy thinking Fearlessness, and Fear will die of his own accord. Fearlessness is positive - Fear is negative, and you may be sure that the positive will prevail. So long as Fear is around with his "but," "if," "suppose," "I'm afraid," "I can't," "what if," and all the rest of his cowardly suggestions, you will not be able to use your Thought Force to the best advantage. Once get him out of the way, you will have clear sailing, and every inch of thought- sail will catch the wind. He is a Jonah. Overboard with him! (The whale that swallows him will have my sympathy.) I advise that you start in to do some of the things which you feel you could do if you were not afraid to try. Start to work to do these things, affirming Courage all the way through, and you will be surprised to see how the changed mental attitude will clear away obstacles from your path, and will make things very much easier than you had anticipated. Exercises of this kind will develop you wonderfully, and you will be much gratified at the result of a little practice along these lines. There are many things before you awaiting accomplishment, which you can master if you will only throw aside the yoke of Fear - if you will only refuse to accept the race suggestion, and will boldly assert the "I" and its power. And the best way to vanquish Fear is to assert "Courage" and stop thinking of Fear. By this plan you will train the mind into new habits of thought, thus eradicating the old negative thoughts which have been pulling you down, and holding you back. Take the word "Courage" with you as your watchword and manifest it in action. Remember, the only thing to fear is Fear, and - well, don't even fear Fear, for he's a cowardly chap at the best, who will run if you show a brave front.

The Transmutation of Negative Thought

WORRY is the child of Fear - if you kill out Fear, Worry will die for want of nourishment. This advice is very old, and yet it is always worthy of repetition, for it is a lesson of which we are greatly in need. Some people think that if we kill out Fear and Worry we will never be able to accomplish anything. I have read editorials in the great journals in which the writers held that without Worry one can never accomplish any of the great tasks of life, because Worry is necessary to stimulate interest and work. This is nonsense, no matter who utters it. Worry never helped one to accomplish anything; on the contrary, it stands in the way of accomplishment and attainment. The motive underlying action and "doing things" is Desire and Interest. If one earnestly desires a thing, he naturally becomes very much interested in its accomplishment, and is quick to seize upon anything likely to help him to gain the thing he wants. More than that, his mind starts up a work on the subconscious plane that brings into the field of consciousness many ideas of value and importance. Desire and Interest are the causes that result in success. Worry is not Desire. It is true that if one's surroundings and environments become intolerable, he is driven in desperation to some efforts that will result in throwing off the undesirable conditions and in the acquiring of those more in harmony with his desire. But this is only another form of Desire - the man desires something different from what he has; and when his desire becomes strong enough his entire interest is given to the task, he makes a mighty effort, and the change is accomplished. But it wasn't Worry that caused the effort. Worry could content itself with wringing its hands and moaning, "Woe is me," and wearing its nerves to a frazzle, and accomplishing nothing. Desire acts differently. It grows stronger as the man's conditions become intolerable, and finally when he feels the hurt so strongly that he can't stand it any longer, he says, "I won't stand this any longer - l will make a change," and lo! Then Desire springs into action. The man keeps on "wanting" a change the worst way (which is the best way) and his Interest and Attention being given to the task of deliverance, he begins to make things move. Worry never accomplished anything. Worry is negative and death producing. Desire and Ambition are positive and life producing. A man may worry himself to death and yet nothing will be accomplished, but let that man transmute his worry and discontent into Desire and Interest, coupled with a belief that he is able to make the change - the "I Can and I Will" idea -then something happens. Yes, Fear and Worry must go before we can do much. One must proceed to cast out these negative intruders, and replace them with Confidence and Hope. Transmute Worry into keen Desire. Then you will find that Interest is awakened, and you will begin to think things of interest to you. Thoughts will come to you from the great reserve stock in your mind and you will start to manifest them in action. Moreover you will be placing yourself in harmony with similar thoughts of others, and will draw to you aid and assistance from the great volume of thought waves with which the world is filled. One draws to himself thought waves corresponding in character with the nature of the prevailing thoughts in his won mind - his mental attitude. Then again he begins to set into motion the great Law of Attraction, whereby he draws to him others likely to help him, and is, in turn, attracted to others who can aid him. This Law of Attraction is no joke, no metaphysical absurdity, but is a great live working principle of Nature, as anyone may learn by experimenting and observing. To succeed in anything you must want it very much - Desire must be in evidence in order to attract. The man of weak desires attracts very little to himself. The stronger the Desire the greater the force set into motion. You must want a thing hard enough before you can get it. You must want it more than you do the things around you, and you must be prepared to pay the price for it. The price is the throwing overboard of certain lesser desires that stand in the way of the accomplishment of the greater one. Comfort, ease, leisure, amusements, and many other things may have to go (not always, though). It all depends on what you want. As a rule, the greater the thing desired, the greater the price to be paid for it. Nature believes in adequate compensation. But if you really Desire a thing in earnest, you will pay the price without question; for the Desire will dwarf the importance of the other things. You say that you want a thing very much, and are doing everything possible toward its attainment? Pshaw! You are only playing Desire. Do you want the thing as much as a prisoner wants freedom - as much as a dying man wants life? Look at the almost miraculous things accomplished by prisoners desiring freedom. Look how they work through steel plates and stonewalls with a bit of stone. Is your desire as strong as that? Do you work for the desired thing as if your life depended upon it? Nonsense! You don't know what Desire is. I tell you if a man wants a thing as much as the prisoner wants freedom, or as much as a strongly vital man wants life, then that man will be able to sweep away obstacles and impediments apparently immovable. The key to attainment is Desire, Confidence, and Will. This key will open many doors. Fear paralyzes Desire - it scares the life out of it. You must get rid of Fear. There have been times in my life when Fear would get hold of me and take a good, firm grip on my vitals, and I would lose all hope; all interest; all ambition; all desire. But, thank the Lord, I have always managed to throw off the grip of the monster and face my difficulty like a man; and lo! Things would seem to be straightened out for me somehow. Either the difficulty would melt away or I would be given means to overcome, or get around, or under or over it. It is strange how this works. No matter how great is the difficulty, when we finally face it with courage and confidence in ourselves, we seem to pull through somehow, and then we begin to wonder what we were scared about. This is not a mere fancy, it is the working of a mighty law, which we do not as yet fully understand, but which we may prove at any time. People often ask: "it's all very well for you New Thought people to say 'Don't worry,' but what's a person to do when he thinks of all the possible things ahead of him, which might upset him and his plans? Well, all that I can say is that the man is foolish to bother about thinking of troubles to come at some time in the future. The majority of things that we worry about don't come to pass at all; a large proportion of the others come in a milder form than we had anticipated, and there are always other things which come at the same time which help us to overcome the trouble. The future holds in store for us not only difficulties to be overcome, but also agents to help us in overcoming the difficulties. Things adjust themselves. We are prepared for any trouble which may come upon us, and when the time comes we somehow find ourselves able to meet it.

It has been well said that nine-tenths of the worries are over things which never comes to pass, and that the other tenth is over things of little or no account. So what's the use in using up all your reserve force in fretting over future troubles, if this be so? Better wait until your troubles really come before you worry. You will find that by this storing up of energy you will be able to meet about any sort of trouble that comes your way. What is it that uses up all the energy in the average man or woman, anyway? Is it the real overcoming of difficulties, or the worrying about impending troubles? It's always "Tomorrow, tomorrow," and yet tomorrow never comes just as we feared it would. Tomorrow is all right; it carries in its grip good things as well as troubles. Bless my soul, when I sit down and think over the things which I once feared might possibly descend upon me, I laugh! Where are those feared things now? I don't know - have almost forgotten that I ever feared them. You do not need fight Worry - that isn't the way to overcome the habit. Just practice concentration, and then learn to concentrate upon something right before you, and you will find that the worry thought has vanished. The mind can think of but one thing at a time, and if you concentrate upon a bright thing, the other thing will fade away. There are better ways of overcoming objectionable thoughts than by fighting them. Learn to concentrate upon thoughts of an opposite character, and you will have solved the problem. When the mind is full of worry thoughts, it cannot find time to work out plans to benefit you. But when you have concentrated upon bright, helpful thoughts, you will discover that it will start to work subconsciously; and when the time comes you will find all sorts of plans and methods by which you will be able to meet the demands upon you. Keep your mental attitude right, and all things will be added unto you. There's no sense in worrying; nothing has ever been gained by it, and nothing ever will be. Bright, cheerful and happy thoughts attract bright, cheerful and happy things to us - worry drives them away. Cultivate the right mental attitude.

The Law of Mental Control

YOUR thoughts are either faithful servants or tyrannical masters - just as you allow them to be. You have the say about it; take your choice. They will either go about your work under direction of the firm will, doing it the best they know how, not only in your waking hours, but when you are asleep - some of our best mental work being performed for us when our conscious mentality is at rest, as is evidenced by the fact that when the morning comes we find troublesome problems have been worked out for us during the night, after we had dismissed them from our minds -apparently; or they will ride all over us and make us their slaves if we are foolish enough to allow them to do so. More than half the people of the world are slaves of every vagrant thought which may see fit to torment them. Your mind is given you for your good and for your own use - not to use you. There are very few people who seem to realize this and who understand the art of managing the mind. The key to the mystery is Concentration. A little practice will develop within every man the power to use the mental machine properly. When you have some mental work to do concentrate upon it to the exclusion of everything else, and you will find that the mind will get right down to business - to the work at hand -and matters will be cleared up in no time. There is an absence of friction, and all waste motion or lost power is obviated. Every pound of energy is put to use, and every revolution of the mental driving wheel counts for something. It pays to be able to be a competent mental engineer. And the man who understands how to run his mental engine knows that one of the important things is to be able to stop it when the work has been done. He does not keep putting coal in the furnace, and maintaining a high pressure after the work is finished, or when the day's portion of the work has been done, and the fires should be banked until the next day. Some people act as if the engine should be kept running whether there was any work to be done or not, and then they complain if it gets worn out and wobbles and needs repairing. These mental engines are fine machines, and need intelligent care. To those who are acquainted with the laws of mental control it seems absurd for one to lie awake at night fretting about the problems of the day, or more often, of the morrow. It is just as easy to slow down the mind as it is to slow down an engine, and thousands of people are learning to do this in these days of New Thought. The best way to do it is to think of something else - as far different from the obtruding thought as possible. There is no use fighting an objectionable thought with the purpose of "downing" it - that is a great waste of energy, and the more you keep on saying, "I won't think of this thing!" the more it keeps on coming into your mind, for you are holding it there for the purpose of hitting it. Let it go; don't give it another thought; fix the mind on something entirely different, and keep the attention there by an effort of the will. A little practice will do much for you in this direction. There is only room for one thing at a time in the focus of attention; so put all your attention upon one thought, and the others will sneak off. Try it for yourself.

Asserting the Life-Force

I have spoken to you of the advantage of getting rid of Fear. Now I wish to put LIFE into you. Many of you have been going along as if you were dead - no ambition - no energy - no vitality - no interest - no life. This will never do. You are stagnating. Wake up and display a few signs of life! This is not the place in which you can stalk around like a living corpse -this is the place for wide-awake, active, live people, and a good general awakening is what is needed; although it would take nothing less than a blast from Gabriel's trumpet to awaken some of the people who are stalking around thinking that they are alive, but who are really dead to all that makes life worthwhile. We must let Life flow through us, and allow it to express itself naturally. Do not let the little worries of life, or the big ones either, depress you and cause you to lose your vitality. Assert the Life Force within you, and manifest it in every thought, act and deed, and before long you will be exhilarated and fairly bubbling over with vitality and energy. Put a little life into your work - into your pleasures - into yourself. Stop doing things in a half-headed way, and begin to take an interest in what you are doing, saying and thinking. It is astonishing how much interest we may find in the ordinary things of life if we will only wake up. There are interesting things all around us - interesting events occurring every moment - but we will not be aware of them unless we assert our life force and begin to actually live instead of merely existing.

No man or woman ever amounted to anything unless he or she put life into the tasks of everyday life - the acts - the thoughts. What the world needs is live men and women. Just look into the eyes of the people whom you meet, and see how few of them are really alive. The most of them lack that expression of conscious life which distinguishes the man who lives from the one who simply exists. I want you to acquire this sense of conscious life so that you may manifest it in your life and show what Mental Science has done for you. I want you to get to work today and begin to make yourselves over according to the latest pattern. You can do this if you will only take the proper interest in the task.

AFFIRMATION AND EXERCISE

Fix in your mind the thought that the "I" within you is very much alive and that you are manifesting life fully, mentally and physically. And keep this though there, aiding yourself with constant repetitions of the watchword. Don't let the thought escape you, but keep pushing it back into the mind. Keep it before the mental vision as much as possible. Repeat the watchword when you awaken in the morning - say it when you retire at night. And say it at meal times, and whenever else you can during the day

- at least once an hour. Form the mental picture of yourself as filled with Life and Energy. Live up to it as far as possible. When you start in to perform a task say "I AM Alive" and mix up as much life as possible in the task. If you find yourself feeling depressed, say "I AM Alive," and then take a few deep breaths, and with each inhalation let the mind hold the thought that you are breathing in Strength and Life, and as you exhale, hold the thought that you are breathing out all the old, dead, negative conditions and are glad to get rid of them. Then finish up with an earnest, vigorous affirmation: "I AM Alive," and mean it when you say it too. And let your thoughts take form in action. Don't rest content with merely saying that you are alive, but prove it with your acts. Take an interest in doing things, and don't go around "mooning" or daydreaming. Get down to business, and LIVE.

Training the Habit-Mind

PROFESSOR William James, the well-known teacher of, and writer upon Psychology very truly says: "The great thing in all education is to make our nervous system our ally instead of our enemy. For this we must make automatic and habitual, as early as possible, as many useful actions as we can and as carefully guard against growing into ways that are likely to be disadvantageous. In the acquisition of a new habit, or the leaving off of an old one we must take care to launch ourselves with as strong and decided initiative as possible. Never suffer an exception to occur until the new habit is securely rooted in your life. Seize the very first possible opportunity to act on every resolution you make and on every emotional prompting you may experience, in the direction of the habits you aspire to gain." This advice is along the lines familiar to all students of Mental Science, but it states the matter more plainly than the majority of us have done. It impresses upon us the importance of passing on to the subconscious mind the proper impulses, so that they will become automatic and "second nature." Our subconscious mentality is a great storehouse for all sorts of suggestions from ourselves and others and, as it is the "habit-mind," we must be careful to send it the proper material from which it may make habits. If we get into the habit of doing certain things, we may be sure that the subconscious mentality will make it easier for us to do just the same thing over and over again, easier each time, until finally we are firmly bound with the ropes and chains of the habit, and find it more or less difficult, sometimes almost impossible, to free ourselves from the hateful thing. We should cultivate good habits against the hour of need. The time will come when we will be required to put forth our best efforts, and it rests with us today whether that hour of need shall find us doing the proper thing automatically and almost without thought, or struggling to do it bound down and hindered with the chains of things opposed to that which we desire at that moment. We must be on guard at all times to prevent the forming of undesirable habits. There may be no special harm in doing a certain thing today, or perhaps again tomorrow, but there may be much harm in setting up the habit of of doing that particular thing. If you are confronted with the question: "Which of these two things should I do?" the best answer is: "I will do that which I would like to become a habit with me." In forming a new habit, or in breaking an old one, we should throw ourselves into the task with as much enthusiasm as possible, in order to gain the most ground before the energy expends itself when it meets with friction from the opposing habits already formed. We should start in by making as strong an impression as possible upon the subconscious mentality. Then we should be constantly on guard against temptations to break the new resolution "just this once." This "just once" idea kills off more good resolutions than any other one cause. The moment you yield "just this once, you introduce the thin edge of the wedge that will, in the end, split your resolution into pieces. Equally important is the fact that each time you resist temptation the stronger does your resolution become. Act upon your resolution as early and as often as possible, as with every manifestation of thought in action, the stronger does it become. You are adding to the strength of your original resolution every time you back it up with action. The mind has been likened to a piece of paper that has been folded. Ever afterwards it has a tendency to fold in the same crease - unless we make a new crease or fold, when it will follow the last lines. And the creases are habits - every time we make one it is so much easier for the mind to fold along the same crease afterward. Let us make our mental creases in the right direction.

The Psychology of Emotion

ONE is apt to think of the emotions as independent from habit. We easily may think of one acquiring habits of action, and even of thinking, but we are apt to regard the emotions as something connected with "feeling" and quite divorced from intellectual effort. Yet, not withstanding the distinction between the two, both are dependent largely upon habit, and one may repress, increase, develop, and change one's emotions, just as one may regulate habits of action and lines of thought. It is an axiom of psychology that "Emotions deepen by repetition." If a person allows a state of feeling to thoroughly take possession of him, he will find it easier to yield to the same emotion the second time, and so on, until the particular emotion or feeling becomes second nature to him. If an undesirable emotion shows itself inclined to take up a permanent abode with you, you had better start to work to get rid of it, or at least to master it. And the best time to do this is at the start; for each repetition renders the habit more firmly entrenched, and the task of dislodging it more difficult. Were you ever jealous? If so, you will remember how insidious was its first approach; how subtly it whispered hateful suggestions into your willing ear, and how gradually it followed up such suggestions, until, finally you began to see green. (Jealousy has an effect upon the bile, and causes it to poison the blood. This is why the idea of green is always associated with it.) Then you will remember how the thing seemed to grow, taking possession of you until you scarcely could shake it off. You found it much easier to become jealous the next time. It seemed to bring before you all sorts of objects apparently justifying your suspicions and feeling. Everything began to look green - the green-eyed monster waxed fat. And so it is with every feeling or emotion. If you give way to a fit of rage, you will find it easier to become angry the next time, on less provocation. The habit of feeling and acting "mean" does not take long to firmly settle itself in its new home if encouraged. Worry is a great habit for growing and waxing fat. People start by worrying about big things, and then begin to worry and fret about some smaller thing. And then the merest trifle worries and distresses them. They imagine that all sorts of evil things are about to befall them. If they start on a journey they are certain there is going to be a wreck. If a telegram comes, it is sure to contain some dreadful tidings. If a child seems a little quiet, the worrying mother is positive it is going to fall ill and die. If the husband seems thoughtful, as he revolves some business plan in his mind, then the good wife is convinced that he is beginning to cease to love her, and indulges in a crying spell. And so it goes - worry, worry, worry - each indulgence making the habit more at home. After a while the continued thought shows itself in action. Not only is the mind poisoned by the blue thoughts, but the forehead shows deep lines between the eyebrows, and the voice takes on that whining, rasping tone so common among worry-burdened people. The condition of mind known as "fault-finding" is another emotion that grows fat with exercise. First, fault is found with this thing, then with that, and finally with everything. The person becomes a chronic "nagger" - a burden to friends and relatives, and a thing to be avoided by outsiders. Women make the greatest naggers. Not because men are any better, but simply because a man nagger apt to have the habit knocked out of him by other men who will not stand his nonsense - he find that he is making things too hot for himself and he reforms; while a woman has more of a chance to indulge in the habit. But this nagging is all a matter of habit. It grows from small beginnings, and each time it is indulged in it throws out another root, branch, or tendril, and fastens itself the closer to the one who has given it soil in which to grow. Envy, uncharitableness, gossip scandal-mongering, are all habits of this kind. The seeds are in every human breast, and only need good soil and a little watering to become lusty and strong. Each time you give way to one of these negative emotions, the easier do you make it for a recurrence of the same thing, or similar ones. Sometimes by encouraging one unworthy emotion, you find that you have given room for the growth of a whole family of these mental weeds. Now, this is not a good old orthodox preachment against the sin of bad thoughts. It is merely a calling of your attention to the law underlying the psychology of emotion. Nothing new about it - old as the hills - so old that many of us have forgotten all about it. If you wish to manifest these constantly disagreeable and unpleasant traits, and to suffer the unhappiness that comes from them, by all means do so -that is your own business, and privilege. It's none of mine, and I am not preaching at you - it keeps me busy minding my own business and keeping an eye on my own undesirable habits and actions. I am merely telling you the law regarding the matter, and you may do the rest. If you wish to choke out these habits, there are two ways open to you. First, whenever you find yourself indulging in a negative thought or feeling, take right hold of it and say to it firmly, and vigorously, "Get out!" It won't like this at first, and will bridle up, curve its back and snarl like an offended cat. But never mind - just say, "Scat" to it. The next time it will not be so confident and aggressive - it will have manifested a little of the fear-habit. Each time you repress and choke out a tendency of this kind, the weaker it will become, and the stronger will your will be. Professor James says: "Refuse to express a passion, and it dies. Count ten before venting your anger, and its occasion seems ridiculous. Whistling to keep up courage is no mere figure of speech. On the other hand, sit all day in a moping posture, sigh, and reply to everything with a dismal voice, and your melancholy lingers. There is no more valuable precept in moral education than this, as all who have experience know: if we wish to conquer emotional tendencies in ourselves, we must assiduously, and in the first instance, cold-bloodedly, go through the outward movements of those contrary dispositions we prefer to cultivate. Smooth the brow, brighten the eye, contract the dorsal rather than the ventral aspect of the frame, and speak in a major key, pass the genial compliment, and your heart must be frigid indeed if it does not gradually thaw.

Developing new Brain Cells

I have spoken of the plan of getting rid of undesirable states of feeling by driving them out. But a far better way is to cultivate the feeling or emotion directly opposed to the one you wish to eradicate. We are very apt to regard ourselves as the creatures of our emotions and feelings, and to fancy that these feelings and emotions are "we." But such is far from being the truth. It is true that the majority of the race are slaves of their emotions and feelings, and are governed by them to a great degree. They think that feelings are things that rule one and from which one cannot free himself, and so they cease to rebel. They yield to the feeling without question, although they may know that the emotion or mental trait is calculated to injure them, and to bring unhappiness and failure instead of happiness and success. They say, "We are made that way," and let it go at that. The new Psychology is teaching the people better things. It tells them that they are masters of their emotions and feelings, instead of being their slaves. It tells them that brain-cells may be developed that will manifest along desirable lines, and that the old brain-cells that have been manifesting so unpleasantly may be placed on the retired list, and allowed to atrophy from want of use. People may make themselves over, and change their entire natures. This is not mere idle theory, but is a working fact which has been demonstrated by thousands of people, and which is coming more and more before the attention of the race.

No matter what theory of mind we entertain, we must admit that the brain is the organ and instrument of the mind, in our present state of existence, at least, and that the brain must be considered in this matter. The brain is like a wonderful musical instrument, having millions of keys, upon which we may play innumerable combinations of sounds. We come into the world with certain tendencies, temperaments, and pre-dispositions, We may account for these tendencies by heredity, or we may account for them upon theories of pre-existence, but the facts remain the same. Certain keys seem to respond to our touch more easily than others. Certain notes seem to sound forth as the current of circumstances sweeps over the strings. And certain other notes are less easily vibrated. But we find that if we but make an effort of the will to restrain the utterance of some of these easily sounded strings, they will grow more difficult to sound, and less liable to be stirred by the passing breeze. And if we will pay attention to some of the other strings that have not been giving forth a clear tone, we will soon get them in good working order; their notes will chime forth clear and vibrant, and will drown the less pleasant sounds. We have millions of unused brain-cells awaiting our cultivation. We are using but a few of them, and some of these we are working to death. We are able to give some of these cells a rest, by using other cells. The brain may be trained and cultivated in a manner incredible to one who has not looked into the subject. Mental attitudes may be acquired and cultivated, changed and discarded, at will. There is no longer any excuse for people manifesting unpleasant and harmful mental states. We have the remedy in our own hands. We acquire habits of thought, feeling, and action, repeated use. We may be born with a tendency in a certain direction, or we may acquire tendencies by suggestions from other; such as the examples of those around us, suggestions from reading, listening to teachers. We are a bundle of mental habits. Each time we indulge in an undesirable thought or habit, the easier does it become for us to repeat that thought or action. Mental scientists are in the habit of speaking of desirable thoughts or mental attitudes as "positive," and of the undesirable ones as "negative." There is a good reason for this. The mind instinctively recognizes certain things as good for the individual to which it belongs, and it clears the path for such thoughts, and interposes the least resistance to them. They have a much greater effect than an undesirable thought possesses, and one positive thought will counteract a number of negative thoughts. The best way to overcome undesirable or negative thoughts and feelings is to cultivate the positive ones. The positive thought is the strongest plant, and will in time starve out the negative one by withdrawing from it the nourishment necessary for its existence. Of course the negative thought will set up a vigorous resistance at first, for it is a fight for life with it. In the slang words of the time, it "sees its finish" if the positive thought is allowed to grow and develop; and, consequently it makes things unpleasant for the individual until he has started well into the work of starving it out. Brain cells do not like to be laid on the shelf any more than does any other form of living energy, and they rebel and struggle until they become too weak to do so. The best way is to pay as little attention as possible to these weeds of the mind, but put in as much time as possible watering, caring for and attending to the new and beautiful plants in the garden of the mind. For instance, if you are apt to hate people, you can best overcome the negative thought by cultivating Love in its place. Think Love, and act it out, as often as possible. Cultivate thoughts of kindness, and act as kindly as you can to everyone with whom you come in contact. You will have trouble at the start, but gradually Love will master Hate, and the latter will begin to droop and wither. If you have a tendency toward the "blues" cultivate a smile, and a cheerful view of things. Insist upon your mouth wearing upturned corners, and make an effort of the will to look upon the bright side of things. The "blue-devils" will set up a fight, of course, but pay no attention to them - just go on cultivating optimism and cheerfulness. Let "Bright, Cheerful and Happy" be your watchword, and try to live it out.

These recipes may seem very old and timeworn, but they are psychological truths and may be used by you to advantage. If you once comprehend the nature of the thing, the affirmations and autosuggestions of the several schools may be understood and taken advantage of. You may make yourself energetic instead of slothful, active instead of lazy, by this method. It is all a matter of practice and steady work. New Thought people often have much to say about "holding the thought;" and, indeed, it is necessary to "hold the thought" in order to accomplish results. But something more is needed. You must "act out" the thought until it becomes a fixed habit with you. Thoughts take form in action; and in turn actions influence thought. So by "acting out" certain lines of thought, the actions react upon the mind, and increase the development of the part of the mind having close relation to the act. Each time the mind entertains a thought, the easier becomes the resulting action - and each time an act is performed, the easier becomes the corresponding thought. So you see the thing works both ways - action and reaction. If you feel cheerful and happy, it is very natural for you to laugh. And if you will laugh a little, you will begin to feel bright and cheerful. Do you see what I am trying to get at? Here it is, in a nutshell: if you wish to cultivate a certain habit of action, begin by cultivating the mental attitude corresponding to it. And as a means of cultivating that mental attitude, start in to "act-out " or go through, the motions of the act corresponding to the thought. Now, see if you cannot apply this rule. Take up something that you really feel should be done, but which you do not feel like doing. Cultivate the thought leading up to it - say to yourself: "I like to do so and so," and then go through the motions (cheerfully, remember!) and act out the thought that you like to do the thing. Take an interest in the doing - study out the best way to do it - put brains into it - take a pride in it - and you will find yourself doing the thing with a considerable amount of pleasure and interest - you will have cultivated a new habit. If you prefer trying it on some mental trait of which you wish to be rid, it will work the same way. Start in to cultivate the opposite trait, and think it out and act it out for all you are worth. Then watch the change that will come over you. Don't be discouraged at the resistance you will encounter at first, but sing gaily: "I Can and I Will," and get to work in earnest. The important thing in this work is to keep cheerful and interested. If you manage to do this, the rest will be easy.

The Attractive Power - Desire Force

WE have discussed the necessity of getting rid of fear, that your desire may have full strength with which to work. Supposing that you have mastered this part of the task, or at least started on the road to mastery, I will now call your attention to another important branch of the subject. I allude to the subject of mental leaks. No, I don't mean the leakage arising from your failure to keep your own secrets - that is also important, but forms another story. The leakage I am now referring to is that occasioned by the habit of having the attention attracted to and distracted by every passing fancy. In order to attain a thing it is necessary that the mind should fall in love with it, and be conscious of its existence, almost to the exclusion of everything else. You must get in love with the thing you wish to attain, just as much as you would if you were to meet the girl or man you wished to marry. I do not mean that you should become a monomaniac upon the subject, and should lose all interest in everything else in the world - that won't do, for the mind must have recreation and change. But, I do mean that you must be so "set" upon the desired thing that all else will seem of secondary importance. A man in love may be pleasant to everyone else, and may go through the duties and pleasures of life with good spirit, but underneath it all he is humming to himself "Just One Girl;" and every one of his actions is bent toward getting that girl, and making a comfortable home for her. Do you see what I mean? You must get in love with the thing you want, and you must get in love with it in earnest - none of this latter-day flirting, "on-today and off-tomorrow" sort of love, but the good old-fashioned kind, that used to make it impossible for a young man to get to sleep unless he took a walk around his best girl's house, just to be sure it was still there. That's the real kind! And the man or woman in search of success must make of that desired thing his ruling passion - he must keep his mind on the main chance. Success is jealous - that's why we speak of her as feminine. She demands a man's whole affection, and if he begins flirting with other fair charmers, she soon turns her back upon him. If a man allows his strong interest in the main chance to be sidetracked, he will be the loser. Mental Force operates best when it is concentrated. You must give to the desired thing your best and most earnest thought. Just as the man who is thoroughly in love will think out plans and schemes whereby he may please the fair one, so will the man who is in love with his work or business give it his best thought, and the result will be that a hundred and one plans will come into his field of consciousness, many of which are very important. The mind works on the subconscious plane, remember, and almost always along the lines of the ruling passion or desire. It will fix up things, and patch together plans and schemes, and when you need them the most it will pop them into your consciousness, and you will feel like hurrahing, just as if you had received some valuable aid from outside. But if you scatter your thought-force, the subconscious mind will not know just how to please you, and the result is that you are apt to be put off from this source of aid and assistance. Beside this, you will miss the powerful result of concentrated thought in the conscious working out of the details of your plans. And then again the man whose mind is full of a dozen interests fails to exert the attracting power that is manifested by the man of the one ruling passion, and he fails to draw to him persons, things, and results that will aid in the working out of his plans, and will also fail to place himself in the current of attraction whereby he is brought into contact with those who will be glad to help him because of harmonious interests. I have noticed, in my own affairs, that when I would allow myself to be side-tracked by anything outside of my regular line of work, it would be only a short time before my receipts dropped off, and my business showed signs of a lack of vitality. Now, many may say that this was because I left undone some things that I would have done if my mind had been centered on the business. This is true; but I have noticed like results in cases where there was nothing to be done - cases in which the seed was sown, and the crop was awaited. And in just such cases, as soon as I directed my thought to the matter the seed began to sprout. I do not man that I had to send out great mental waves with the idea of affecting people - not a bit of it. I simply began to realize what a good thing I had, and how much people wanted it, and how glad they would be to know of it and all that sort of thing, and lo! My thought seemed to vitalize the work, and the seed began to sprout. This is no mere fancy, for I have experienced it on several occasions; I have spoken to many others on the subject, and I find that our experiences tally perfectly. So don't get into the habit of permitting these mental leaks. Keep your Desire fresh and active, and let it get in its work without interference from conflicting desires. Keep in love with the thing you wish to attain - feed your fancy with it - see it as accomplished already, but don't lose your interest. Keep your eye on the main chance, and keep your one ruling passion strong and vigorous. Don't be a mental polygamist - one mental love is all that a man needs - that is, one at a time.

Some scientists have claimed that something that might as well be called "Love" is at the bottom of the whole of life. They claim that the love of the plant for water causes it to send forth its roots until the loved thing is found. They say that the love of the flower for the sun causes it to grow away from the dark places, so that it may receive the light. The so-called "chemical affinities" are really a form of love. And Desire is a manifestation of this Universal Life Love. So I am not using a mere figure of speech when I tell you that you must love the thing you wish to attain. Nothing but intense love will enable you to surmount the many obstacles placed in your path. Nothing but that love will enable you to bear the burdens of the task. The more Desire you have for a thing, the more you Love it; and the more you Love it, the greater will be the attractive force exerted toward its attainment - both within yourself, and outside of you. So love but one thing at a time - don't be a mental Mormon.

The Great Dynamic Forces

YOU have noticed the difference between the successful and strong men in any walk of life, and the unsuccessful weak men around them. You are conscious of the widely differing characteristics of the two classes, but somehow find it difficult to express just in what the difference lies. Let us take a look at the matter. Burton said: "The longer I live, the more certain I am that the great difference between men, the feeble and the powerful, the great and the insignificant, is energy and invincible determination - a purpose once fixed and then Death or Victory. That quality will do anything that can be done in this world - and no talents, no circumstances, no opportunities will make a two-legged creature a man without it." I do not see how the idea could be more clearly expressed than Burton has spoken. He has put his finger right in the center of the subject - his eye has seen into the heart of it. Energy and invincible determination - these two things will sweep away mighty barriers, and will surmount the greatest obstacles. And yet they must be used together. Energy without determination will go to waste. Lots of men have plenty of energy - they are full to overflowing with it; and yet they lack concentration - they lack the concentrated force that enables them to bring their power to bear upon the right spot. Energy is not nearly so rare a thing as many imagine it to be. I can look around me at any lime, and pick out a number of people I know who are full of energy many of them are energy plus - and yet, somehow, they do not seem to make any headway. They are wasting their energy all the time. Now they are fooling with this thing - now meddling with that. They will take up some trifling thing of no real interest or importance, and waste enough energy and nervous force to carry them through a hard day's work, and yet when they are through, nothing has been accomplished. Others who have plenty of energy, fail to direct it by the power of the Will toward the desired end. "Invincible determination" - those are the words. Do they not thrill you with their power? If you have something to do, get to work and do it. Marshal your energy, and then guide and direct it by your Will - bestow upon it that "invincible determination" and you will do the thing. Everyone has within him a giant will, but the majority of us are too lazy to use it. We cannot get ourselves nerved up to the point at which we can say, truthfully: "I Will. If we can but pluck up our courage to that point, and will then pin it in place so that it will not slip back, we will be able to call into play that wonderful power - the Human Will. Man, as a rule, has but the faintest conception of the power of the Will, but those who have studied along the occult teachings, know that the Will is one of the great dynamic forces of the universe, and if harnessed and directed properly it is capable of accomplishing almost miraculous things. "Energy and Invincible Determination: -- aren't they magnificent words? Commit them to memory - press them like a die into the wax of your mind, and they will be a constant inspiration to you in hours of need. If you can get these words to vibrating in your being, you will be a giant among pygmies. Say these words over and over again, and see how you are filled with new life - see how your blood will circulate - how your nerves will tingle. Make these words a part of yourself, and then go forth anew to the battle of life, encouraged and strengthened. Put them into practice. "Energy and Invincible Determination" - let that be your motto in your work-a-day life, and you will be one of those rare men who are able to "do things." Many persons are deterred from doing their best by the fact that they underrate themselves by comparison with the successful ones of life, or rather, overrate the successful ones by comparison with themselves. One of the curious things noticed by those who are brought in contact with the people who have "arrived" is the fact that these successful people are not extraordinary after all. You meet with some great writer, and you are disappointed to find him very ordinary indeed. He does not converse brilliantly, and, in fact, you know a score of everyday people who seem far more brilliant than this man who dazzles you by his brightness in his books. You meet some great statesman, and he does not seem nearly so wise as lots of old fellows in your own village, who waste their wisdom upon the desert air. You meet some great captain of industry, and he does not give you the impression of the shrewdness so marked in some little bargain-driving trader in your own town. How is this, anyway? Are the reputations of these people fictitious, or what is the trouble The trouble is this: you have imagined these people to be made of superior metal, and are disappointed to find them made of the same stuff as yourself and those about you. But, you ask, wherein does their greatness of achievement lie? Chiefly in this: Belief in themselves and in their inherent power, in their faculty to concentrate on the work in hand, when they are working, and in their ability to prevent leaks of power when they are not working. They believe in themselves, and make every effort count.

Your village wise man spills his wisdom on every corner, and talks to a lot of fools; when if he really were wise he would save up his wisdom and place it where it would do some work. The brilliant writer does not waste his wit upon every corner; in fact, he shuts the drawer in which he contains his wit, and opens it only when he is ready to concentrate and get down to business. The captain of industry has no desire to impress you with his shrewdness and "smartness. He never did, even when he was young. While his companions were talking and boasting, and "blowing," this future successful financier was "sawin' wood and sayin' nuthin'." The great people of the world - that is, those who have "arrived" - are not very different from you, or me, or the rest of us - all of us are about the same at the base. You have only to meet them to see how very "ordinary" they are, after all. But, don't forget the fact that they know how to use the material that is in them; while the rest of the crowd does not, and, in fact, even doubts whether the true stuff is there. The man or woman who "gets there", usually starts out by realizing that he or she is not so very different, after all, from the successful people that they hear so much about. This gives them confidence, and the result is they find out that they are able to "do things." Then they learn to keep their mouths closed, and to avoid wasting and dissipating their energy. They store up energy, and concentrate it upon the task at hand; while their companions are scattering their energies in every direction, trying to show off and let people know how smart they are. The man or woman who "gets there," prefers to wait for the applause that follows deed accomplished, and cares very little for the praise that attends promises of what we expect to do "some day," or an exhibition of "smartness" without works.

One of the reasons that people who are thrown in with successful men often manifest success themselves, is that they are able to watch the successful man and sort of "catch the trick" of his greatness. They see that he is an everyday sort of man, but that he thoroughly believes in himself, and also that he does not waste energy, but reserves all his force for the actual tasks before him. And, profiting by example, they start to work and put the lesson into practice in their own lives. Now what is the moral of this talk? Simply this: Don't undervalue yourself, or overvalue others. Realize that you are made of good stuff, and that locked within your mind are many good things. Then get to work and unfold those good things, and make something out of that good stuff. Do this by attention to the things before you, and by giving to each the best that is in you, knowing that plenty of more good things are in you ready for the fresh tasks that will come. Put the best of yourself into the undertaking on hand, and do not cheat the present task in favor of some future one. Your supply is inexhaustible. And don't waste your good stuff on the crowd of gapers, watchers and critics who are standing around watching you work. Save your good stuff for your job, and don't be in too much of a hurry for applause. Save up your good thoughts for "copy" if you are a writer; save up your bright schemes for actual practice, if you are a business man; save up your wisdom for occasion, if you are a statesman; and, in each case, avoid the desire to scatter your pears before - well, before the gaping crowd that wants to be entertained by a "free show." Nothing very "high" about this teaching, perhaps, but it is what many of you need very much. Stop fooling, and get down to business. Stop wasting good raw material, and start to work making something worthwhile.

Claiming your Own

IN a recent conversation, I was telling a woman to pluck up courage and to reach out for a certain good thing for which she had been longing for many years, and which, at last, appeared to be in sight. I told her that it looked as if her desire was about to be gratified - that the Law of Attraction was bringing it to her. She lacked faith, and kept on repeating, "Oh! It's too good to be true - it's too good for me! She had not emerged from the worm-of-the-dust stage, and although she was in sight of the Promised Land she refused to enter it because it "was too good for her." l think I succeeded in putting sufficient "ginger" into her to enable her to claim her own, for the last reports indicate that she is taking possession. But that is not what I wish to tell you. I want to call your attention to the fact that nothing is too good for YOU - no matter how great the thing may be - no matter how undeserving you may seem to be. You are entitled to the best there is, for it is your direct inheritance. So don't be afraid to ask -demand - and take. The good things of the world are not the portion of any favored sons. They belong to all, but they come only to those who are wise enough to recognize that the good things are theirs by right, and who are sufficiently courageous to reach out for them. Many good things are lost for want of the asking. Many splendid things are lost to you because of your feeling that you are unworthy of them. Many great things are lost to you because you lack the confidence and courage to demand and take possession of them.

"None but the brave deserves the fair," says the old adage, and the rule is true in all lines of human effort. If you keep on repeating that you are unworthy of the good thing - that it is too good for you - the Law will be apt to take you at your word and believe what you say. That's a peculiar thing about the Law - it believes - what you say - it takes you in earnest. So beware what you say to it, for it will be apt to give credence. Say to it that you are worthy of the best there is, and that there is nothing too good for you, and you will be likely to have the Law take you in earnest, and say, "I guess he is right; I'm going to give him the whole bakeshop if he wants it - he knows his rights, and what's the use of trying to deny it to him?" But if you say, "Oh, it's too good for me! The Law will probably say, "Well, I wouldn't wonder but that that is so. Surely he ought to know, and it isn't for me to contradict him." And so it goes. Why should anything be too good for you? Did you ever stop to think just what you are? You are a manifestation of the Whole Thing, and have a perfect right to all there is. Or, if you prefer it this way, you are a child of the Infinite, and are heir to it all. You are telling the truth in either statement, or both. At any rate, no matter for what you ask, you are merely demanding your own. And the more in earnest you are about demanding it - the more confident you are of receiving it - the more will you use in reaching out for it - the surer you will be to obtain it. Strong desire - confident expectation - courage in action - these things bring to you your own. But before you put these forces into effect, you must awaken to a realization that you are merely asking for your own, and not for something to which you have no right or claim. So long as there exists in your mind the last sneaking bit of doubt as to your right to the things you want, you will be setting up a resistance to the operation of the Law. You may demand as vigorously as you please, but you will lack the courage to act, if you have a lingering doubt of your right to the thing you want. If you persist in regarding the desired thing as if it belonged to another, instead of to yourself, you will be placing yourself in the position of the covetous or envious man, or even in the position of a tempted thief. In such a case your mind will revolt at proceeding with the work, for it instinctively will recoil from the idea of taking what is not your own - the mind is honest. But when your realize that the best the Universe holds belongs to you as a Divine Heir, and that there is enough for all without your robbing anyone else; then the friction is removed, and the barrier broken down, and the Law proceeds to do its work. I do not believe in this "humble" business. This meek and lowly attitude does not appeal to me - there is no sense in it, at all. The idea of making a virtue of such things, when Man is the heir of the Universe, and is entitled to whatever he needs for his growth, happiness and satisfaction! I do not mean that one should assume a blustering and domineering attitude of mind - that is also absurd, for true strength does not so exhibit itself. The blusterer is a self-confessed weakling - he blusters to disguise his weakness. The truly strong man is calm, self-contained, and carries with him a consciousness of strength which renders unnecessary the bluster and fuss of assumed strength. But get away from this hypnotism of "humility" - this "meek and lowly" attitude of mind. Remember the horrible example of Uriah Heep, and beware of imitating him. Throw back you head, and look the world square in the face. There's nothing to be afraid of - the world is apt to be as much afraid of you, as yell are of it, anyway. Be a man, or woman, and not a crawling thing. And this applies to your mental attitude, as well as to your outward demeanor. Stop this crawling in your mind. See yourself as standing erect and facing life without fear, and you will gradually grow into your ideal. There is nothing that is too good for you - not a thing. The best there is, is not beginning to be good enough for you; for there are still better things ahead. The best gift that the world has to offer is a mere bauble compared to the great things in the Cosmos that await your coming of age. So don't be afraid to reach out for these playthings of life - these baubles of this plane of consciousness. Reach out for them - grab a whole fistful - play with them until you are tired; that's what they are made for, anyway. They are made for our express use - not to look at, but to be played with, if you desire. Help yourself - there's a whole shopful of these toys awaiting your desire, demand and taking. Don't be bashful! Don't let me hear any more of this silly talk about things being too good for you. Pshaw! You have been like the Emperor's little son thinking that the tin soldiers and toy drum were far too good for him, and refusing to reach out for them. But you don't find this trouble with children as a rule. They instinctively recognize that nothing is too good for them. They want all that is in sight to play with, and they seem to feel that the things are theirs by right. And that is the condition of mind that we seekers after the Divine Adventure must cultivate. Unless we become as little children we cannot enter the Kingdom of Heaven.

Help yourself to them - ask for them without bashfulness demand as many as you can make use of - they are yours. And if you don't see just what you want, ask for it - there's a big reserve stock on the shelves, and in the closets. Play, play, play, to your heart's content. Learn to weave mats - to build houses with the blocks - to stitch outlines on the squares - play the game through, and play it well. And demand all the proper materials for the play - don't be bashful - there's enough to go round. But - remember this! While all this be true, the best things are still only game-things - toys, blocks, mats, cubes, and all the rest. Useful, most useful for the learning of the lessons - pleasant, most pleasant with which to play - and desirable, most desirable, for these purposes. Get all the fun and profit out of the use of things that is possible. Throw yourself heartily into the game, and play it out - it is Good. But, here's the thing to remember - never lose sight of the fact that these good things are but playthings - part of the game - and you must be perfectly willing to lay them aside when the time comes to pass into the next class, and not cry and mourn because you must leave your playthings behind you. Do not allow yourself to become unduly attached to them - they are for your use and pleasure, but are not a part of you - not essential to your happiness in the next stage. Despise them not because of their lack of Reality - they are great things relatively, and you may as well have all the fun out of them that you can - don't be a spiritual prig, standing aside and refusing to join in the game. But do not tie yourself to them - they are good to use and play with, but not good enough to use you and to make you a plaything. Don't let the toys turn the tables on you. This is the difference between the master of Circumstances and the Slave of Circumstances. The Slave thinks that these playthings are real, and that he is not good enough to have them. He gets only a few toys, because he is afraid to ask for more, and he misses most of the fun. And then, considering the toys to be real, and not realizing that there are plenty more where these came from, he attaches himself to the little trinkets that have come his way, and allows himself to be made a slave of them. He is afraid that they may be taken away from him and he is afraid to toddle across the floor and help himself to the others. The Master knows that all are his for the asking. He demands that which he needs from day to day, and does not worry about over-loading himself; for he knows that there are "lots more," and that he cannot be cheated out of them. He plays, and plays well, and has a good time in the play - and he learns his Kindergarten lessons in the playing. But he does not become too much attached to his toys. He is willing to fling away the worn-out toys, and reach out for a new one. And when he is called into the next room for promotion, he drops on the floor the worn-out toys of the day, and with glistening eyes and confident attitude of mind, marches into the next room - into the Great Unknown -with a smile on his face. He is not afraid, for he hears the voice of the Teacher, and knows that she is there waiting for him - in that Great Next Room.

Law, not Chance

SOME time ago I was talking to a man about the Attractive Power of Thought. He said that he did not believe that Thought could attract anything to him, and that it was all a matter of luck. He had found, he said, that ill luck relentlessly pursued him, and that everything he touched went wrong. It always had, and always would, and he had grown to expect it. When he undertook a new thing he knew beforehand that it would go wrong and that no good would come of it. Oh, no! There wasn't anything in the theory of Attractive Thought, so far as he could see; it was all a matter of luck!

This man failed to see that by his own confession he was giving a most convincing argument in favor of the Law of Attraction. He was testifying that he was always expecting things to go wrong, and that they always came about as he expected. He was a magnificent illustration of the Law of Attraction - but he didn't know it, and no argument seemed to make the matter clear to him. He was "up against it," and there was no way out of it - he always expected the ill luck. and every occurrence proved that he was right, and that the Mental Science position was all nonsense.

There are many people who seem to think that the only way in which the Law of Attraction operates is when one wishes hard, strong and steady. They do not seem to realize that a strong belief is as efficacious as a strong wish. The successful man believes in himself and his ultimate success, and, paying no attention to little setbacks, stumbles, tumbles and slips, presses on eagerly to the goal, believing all the time that he will get there. His views and aims may alter as he progresses, and he may change his plans or have them changed for him, but all the time he knows in his heart that he will eventually "get there." He is not steadily wishing he may get there - he simply feels and believes it, and thereby sets to operation the strongest forces known in the world of thought.

The man who just as steadily believes he is going to fail will invariably fail. How could he help it? There is no special miracle about it. Everything he does, thinks and says is tinctured with the thought of failure. Other people catch his spirit, and fail to trust him or his ability, which occurrences he in turn sets down as but other exhibitions of his ill luck, instead of ascribing them to his belief and expectation of failure. He is suggesting failure to himself all the time, and he invariably takes on the effect of the autosuggestion. Then, again, he by his negative thoughts shuts up that portion of his mind from which should come the ideas and plans conducive to success and which do come to the man who is expecting success because he believes in it. A state of discouragement is not the one in which bright ideas come to us. It is only when we are enthused and hopeful that our minds work out the bright ideas which we may turn to account.

Men instinctively feel the atmosphere of failure hovering around certain of their fellows, and on the other hand recognize something about others which leads them to say, when they hear of a temporary mishap befalling such a one: "Oh, he'll come out all right somehow - you can't down him." It is the atmosphere caused by the prevailing Mental Attitude. Clear up your Mental Atmosphere!

223

There is no such thing as chance. Law maintains everywhere, and all that happens because of the operation of Law. You cannot name the simplest thing that ever occurred by chance - try it, and then run the thing down to a final analysis, and you will see it as the result of law. It is as plain as mathematics. Plan and purpose; cause and effect. From the movements of worlds to the growth of the grain of mustard seed - all the result of Law. The fall of the stone down the mountainside is not chance - forces which had been in operation for centuries caused it. And back of that cause were other causes, and so on until the Causeless Cause is reached.

And Life is not the result of chance - the Law is here, too. The Law is in full operation whether you know it or not - whether you believe in it or not. You may be the ignorant object upon   which the Law operates, and bring yourself all sorts of trouble because of your ignorance of or opposition to the Law. Or you may fall in with the operations to the Law - get into its current,   as it were - and Life will seem a far different thing to you. You cannot get outside of the Law,   by refusing to have anything to do with it. You are at liberty to oppose it and produce all the   friction you wish to - it doesn't' hurt the Law, and you may keep it up until you learn your lesson.

The Law of Thought Attraction is one name for the law, or rather for one manifestation of it. Again I say, your thoughts are real things. They go forth from you in all directions, combining with thoughts of like kind - opposing thoughts of a different character - forming combinations - going where they are attracted - flying away from thought centers opposing them. And your mind attracts the thought of others, which have been sent out by them conscious or unconsciously. But it attracts only those thoughts which are in harmony with its own. Like attracts like, and opposites repel opposites, in the world of thought.

If you set your mind to the keynote of courage, confidence, strength and success, you attract to yourself thoughts of like nature; people of like nature; things that fit in the mental tune. Your prevailing thought or mood determines that which is to be drawn toward you - picks out your mental bedfellow. You are today setting into motion thought currents which will in time attract toward you thoughts, people and conditions in harmony with the predominant note of your thought. Your thought will mingle with that of others of like nature and mind, and you will be attracted toward each other, and will surely come together with a common purpose sooner or later, unless one or the other of you should change the current of his thoughts.

Fall in with the operations of the law. Make it a part of yourself. Get into its currents. Maintain your poise. Set your mind to the keynote of Courage, Confidence and Success. Get in touch with all the thoughts of that kind that are emanating every hour from hundreds of minds. Get the best that is to be had in the thought world. The best is there, so be satisfied with nothing less. Get into partnership with good minds. Get into the right vibrations. You must be tired of being tossed about by the operations of the Law - get into harmony with it.

Feeling is the Secret

Neville Goddard

© Copyright 2007 – BN Publishing

www.bnpublishing.com

info@bnpublishing.com

Printed in the U.S.A.

TABLE OF CONTENTS

Foreword

THIS book is concerned with the art of realizing your desire. It gives you an account of the mechanism used in the production of the visible world. It is a small book but not slight. There is a treasure in it, a clearly defined road to the realization of your dreams.

Were it possible to carry conviction to another by means of reasoned arguments and detailed instances this book would be many times its size. It is seldom possible, however, to do so by means of written statements or arguments since to the suspended judgment it always seems plausible to say that the author was dishonest or deluded, and, therefore, his evidence was tainted.

Consequently, I have purposely omitted all arguments and testimonials, and simply challenge the open-minded reader to practice the law of consciousness as revealed in this book. Personal success will prove far more convincing than all the books that could be written on the subject.

NEVILLE.

Chapter 1 – LAW AND ITS OPERATION

THE world, and all within it, is man's conditioned consciousness objectified. Consciousness is the cause as well as the substance of the entire world. So it is to consciousness that we must turn if we would discover the secret of creation.

Knowledge of the law of consciousness and the method of operating this law will enable you to accomplish all you desire in life. Armed with a working knowledge of this law, you can build and maintain an ideal world.

Consciousness is the one and only reality, not figuratively but actually. This reality may for the sake of clarity be likened unto a stream which is divided into two parts, the conscious and the subconscious. In order to intelligently operate the law of consciousness it is necessary to understand the relationship between the conscious and the subconscious. The conscious is personal and selective; the subconscious is impersonal and nonselective. The conscious is the realm of effect; the subconscious is the realm of cause. These two aspects are the male and female divisions of consciousness. The conscious is male; the subconscious is female. The conscious generates ideas and impresses these ideas on the subconscious; the subconscious receives ideas and gives form and expression to them.

By this law—first conceiving an idea and then impressing the idea conceived on the subconscious—all things evolve out of consciousness; and without this sequence there is not anything made that is made. The conscious impresses the subconscious while the subconscious expresses all that is impressed upon it.

The subconscious does not originate ideas but accepts as true those which the conscious mind feels to be true and in a way known only to itself objectifies the accepted ideas.

Therefore, through his power to imagine and feel and his freedom to choose the idea he will entertain, man has control over creation. Control of the subconscious is accomplished through control of your ideas and feelings.

The mechanism of creation is hidden in the very depth of the subconscious, the female aspect or womb of creation. The subconscious transcends reason and is independent of induction. It contemplates a feeling as a fact existing within itself and on this assumption proceeds to give expression to it. The creative process begins with an idea and its cycle runs its course as a feeling and ends in a volition to act.

Ideas are impressed on the subconscious through the medium of feeling. No idea can be impressed on the subconscious until it is felt, but once felt—be it good, bad or indifferent—it must be expressed. Feeling is the one and only medium through which ideas are conveyed to the subconscious. Therefore, the man who does not control his feeling may easily impress the subconscious with undesirable states. By control of feeling is not meant restraint or suppression of your feeling, but rather the disciplining of self to imagine and entertain only such feeling as contributes to your happiness. Control of your feeling is all-important to a full and happy life. Never entertain an undesirable feeling nor think sympathetically about wrong in any shape or form. Do not dwell on the imperfection of yourself or others. To do so is to impress the subconscious with these limitations. What you do not want done unto you, do not feel that it is done unto you or another. This is the whole law of a full and happy life. Everything else is commentary.

Every feeling makes a subconscious impression and unless it is counteracted by a more powerful feeling of an opposite nature it must be expressed. The dominant of two feelings is the one expressed. I am healthy is a stronger feeling than I will be healthy. To feel I will be is to confess I am not; I am is stronger than I am not. What you feel you are always dominates what you feel you would like to be; therefore, to be realized, the wish must be felt as a state that is rather than a state that is not.

Sensation precedes manifestation and is the foundation upon which all manifestation rests. Be careful of your moods and feelings, for there is an unbroken connection between your feelings and your visible world. Your body is an emotional filter and bears the unmistakable marks of your prevalent emotions. Emotional disturbances, especially suppressed emotions, are the causes of all disease. To feel intensely about a wrong without voicing or expressing that feeling, is the beginning of disease— dis-ease—in both body and environment. Do not entertain the feeling of regret or failure for frustration or detachment from your objective results in disease.

Think feelingly only of the state you desire to realize. Feeling the reality of the state sought and living and acting on that conviction is the way of all seeming miracles. All changes of expression are brought about through a change of feeling. A change of feeling is a change of destiny. All creation occurs in the domain of the subconscious. What you must acquire, then, is a reflective control of the operation of the subconscious, that is, control of your ideas and feelings.

Chance or accident is not responsible for the things that happen to you, nor is predestined fate the author of your fortune or misfortune. Your subconscious impressions determine the conditions of your world. The subconscious is not selective; it is impersonal and no respecter of persons. The subconscious is not concerned with the truth or falsity of your feeling. It always accepts as true that which you feel to be true. Feeling is the assent of the subconscious to the truth of that which is declared to be true. Because of this quality of the subconscious there is nothing impossible to man. Whatever the mind of man can conceive and feel as true, the subconscious can and must objectify. Your feelings create the pattern from which your world is fashioned, and a change of feeling is a change of pattern.

The subconscious never fails to express that which has been impressed upon it. The moment it receives an impression it begins to work out the ways of its expression. It accepts the feeling impressed upon it, your feeling, as a fact existing within itself and immediately sets about to produce in the outer or objective world the exact likeness of that feeling. The subconscious never alters the accepted beliefs of man. It out-pictures them to the last detail whether or not they are beneficial.

To impress the subconscious with the desirable state you must assume the feeling that would be yours had you already realized your wish. In defining your objective you must be concerned only with the objective itself. The manner of expression or the difficulties involved are not to be considered by you. To think feelingly on any state impresses it on the subconscious. Therefore, if you dwell on difficulties, barriers or delay, the subconscious, by its very non-selective nature, accepts the feeling of difficulties and obstacles as your request and proceeds to produce them in your outer world.

The subconscious is the womb of creation. It receives the idea unto itself through the feelings of man. It never changes the idea received, but always gives it form. Hence the subconscious out-pictures the idea in the image and likeness of the feeling received. To feel a state as hopeless or impossible is to impress the subconscious with the idea of failure. Although the subconscious faithfully serves man it must not be inferred that the relation is that of a servant to a master as was anciently conceived. The subconscious has a distinct distaste for compulsion and responds to persuasion rather than to command; consequently, it resembles the beloved wife more than the servant.

The conscious (objective) or male aspect truly is the head and dominates the subconscious (subjective) or female aspect. However, this leadership is not that of the tyrant but of the lover. So by assuming the feeling that would be yours were you already in possession of your objective, the subconscious is moved to build the exact likeness of your assumption. Your desires are not subconsciously accepted until you assume the feeling of their reality, for only through feeling is an idea subconsciously accepted and only through this subconscious acceptance is it ever expressed.

It is easier to ascribe your feeling to events in the world than to admit that the conditions of the world reflect your feeling. However, it is eternally true that the outside mirrors the inside. "As within so without." "A man can receive nothing unless it is given him from heaven," and "The kingdom of heaven is within you." Nothing comes from without; all things come from within— from the subconscious. It is impossible for you to see other than the contents of your consciousness. Your world in its every detail is your consciousness objectified. Objective states bear witness of subconscious impressions. A change of impression results in a change of expression.

The subconscious accepts as true that which you feel as true, and because creation is the result of subconscious impressions, you, by your feeling, determine creation. You are already that which you want to be, and your refusal to believe this is the only reason you do not see it. To seek on the outside for that which you do not feel you are is to seek in vain, for we never find that which we want; we find only that which we are. In short, you express and have only that which you are conscious of being or possessing. Denying the evidence of the senses and appropriating the feeling of the wish fulfilled is the way to the realization of your desire.

Mastery of self-control of your thoughts and feelings is your highest achievement. However, until perfect self-control is attained so that in spite of appearances you feel all that you want to feel, use sleep and prayer to aid you in realizing your desired states. These are the two gateways into the subconscious.

Chapter Two – SLEEP

SLEEP, the life that occupies one-third of our stay on earth, is the natural door into the subconscious. So it is with sleep that we are now concerned. The conscious two-thirds of our life on earth is measured by the degree of attention we give sleep. Our understanding of and delight in what sleep has to bestow will cause us, night after night, to set out for it as though we were keeping an appointment with a lover.

"In a dream, in a vision of the night, when deep sleep falleth upon men, in slumbering upon the bed; then he openeth the ears of men and sealeth their instruction." Job 33.

It is in sleep and in prayer, a state akin to sleep, that man enters the subconscious to make his impressions and receive his instructions. In these states the conscious and subconscious are creatively joined. The male and female become one flesh.

Sleep is the time when the male or conscious mind turns from the world of sense to seek its lover or subconscious self. The subconscious—unlike the woman of the world who marries her husband to change him—has no desire to change the conscious, waking state, but loves it as it is and faithfully reproduces its likeness in the outer world of form. The conditions and events of your life are your children formed from the molds of your subconscious impressions in sleep. They are made in the image and likeness of your innermost feeling that they may reveal you to yourself.

"As in heaven so on earth." As in the subconscious so on earth. Whatever you have in consciousness as you go to sleep is the measure of your expression in the waking two-thirds of your life on earth. Nothing stops you from realizing your objective save your failure to feel that you are already that which you wish to be, or that you are already in possession of the thing sought. Your subconscious gives form to your desires only when you feel your wish fulfilled.

The unconsciousness of sleep is the normal state of the subconscious. Because all things come from within yourself, and your conception of yourself determines that which comes, you should always feel the wish fulfilled before you drop off to sleep. You never draw out of the deep of yourself that which you want; you always draw that which you are, and you are that which you feel yourself to be as well as that which you feel as true of others.

To be realized, then, the wish must be resolved into the feeling of being or having or witnessing the state sought. This is accomplished by assuming the feeling of the wish fulfilled. The feeling which comes in response to the question "How would I feel were my wish realized?" is the feeling which should monopolize and immobilize your attention as you relax into sleep. You must be in the consciousness of being or having that which you want to be or to have before you drop off to sleep.

Once asleep man has no freedom of choice. His entire slumber is dominated by his last waking concept of self. It follows, therefore, that he should always assume the feeling of accomplishment and satisfaction before he retires in sleep. Your mood prior to sleep defines your state of consciousness as you enter into the presence of your everlasting lover, the subconscious. She sees you exactly as you feel yourself to be. If, as you prepare for sleep, you assume and maintain the consciousness of success by feeling "I am successful," you must be successful. Lie flat on your back with your head on a level with your body. Feel as you would were you in possession of your wish and quietly relax into unconsciousness.

"He that keepeth Israel shall neither slumber nor sleep." Nevertheless "He giveth his beloved sleep." The subconscious never sleeps. Sleep is the door through which the conscious, waking mind passes to be creatively joined to the subconscious. Sleep conceals the creative act while the objective world reveals it. In sleep man impresses the subconscious with his conception of himself.

What more beautiful description of this romance of the conscious and subconscious is there than that told in the "Song of Solomon"! "By night on my bed I sought him whom my soul loveth. . . . I found him whom my soul loveth; I held him and I would not let him go, until I had brought him into my mother's house, and into the chamber of her that conceived me." Preparing to sleep, you feel yourself into the state of the answered wish, and then relax into unconsciousness. Your realized wish is he whom you seek. By night on your bed you seek the feeling of the wish fulfilled that you may take it with you into the chamber of her that conceived you, into sleep or the subconscious which gave you form, that this wish also may be given expression. This is the way to discover and conduct your wishes into the subconscious. Feel yourself in the state of the realized wish and quietly drop off to sleep.

Night after night you should assume the feeling of being, having and witnessing that which you seek to be, possess and see manifested. Never go to sleep feeling discouraged or dissatisfied. Never sleep in the consciousness of failure. Your subconscious, whose natural state is sleep, sees you as you believe yourself to be, and whether it be good, bad, or indifferent, the subconscious will faithfully embody your belief. As you feel so do you impress her; and she, the perfect lover, gives form to these impressions and out-pictures them as the children of her beloved.

"Thou art all fair, my love;" is the attitude of mind to adopt before dropping off to sleep. Disregard appearances and feel that things are as you wish them to be, for "He calleth things that are not seen as though they were, and the unseen becomes seen." To assume the feeling of satisfaction is to call conditions into being which will mirror satisfaction. Proof that you are will follow the consciousness that you are; it will not precede it.

You are an eternal dreamer dreaming non-eternal dreams. Your dreams take form as you assume the feeling of their reality. Do not limit yourself to the past. Knowing that nothing is impossible to consciousness begin to imagine states beyond the experiences of the past. Whatever the mind of man can imagine man can realize. All objective (visible) states were first subjective (invisible) states, and you called them into visible states by assuming the feeling of their reality. The creative process is first imagining and then believing the state imagined. Always imagine and expect the best.

The world cannot change until you change your conception of it. "As within so without." Nations as well as people are only what you believe them to be. No matter what the problem is, no matter where it is, no matter whom it concerns, you have no one to change but yourself, and you have neither opponent nor helper in bringing about the change within yourself. You have nothing to do but convince yourself of the truth of that which you desire to see manifested. As soon as you succeed in convincing yourself of the reality of the state sought, results follow to confirm your fixed belief. You never suggest to another the state which you desire to see him express; instead you convince yourself that he is already that which you desire him to be.

Realization of your wish is accomplished by assuming the feeling of the wish fulfilled. You cannot fail unless you fail to convince yourself of the reality of your wish. A change of belief is confirmed by a change of expression. Every night as you drop off to sleep feel satisfied and spotless, for your subjective lover always forms the objective world in the image and likeness of your conception of it, the conception defined by your feeling.

The waking two-thirds of your life on earth ever corroborates or bears witness to your subconscious impressions. The actions and events of the day are effects; they are not causes. Free will is only freedom of choice. You are free to choose the kind of mood you assume; but the expression of the mood is the secret of the subconscious. The subconscious receives impressions only through the feelings of man and in a way known only to itself gives these impressions form and expression. The actions of man are determined by his subconscious impressions. His illusion of free will, his belief in freedom of action, is but ignorance of the causes which make him act. He thinks himself free because he has forgotten the link between himself and the event.

Man awake is under compulsion to express his subconscious impressions. If in the past he unwisely impressed himself, then let him begin to change his thought and feeling, for only as he does so will he change his world. Do not waste one moment in regret, for to think feelingly of the mistakes of the past is to re-infect yourself. Turn from appearances and assume the feeling that would be yours were you already the one you wish to be.

Feeling a state produces that state. The part you play on the world's stage is determined by your conception of yourself. By feeling your wish fulfilled and quietly relaxing into sleep, you cast yourself in a star role to be played on earth tomorrow, and while asleep you are rehearsed and instructed in your part.

The acceptance of the end automatically wills the means of realization. Make no mistake about this. If, as you prepare for sleep, you do not consciously feel yourself into the state of the answered wish, then you will take with you into the chamber of her who conceived you the sum total of the reactions and feelings of the waking day; and while asleep you will be instructed in the manner in which they will be expressed tomorrow. You will rise believing that you are a free agent, not realizing that every action and event of the day is predetermined by your concept of self as you fell asleep. Your only freedom then is your freedom of reaction. You are free to choose how you feel and react to the day's drama, but

243

the drama—the actions, events and circumstances of the day—have already been determined.

Unless you consciously and purposely define the attitude of mind with which you go to sleep, you unconsciously go to sleep in the composite attitude of mind made up of all feelings and reactions of the day. Every reaction makes a subconscious impression and, unless counteracted by an opposite and more dominant feeling, is the cause of future action. Ideas enveloped in feeling are creative actions. Use your divine right wisely. Through your ability to think and feel you have dominion over all creation.

While you are awake you are a gardener selecting seed for your garden. Your conception of yourself as you fall asleep is the seed you drop into the ground of the subconscious. Dropping off to sleep feeling satisfied and happy compels conditions and events to appear in your world which confirm these attitudes of mind. Sleep is the door into heaven. What you take in as a feeling you bring out as a condition, action, or object in space. So sleep in the feeling of the wish fulfilled. "As in consciousness so on earth."

Chapter Three – PRAYER

PRAYER like sleep is also an entrance into the subconscious. Prayer is an illusion of sleep which diminishes the impression of the outer world and renders the mind more receptive to suggestion from within. The mind in prayer is in a state of relaxation and receptivity akin to the feeling attained just before dropping off to sleep.

Prayer is not so much what you ask for, as how you prepare for its reception. The only condition required is that you believe that your prayers are already realized.

Your prayer must be answered if you assume the feeling that would be yours were you already in possession of your objective. The moment you accept the wish as an accomplished fact the subconscious finds means for its realization. To pray successfully then, you must yield to the wish, that is, feel the wish fulfilled.

The perfectly disciplined man is always in tune with the wish as an accomplished fact. He knows that consciousness is the one and only reality, that ideas and feelings are facts of consciousness and are as real as objects in space; therefore he never entertains a feeling which does not contribute to his happiness for feelings are the causes of the actions and circumstances of his life. On the other hand, the undisciplined man finds it difficult to believe that which is denied by the senses and usually accepts or rejects solely on appearances of the senses. Because of this tendency to rely on the evidence of the senses, it is necessary to shut them out before starting to pray, before attempting to feel that which they deny. Whenever you are in the state of mind, "I should like to but I cannot," the harder you try the less you are able to yield to the wish. You never attract that which you want but always attract that which you are conscious of being.

Prayer is the art of assuming the feeling of being and having that which you want. When the senses confirm the absence of your wish, all conscious effort to counteract this suggestion is futile and tends to intensify the suggestion.

Prayer is the art of yielding to the wish and not the forcing of the wish. Whenever your feeling is in conflict with your wish, feeling will be the victor. The dominant feeling invariably expresses itself. Prayer must be without effort. In attempting to fix an attitude of mind which is denied by the senses, effort is fatal.

To yield successfully to the wish as an accomplished fact, you must create a passive state, a kind of reverie or meditative reflection similar to the feeling which precedes sleep. In such a relaxed state the mind is turned from the objective world and easily senses the reality of a subjective state. It is a state in which you are conscious and quite able to move or open your eyes but have no desire to do so. An easy way to create this passive state is to relax in a comfortable chair or on a bed. If on a bed, lie flat on your back with your head on a level with your body, close the eyes and imagine that you are sleepy. Feel—I am sleepy, so sleepy, so very sleepy. In a little while a faraway feeling accompanied by a general lassitude and loss of all desire to move envelops you. You feel a pleasant, comfortable rest and not inclined to alter your position, although under other circumstances you would not be at all comfortable. When this passive state is reached, imagine that you have realized your wish—not how it was realized—but simply the wish fulfilled. Imagine in picture form what you desire to achieve in life; then feel yourself as having already achieved it. Thoughts produce tiny little speech movements which may be heard in the passive state of prayer as pronouncements from without. However, this degree of passivity is not essential to the realization of your prayers. All that is necessary is to create a passive state and feel the wish fulfilled.

All you can possibly need or desire is already yours. You need no helper to give it to you; it is yours now. Call your desires into being by imagining and feeling your wish fulfilled. As the end is accepted you become totally indifferent as to possible failure, for acceptance of the end wills the means to that end. When you emerge from the moment of prayer it is as though you were shown the happy and successful end of a play although you were not shown how that end was achieved. However, having witnessed the end, regardless of any anticlimactic sequence you remain calm and secure in the knowledge that the end has been perfectly defined.

Chapter 4   Spirit - Feeling

"NOT by might, nor by power, but by my spirit, saith the Lord of hosts." Get into the spirit of the state desired by assuming the feeling that would be yours were you already the one you want to be. As you capture the feeling of the state sought, you are relieved of all effort to make it so, for it is already so. There is a definite feeling associated with every idea in the mind of man. Capture the feeling associated with your realized wish by assuming the feeling that would be yours were you already in possession of the thing you desire, and your wish will objectify itself.

Faith is feeling, "According to your faith (feeling) be it unto you." You never attract that which you want but always that which you are. As a man is, so does he see. That which you feel yourself to be you are, and you are given that which you are. So assume the feeling that would be yours were you already in possession of your wish, and your wish must be realized. "So God created man in his own image, in the image of God created he him." You are that which you believe yourself to be.
It is natural to do the works of the one you believe yourself to be. So live in the feeling of being the one you want to be and that you shall be.

When a man believes in the value of the advice given him and applies it, he establishes within himself the reality of success.

THE END

We suggest you now read the book,

"Automatic Wealth I : the Secrets of the Millionaire Mind" - Including: As a Man Thinketh, the Science of Getting Rich, the Way to Wealth & Think and Grow Rich [UNABRIDGED] (Paperback)
by Napoleon Hill, James Allen, Wallace D. Wattles, Benjamin Franklin, carefully.

We hope that after you have the opportunity to practice the principles involved in these lessons, you will write to us and let us know of the results in your life.

BN Publishing

Improving People's Life

info@bnpublishing.com

www.bnpublishing.com

We Have Book Recommendations for You

The Strangest Secret by Earl Nightingale (Audio CD - Jan 2006)

Acres of Diamonds [MP3 AUDIO] [UNABRIDGED] (Audio CD) by Russell H. Conwell

Automatic Wealth: The Secrets of the Millionaire Mind - Including: Acres of Diamonds, As a Man Thinketh, I Dare you!, The Science of Getting Rich, The Way to Wealth, and Think and Grow Rich [UNABRIDGED]
by Napoleon Hill, et al (CD-ROM)

Think and Grow Rich [MP3 AUDIO] [UNABRIDGED]
by Napoleon Hill, Jason McCoy (Narrator)   (Audio CD - January 30, 2006)

As a Man Thinketh [UNABRIDGED]
by James Allen, Jason McCoy (Narrator) (Audio CD)

Your Invisible Power: How to Attain Your Desires by Letting Your Subconscious Mind Work for You [MP3 AUDIO] [UNABRIDGED]

Thought Vibration or the Law of Attraction in the Thought World [MP3 AUDIO] [UNABRIDGED]
by William Walker Atkinson, Jason McCoy (Narrator) (Audio CD - July 1, 2005)

The Law of Success Volume I: The Principles of Self-Mastery by Napoleon Hill (Audio CD - Feb 21, 2006)

The Law of Success, Volume I: The Principles of Self-Mastery (Law of Success, Vol. 1) (The Law of Success) by Napoleon Hill (Paperback - Jun 20, 2006)

The Law of Success, Volumes II & III: A Definite Chief Aim & Self -Confidence by Napoleon Hill (Paperback - Jun 20, 2006)

Thought Vibration or the Law of Attraction in the Thought World & Your Invisible Power (Paperback)

Automatic Wealth, The Secrets of the Millionaire Mind - Including: As a Man Thinketh, The Science of Getting Rich, The Way to Wealth and Think and Grow Rich (Paperback)

The Bestsellers in this Book give sound advice about money and how to obtain it. Just reach for the stars, stay focused on your dreams, and watch them come true. There is nothing we can imagine that we can't do. So what are we waiting for? Let's begin the journey of self-fulfillment.

4 Bestsellers in 1 Book:

As a Man Thinketh by James Allen

The Science of Getting Rich by Wallace D. Wattles

The Way to Wealth by Benjamin Franklin

Think and Grow Rich by Napoleon Hill

BN Publishing

Improving People's Life

www.bnpublishing.com

Get Published!

BN Publishing helped authors publish more titles. So whether you're writing a romance novel, historical fiction, mystery, action and suspense, poetry, children's or any other genre, we can help you reach your publishing goals.

Paperback

Reach 20,000 retail accounts in the U.S. (including chains, independents, specialty stories, and libraries).

Including:

www.amazon.com

www.amazon.co.uk

www.amazon.ca

www.bn.com

www.powells.com

www.ebay.com

and more...

Your book will be included in a physical catalog that will go out to over 20,000 retail stores.

When your title is entered into our library it will automatically appear in the bookstore and library databases.

Our United States and United Kingdom based sales teams works with publisher clients based throughout the world who want to print books in the United States and United Kingdom, or reach the North American, UK and wider European markets through our broad distribution channel partners.

If we decide to publish it:

we will send you 2 free copies of the finished book;

we will give you 10% royalty of the selling price of each book copy sold (selling price = the price the book is sold by BN Publishing to wholesalers or other resellers);

 and if you wish to have more copies of your book, we will sell you the book for two thirds of the list price.

Please send us more information about your book to info@bnpublishing.com

Printed in the United States
119755LV00003B/59/A